HEROIC VOICES
OF THE SPANISH CIVIL WAR

HEROIC VOICES
OF THE SPANISH CIVIL WAR

Memories from the
International Brigades

PETER DARMAN

NEW
HOLLAND

Published in 2009 by New Holland Publishers (UK) Ltd
London • Cape Town • Sydney • Auckland
www.newhollandpublishers.com
Garfield House, 86–88 Edgware Road, London W2 2EA, United Kingdom
80 McKenzie Street, Cape Town 8001, South Africa
Unit 1, 66 Gibbes Street, Chatswood, NSW 2067, Australia
218 Lake Road, Northcote, Auckland, New Zealand

10 9 8 7 6 5 4 3 2 1

A catalogue record for this book is available from the British Library

ISBN 978 1 84773 469 3

Publishing Director: Rosemary Wilkinson
Publisher: Aruna Vasudevan
Project Editor: Julia Shone
Editor: Fiona Plowman
Editorial Assistant: Cosima Hibbert
Design and cover design: 2M Design
Illustrator: Stephen Dew
DTP: Pete Gwyer
Production: Melanie Dowland

Printed and bound by Athenaeum Press Ltd, Gateshead, United Kingdom

Note: Imperial measurements are used throughout this book, as used in original
archive material.

Contents

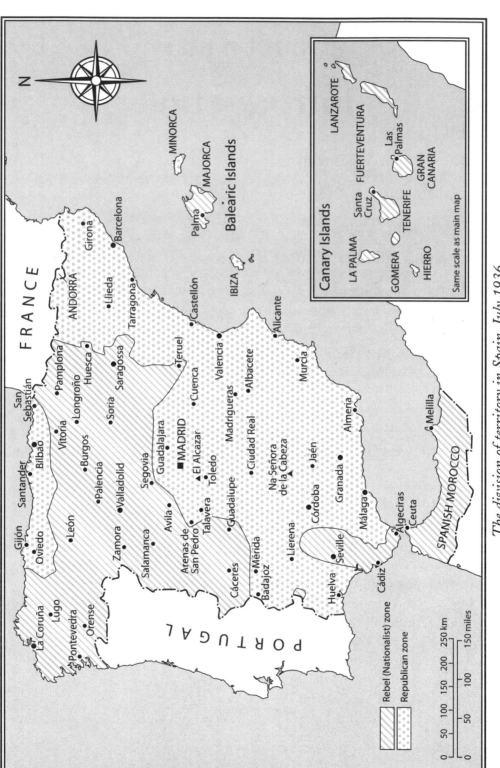

The division of territory in Spain, July 1936.

Introduction

'It's better to die on your feet than to live forever on your knees.'
– Dolores Ibárruri, La Pasionaria.

This book is concerned with the first-hand accounts of those who fought in the International Brigades in the Spanish Civil War (1936–39). As such, the war itself necessarily becomes a back-drop to the eyewitness narratives. That said, a broad outline of the war and the international events around it are useful to place those eyewitness accounts into context, and to explain why so many foreigners were fighting in Spain during the civil war.

The civil war in Spain occurred at a time of great political and economic change in Europe. The Great Depression which began in 1929 had ravaged the economies of the industrial nations, resulting in unprecedented levels of unemployment. Traditional political parties appeared to be incapable of solving society's problems, and so people looked to new political ideologies for answers. In Russia in 1917, the Bolsheviks had seized power and set about establishing a communist society, which later became the Soviet Union. Two years later, in 1919, they set up the Comintern, an association of national communist parties whose purpose was to promote world revolution. In reality the Comintern acted as an organ through which the Soviet Union could control the international communist movement. After emerging victorious in the Russian Civil War, the Bolsheviks set about exporting their brand of communism to other countries during the 1920s and 1930s.

Under Vladimir Ilyich Lenin (1870–1924; leader of Soviet State 1917–24) and then Josef Stalin (1878–1953; leader of Soviet Union, 1924–53), this government was feared in Western and Eastern Europe because it represented political revolution and the destruction of the existing social order. European governments were naturally worried by this prospect. For a time in 1919, after the trauma of World War I (1914–18), it had seemed that communist regimes might establish themselves in many other European countries. Indeed, in the 1920s and 1930s, communist groups were involved in civil wars and political violence in various European states.

At the other end of the political spectrum stood fascism. This ultra right-wing ideology was spawned in the years after World War I, when nationalist parties sought to right supposed wrongs that had been committed against their homelands. This was especially true in defeated Germany, which seethed with resentment about both losing the war and losing territory to the new nations created by the detested Treaty of Versailles. In Italy, too, the failure of the government to maintain order led to violence between Benito Mussolini's fascists and the communists, a problem solved when Mussolini came to power in 1922 and set about establishing a totalitarian state.

Whereas communism wanted to unite the world's working class in economic and social equality (in theory at least), fascism sought to establish a centrist repressive state with an ultra nationalist ideology violently opposed to liberal democracy, communism and socialism. Fascism encouraged the glorification of war and the armed forces, the persecution of political opponents, extreme nationalism shading into overt racism, and the belief that only nations that were militarily strong and 'tough' could get ahead, or indeed deserved to survive. All this was closely connected to a visceral fear of communism, which was seen as the biggest menace to their essentially conservative view of society.

According to fascism all means were justified to preserve the nation, or a particular race. In Germany, Adolf Hitler's Nazi Party came to power in January 1933. German fascism, or national socialism, also promoted the idea of 'racial purity', the belief that the 'Aryan race' must be protected from, and be allowed to expand at the expense of, 'lesser' races, especially the Jews and the Slavs who populated Eastern Europe and the Soviet Union.

As soon as they gained power in Germany, the Nazis embarked on a campaign to reclaim all the lands that had been 'lost' as a result of the Treaty of Versailles. In March 1935, Hitler renounced the treaty's disarmament clauses and reintroduced military conscription. In the same month German troops marched into the Saar region of Germany, which had been detached from Germany by the Treaty of Versailles. In November 1935, the Nazis introduced the so-called Nuremberg Laws, which reduced German Jews to second-class citizens. In March 1936, German troops marched into the demilitarized Rhineland.

In Italy, Mussolini sought to become a 20th-century Julius Caesar by increasing the size of the Italian overseas empire. In October 1935, to the disgust of most of the international community, he ordered his troops to invade Ethiopia. The ill-armed Ethiopians proved no match for tanks and aircraft, and the country soon became part of Italian East Africa. The League of Nations, led by Britain, condemned the invasion and voted to impose sanctions on Italy. Germany did not condemn Italy's aggression, with the result that Hitler won the gratitude of the Italian dictator. Henceforth the two fascist powers would become ever closer allies.

It was against this background that civil war broke out in Spain in July 1936. The country had been wracked by strife between political extremists on the right and left since the 1920s. The onset of the Great Depression in 1929 aggravated these divisions still further, with the result that the country's centrist republic was doomed by 1931. The left-wing Popular Front won the 1936 elections, prompting the launching of a coup against the government by right-wing military officers in Spanish Morocco. The coup was led by the Army of Africa's commander, General Francisco Franco, and when it broke out there were immediate revolts by the garrisons at Cádiz, Seville, Burgos, Saragossa, Huesca and other places on the Spanish mainland.

Initially, the Republican government was in a strong position to crush the coup. It held the heart of the country's communications network, the capital Madrid (where the nation's gold reserves were stored), plus most of the other large urban centres. And the strongest rebel force, the Army of Africa, was marooned in Morocco. Between 18 and 20 July the rebellion was crushed in Madrid and Barcelona. The right-wing Nationalists faced defeat, and in desperation they appealed for help from Hitler and Mussolini. On 28 July 1936, each decided independently to aid the Nationalists by providing transport aircraft to ferry the Army of Africa across the Straits of Gibraltar to southern Spain. The coup had now turned into a full-blown civil war.

When the coup had taken place, the Republican government had requested military aid from Britain and France. However, both countries were reluctant and instead proposed and established a Non-Intervention Treaty in September 1936. The purpose of the treaty was to contain the war within Spain by prohibiting the signatories from supplying weapons to either side. Two of the countries that signed the treaty were Germany and Italy, though they instantly ignored it and continued to support the Nationalists. Only Britain abided by the agreement, while France prevaricated between lukewarm support for the Spanish Republic and enforcing the arms embargo. Thus though Russia sent the most aid to the Republic, most of the supplies were confiscated by the French at the border with Spain.

With hindsight the attitude of the Western democracies might appear weak; however, their position must be placed in context. The politicians running Britain and France in the 1930s had experienced the full horrors of World War I, a war in which there had been years of fighting and millions of deaths with no decisive result. France in particular had suffered severely, and a major objective of French foreign policy was to ensure that there would no repeat of the 1914–18 conflict. Almost instinctively, French and British politicians believed that Germans and Italians must share their feelings about the need to avoid war. While it was true that most Germans and Italians did not want war, Hitler particularly and many of his senior Nazi Party colleagues were actually enthused by the idea of war. Hitler had experienced what he recognized as the best moments of his life up to then when he had served in the German Army in World War I. The Nazis also viewed war as a purifying force, in that it would sift out the weak to enable the strong to emerge victorious.

In addition, there were many conservative politicians in Britain and France who viewed Republican Spain as akin to Stalin's Soviet

Union, a nation they both detested and feared. For centuries, a conservative Russia had been a major part of the balance of power in Europe, and a natural ally of France against Germany. Now, the new Soviet Union was (particularly from the perspective of Britain and France) a dangerous, rogue element in international affairs, and one certainly not to be trusted. And what of the Soviet Union? At first Moscow had ignored a plea from Madrid for aid, and had backed the British and French policy of non-intervention. For his part, Stalin had to deal with the large-scale upheavals occurring inside the Soviet Union. Internationally he was more concerned with containing an expansionist Nazi Germany than preventing Spain falling to the fascists. He certainly had no desire to alienate Britain and France by backing the Spanish Republic. Indeed, he wanted the USSR and the two Western democracies to enter into a defensive alliance to contain Germany.

However, it soon became clear that non-intervention was not working, and that the Nationalists were receiving large amounts of military aid from Germany and Italy. Stalin therefore decided the Republic would soon be defeated if it received no outside help. He ordered military aid to be sent to the Republicans, though it remained covert as he was still wary of alienating Britain and France.

Soviet tanks, aircraft, weapons and ammunition arrived just in time. The Nationalists had taken control of the south and west of the country by August 1936, but were turned back from the gates of Madrid in November. The Republic, for the moment, had been saved. Soviet aid did not come cheap, however: the entire Spanish gold reserve was shipped to the USSR for 'safekeeping'. And Moscow made sure that the Republicans paid top prices for the weapons and equipment they purchased from the Soviets.

Outside international diplomacy, the outbreak of the Spanish Civil War had galvanized thousands of supporters of the Republic. Communists, anarchists, trade unionists, anti-fascists and idealists decided to go to Spain to defend democracy against Franco's forces. These foreign volunteers would eventually be formed into International Brigades, but prior to their establishment there were already hundreds of foreigners fighting in Spanish workers' militias. Most enlisted in Barcelona and joined the anarchist, communist and Marxist POUM (Partido Obrero de Unificación Marxista) militias during the first weeks of the war. They numbered around 1,500 in total, but the numbers of foreign volunteers increased rapidly with the decision of the Soviet-backed Comintern, on 18 September 1936, to form the International Brigades. Only the Comintern, with links to communist parties throughout the world, had the organizational ability to recruit large numbers of foreign volunteers. And a key role would be provided by the French Communist Party (PCF) in actually getting volunteers into Spain.

In Spain itself Albacete was selected as the base for the International Brigades, with the first volunteers arriving there on 13 October 1936. Two days later the first Soviet arms ship docked in Cartagena. On 22 October the Republican government formally recognized the International Brigades as being part of the Republican Army (though they retained their own commanders and organization). From the beginning the brigades contained a high proportion of Communist Party members: 80–90 percent of the Germans, around 85 percent of the Latin Americans, 75 percent of the Polish and Balkan volunteers, and 60 percent of French volunteers were members of the party. In the end over 50 countries supplied volunteers to the International Brigades – around 35,000 volunteers in total. The largest contingent was French – around 9,000. There were also 5,000 Germans and Austrians, 3,000 Poles, 3,000 Italians, 2,800 Americans, 1,800 British, 1,600 Belgians, 1,660 Yugoslavs and 1,500 Czechs. Many of these were already political exiles from their own countries, where right-wing regimes had forced them to flee abroad. For many in the International Brigades, fighting fascism in Spain was symbolic of fighting oppression across the whole European continent. Mention must also be made of Jewish volunteers, who comprised up to 7,000 of the International Brigades as a whole (a staggering 20 percent of all recruits).

Not all foreign volunteers fighting for the Republic were members of the Communist Party, though. Many could be found in the anarchist-syndicalist National Confederation of Labour (CNT), or the POUM. The author George Orwell fought with the latter, which numbered 10,000 members in total, of which 700 were foreign volunteers. The vast majority of foreign volunteers, however, served in the International Brigades.

The first unit was the 11th International Brigade, formed in October 1936, followed by the 12th International Brigade (formed November 1936), 13th International Brigade (formed December 1936), 14th International Brigade (formed December 1936), 15th International Brigade (formed January 1937), 86th International Brigade (formed February 1938), 129th International Brigade (formed February 1938), and the 150th International Brigade (formed May 1937). The majority of British volunteers fought in the British Battalion as part of the 15th International Brigade.

Taking the 15th International Brigade as typical, in January 1937 it was organized as follows. It contained four battalions: the British Battalion, the Yugoslav Dimitrov Battalion, the Franco-Belgian Battalion and the American Abraham Lincoln Battalion. The British Battalion was made up of four companies: three infantry companies and a machine-gun company. The battalion numbered 500 men, giving the brigade a total strength of 2,000 troops. At the same time there were 250 other British volunteers serving in different Republican units. One aspect of the organization of the International Brigades, which reflected Soviet influence, was the appointment of political commissars. These individuals worked alongside military officers to ensure the political and ideological zeal of the volunteers. Thus in the British Battalion the battalion commander at the beginning of 1937 was Wilf McCartney. Working alongside him was the battalion political commissar, Dave Springhall, the secretary of the London district of the Communist Party and a member of the party's political bureau who had studied at the Lenin School in Moscow. McCartney also had excellent left-wing credentials, having been imprisoned in Parkhurst Prison for spying for Russia. In general the International Brigades, composed of foreigners who had travelled to Spain with the sole intention of fighting fascists, were highly motivated. As such they were often used as shock troops on the battlefield, either to lead an attack or plug a hole in defences. This invariably meant they suffered high casualties. An estimated third of all foreign volunteers were killed during the war; indeed, it is reckoned that only around 7 percent of the International Brigades left Spain unscathed. Different nationalities suffered higher losses. For example, the casualty rate among American, British and French fighters was around 30 percent, while among the Germans it was 40 percent, among the Yugoslavs 48 percent and among the Hungarians 42 percent. One theory for this disparity is that those volunteers who were refugees from right-wing regimes were considered to be more reliable, and more expendable.

The majority of those who fought in the International Brigades did so as infantry armed with bolt-action rifles. Many brigaders had Soviet rifles, which had five-round magazines (though some rifles used by the Republicans were single-shot weapons). Like most rifles of that time, they had an effective range of around 500m. Beyond this range their effectiveness dropped considerably, the more so if those firing them were poorly trained. For the International Brigades in general, ammunition shortages reduced their firepower on the battlefield still further. Machine guns were much more effective, being fire support weapons that were able to lay down fire over specific areas to prevent enemy movement. In offensive operations they provided support for advancing infantry. The rate of fire, over 500 rounds per minute, and range, around 1500m, made them deadly against infantry. As both sides were to discover in the war, a well-sited machine gun in the hands of an experienced gunner could cut an infantry attack to ribbons in seconds.

Handguns tended to be fairly useless at ranges beyond 50m and were usually carried as symbols of officer rank. It was similar with hand grenades, which had a range of around 30m (depending on the strength of the thrower).

The armoured fighting vehicles used by both sides in Spain were in the main light tanks, which were armed with machine guns and small-calibre guns. The Germans sent 200 tanks to fight for Franco, a mix of Panzer I and II light tanks. The former was armed with two machine guns and the latter with a 20mm cannon and a machine gun. Italian tanks were really tankettes: light vehicles with a crew of two and armed only with machine guns. The L3/33 was armed with a single 6.5mm machine gun while the L3/35 tankette had two 6.5mm machine guns. The best tank in Spain was on the Republican side and was the Russian-supplied T-25, which had a 45mm cannon.

Ground-attack aircraft and bombers could wreak havoc on the battlefield, especially against infantry. Fighters and ground-attack aircraft could strafe enemy troops with machine-gun fire and decimate men and vehicles with bombs, while bombers could rain devastation on towns and cities behind the lines. The Basque town of Guernica, for example, was bombed by 26 German aircraft in April 1937. In a matter of minutes over 1000 civilians were killed and 80 percent of the houses were either destroyed or seriously damaged. It was a horrifying foretaste of what was to come in World War II.

The mystique of the International Brigades was established early in the war, when the 11th and 12th International Brigades took part in the siege of Madrid in November 1936. Their baptism of fire was a brutal affair, and after two days of fighting half the 11th Brigade were dead. The 12th Brigade also suffered heavy casualties. In fact it was not the intervention of the International Brigades that had saved the city; the militias and population had turned back the fascists. But the Brigades' bravery and example inspired Republicans at home and supporters abroad. Recruitment soared, and from then on the brigades would fight in all of the civil war's major battles. Yet, after the victorious Battle of Guadalajara in March 1937, in which the International Brigades played a crucial part, they were hardly mentioned in the Republican press. The Republican government was desperate to win support from the Western democracies, and did not want to draw attention to foreign involvement in its cause, especially after the Non-Intervention Committee had prohibited all recruitment for Spain in February 1937. In addition, Republicans were keen to emphasize the 'national' element of their struggle. This patriotism sat ill at ease with the presence of an internationalist and communist-led force on Spanish soil. Finally, the Republic's Popular Army was also growing in capability, which further sidelined the International Brigades.

In September 1938, in a final attempt to win support from the Western democracies, and indeed save his government, Republican President Juan Negrín announced his government's decision to withdraw all foreign fighters from the Republican zone (at that time there were 12,673 foreign volunteers left in the Popular Army). The farewell parade of the International Brigades took place in Barcelona at the end of October 1938. Six months later the Republic fell to Franco's Nationalists.

Though they had failed to prevent a fascist takeover in Spain, the men and women of the International Brigades could feel justifiably proud of what they had achieved. With hindsight their efforts are all the more remarkable when one considers that in the 1930s it was no small matter to make the decision to travel to a foreign country to fight for a political cause. In an age when the majority of the population did not undertake foreign travel, one must marvel at the courage of individuals who took the decision to go to Spain. Admiration is increased when the age of volunteers is considered: most were in their twenties, and some were teenagers. Being in the main working-class men and women, they would have had little if any money, especially if they were unemployed. And when they arrived in Spain they faced death on the battlefield.

Most of the accounts in this book are taken from the Spanish Civil War Sound Archive Collection held at the Imperial War Museum, London. As such, they are mostly concerned with the activities of the British Battalion, 15th International Brigade. These recordings were made in the mid-1970s, and sadly all those who were interviewed are no longer with us.

Although each account is different, the qualities that they all share shine through: tenacity, fortitude, humility, an absolute belief that their cause was just, and, above all, courage. Reading the eyewitness accounts, it quickly becomes apparent that the brigaders for the most part had no military training, were poorly supplied with arms and ammunition, often went without rations and pay, and had threadbare clothing. However, they carried on fighting, often for long periods and in atrocious weather conditions. Many were killed, most were wounded or suffered debilitating illnesses. But after recovering they went back to the front.

The first-hand accounts in this book do not include those from famous authors or poets who either took part in the Spanish Civil War or who observed it at close quarters, such as George Orwell, Ernest Hemingway and T. S. Eliot. There are two reasons for this. First, the writings of these individuals are readily available both in print and on the internet. Indeed, Orwell's *Homage to Catalonia* is available to download in its entirety. Secondly, despite the enduring myth that the International Brigades were full of young poets and writers, the reality is that they were overwhelmingly composed of working-class volunteers. It is therefore appropriate that those voices should be heard. This is their story, in their own words.

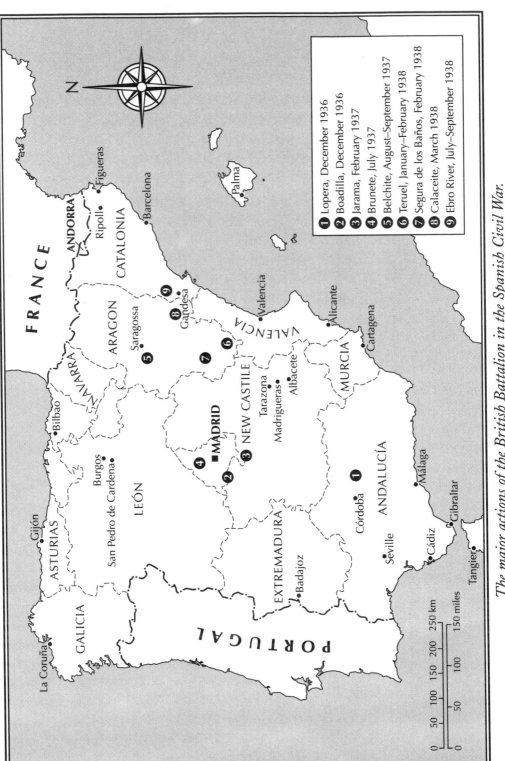

The major actions of the British Battalion in the Spanish Civil War.

Legend:
1 Lopera, December 1936
2 Boadilla, December 1936
3 Jarama, February 1937
4 Brunete, July 1937
5 Belchite, August–September 1937
6 Teruel, January–February 1938
7 Segura de los Baños, February 1938
8 Calaceite, March 1938
9 Ebro River, July–September 1938

Reasons for Volunteering

The reasons that thousands of individuals decided to go to Spain were many and varied. Obviously the desire to fight fascism ranks highest, and the decision of the Comintern to support the Republic meant communists across the world would be mobilized to fight in Spain. Also, the Spanish Civil War inflamed political passions across Europe. Spain was the focal point of international politics, with Germany and Italy on one side and Soviet Russia on the other, and with the Western democracies on the sidelines. For many working-class people, to be part of such an historic event was also a reason to go to Spain. For idealists, especially, Spain was an irresistible attraction.

For a large part of the European working class the issue was clear: in Spain the fascist one-party state system confronted a left-wing coalition of workers and peasants. If the left won then Spain would become a proletarian paradise, similar to the one that many believed (wrongly as it happens) existed in the Soviet Union. In reality, Marxism and Leninism in the USSR had been supplanted by Stalinism, a ruthless centralized system akin to Hitler's Germany. Stalinism tolerated no dissent, as anarchists and Trotskyists would discover to their cost while fighting for the Spanish Republic, and where Stalin's People's Commissariat for Internal Affairs (NKVD) operated behind Republican lines.

But that was in the future. For thousands of foreign volunteers, Spain was where the battle between good and evil would be fought. And victory would bring about a better world. Abe Osheroff, an American citizen, was born in 1915 to parents who had fled from the extreme poverty and anti-Semitism of Czarist Russia. Osheroff was then 'raised in an atmosphere mildly socialistic' in a Brooklyn ghetto of New York, where people 'worked together to build trade unions'.[1] At an early age, he became a 'radical humanist' who was 'deeply moved by anything unjust, unfair' and realized that 'it would take drastic changes to improve the world'.[2] Osheroff was a pacifist, but he still went to Spain to fight.

Across the Atlantic, in Britain, others shared the dream of a better world. Alun Menai Williams was a Welsh miner in the 1930s. He lived in South Wales, in the same region where he was born and grew up. When he finished school, and against his parents' wishes, he decided to become a miner. During his work as a miner an accident left him buried alive for several hours. After being pulled from the rubble he decided that he had had enough of mining and set off for London in search of a better life. His childhood friend, Billy, had introduced him to the anti-fascist movement and went to Spain before Alun. 'The reasons why I volunteered to go to Spain are complex. I was unemployed, a bit of an adventurer, a dedicated anti-fascist.'[3]

Perhaps more than any other group, the Jews realized the danger that Nazi Germany and fascist Italy posed. The German concentration camp at Dachau had opened in 1933, and gradually Germany's Jews were being excluded from society. Communist and Jew Sam Russell (real name Manassah Lesser) had battled Mosley's Blackshirts on the streets of London before he went to Spain. 'The word went out to stop Mosley marching through the East End. There was the most violent anti-Semitism among the police; they sympathized totally with the blackshirts to "get these fucking Jews out of the way". At university I did something that I always have great difficulty explaining ... I joined the OTC, the officer training corps. They were so hard up they'd take anybody. I came across some phrase in Lenin and I've never been able to find it since ... a working class that doesn't learn the use of arms deserves to be slaves.'[4]

Lou Kenton's Jewish parents fled the Ukraine during the pogroms. He was the first of nine children to be born in Britain, in 1908. They shared a three-roomed flat in Stepney, east London. His father, a tailor, died of TB. After leaving school at 14, Kenton got a job in a paper factory. 'My mother wanted me to work in a shop but I hated it. Jews were constantly being attacked [by Blackshirts]. On my first day at the factory, I was involved in seven fights. I reacted very badly to being called a "Jew bastard".'[5] One evening, Kenton and his first wife, an Austrian nurse who fled Hitler's Germany in 1933, attended an anti-fascist meeting. 'We were so inspired that we walked all night talking about it and having a coffee in every place we stopped. We got to a coffee shop at about four in the morning and we looked at each other and said: "We've got to go."'[6]

Canute Frankson

African American volunteer from the United States. Automobile worker. Served in the Abraham Lincoln Battalion, June 1937–July 1938.

Writing to a friend from Albacete in Spain, July 1937.

I'm sure that by this time you are still waiting for a detailed explanation of what has this international struggle to do with my being here. Since this is a war between whites who for centuries have held us in slavery, and have heaped every kind of insult and abuse upon us, segregated and Jim-Crowed us; why I, a Negro who have fought through these years for the rights of my people, am here in Spain today?

Because we are no longer an isolated minority group fighting hopelessly against an immense giant. Because, my dear, we have joined with, and become an active part of, a great progressive force, on whose shoulders rests the responsibility of saving human civilization from the planned destruction of a small group of degenerates gone mad in their lust for power. Because if we crush fascism here we'll save our people in America, and in other parts of the world from the vicious persecution, wholesale imprisonment and slaughter which the Jewish people suffered and are suffering under Hitler's fascist heels.

All we have to do is to think of the lynching of our people. We can but look back at the pages of American history stained with the blood of Negroes; stink with the burning bodies of our people hanging from trees; bitter with the groans of our tortured loved ones from whose living bodies ears, fingers, toes have been cut for souvenirs – living bodies into which red-hot pokers have been thrust. All because of a hate created in the minds of men and women by their masters who keep us all under their heels while they suck our blood, while they live in their bed of ease by exploiting us.

But these people who howl like hungry wolves for our blood, must we hate them? Must we keep the flame which these masters kindled constantly fed? Are these men and women responsible for the programmes of their masters, and the conditions which force them to such degraded depths? I think not. They are tools in the hands of unscrupulous masters. These same people are as hungry as we are. They live in dives and wear rags the same as we do. They, too, are robbed by the masters, and their faces kept down in the filth of a decayed system. They are our fellow men. Soon, and very soon, they and we will understand. Soon, many Angelo Herndons [African American communist organiser] will rise from among them, and from among us, and will lead us both against those who live by the stench of our burnt flesh. We will crush them. We will build us a new society – a society of peace and plenty. There will be no color line, no Jim-Crow trains, no lynching. That is why, my dear, I'm here in Spain.[7]

Tommy Nicholson

Volunteer from Glasgow, Scotland. Served in the British Battalion, 15th International Brigade, May–November 1937.

Some of the young comrades want to know why I and others like me joined the International Brigades and went to fight in Spain. From the first rising of the Spanish workers, our hearts and minds were in Spain. We fought alongside them, even though we weren't there.

I worked in the Govan wireworks in 1937. In Glasgow then you couldn't but be active in the class struggle. Poverty was rife. Glasgow had a strong workers' movement then as now and we all fervently believed in the emancipation of the working class across the world.

I was anxious to get to Spain. Like many another I believed that the whole future of humanity was being fought out there. Either socialism or fascism would win through. That's why we felt that we had to go. Spain became your lifeblood.

But I was not a member of the Communist Party, having disagreements then as I do now. So I wasn't allowed to go. But, come 1937, they relented. There were conditions attached of course.

The conditions were that I should not discuss politics. Needless to say, I accepted and went on my way to fight for what I believed in then, and still believe in just as fervently now. For socialism. For the revolution. For a society where the workers rule their own lives and where production is undertaken to meet the needs of all.[8]

James Lardner

Volunteer from Long Island, United States. Served as a corporal and squad leader with the Abraham Lincoln Battalion, April–September 1938 (died following his capture in the Sierra Pandols in September 1938).

Letter to his mother explaining his reasons for going to Spain.

... Because I believe that fascism is wrong and must be exterminated, and that liberal democracy or more probably communism is right. Because my joining the I.B. [International Brigades] might have an effect on the amendment of the neutrality act in the United States. Because after the war is over I shall be a more effective anti-fascist. Because in my ambitious quest for knowledge in all fields, I cannot afford in this age to overlook war.

Because I shall come into contact with a lot of communists, who are very good company and from whom I expect to learn things. Because I am mentally lazy and should like to do some physical work for a change. Because I need something remarkable in my background to make up for my unfortunate self-consciousness in social relations. Because I am tired of working for the *Herald Tribune* in particular and newspapers in general.

Because I think it will be good for my soul. Because there is a girl in Paris who will have to learn that my presence is not necessary to her existence. Because I want to impress various people, Bill for one. Because I hope to find material for some writing, probably a play. Because I want to improve my Spanish as well as my French. Because I want to know what it is like to be afraid of something and I want to see how other people react to danger. Because there may be a chance to do some reading and I won't have to wear a necktie. Because I should like once more to get in good physical condition.

The first four reasons and the ninth, especially the first, are the most important ones in my opinion, but you may decide for yourself. I have also considered a few reasons why I should not join the army, such as that I might get seriously wounded or killed and that I shall cause you many weeks of worry. I am sorry for your sake that they are not enough to dissuade me. If it is any comfort to you at all, I still hate violence and cruelty and suffering and if I survive this war do not expect to take any dangerous part in the next.

If you still consider me one of your sons, you can send me an occasional letter and possibly a package now and then. My address here, I think, will be in the care of the Brigadas Internacionales, but for a while I think it will be simpler to communicate through the Sheeans. Anything edible would be appreciated, milk, chocolate or raisins, or anything in cans that does not require preparation.

Love
Jim[9]

Frederick Arthur Thomas

*Volunteer from London, England. Served with the Anti-Tank Battery, 15th International Brigade, May 1937–October 1938 (*see plate 7*).*

We organized a local Aid Spain Committee in Hackney and that meant we held meetings in the neighbourhood generally. We organized collections in which we went round the houses, knocking on doors and asking people to give money and tins of food, anything that they could. Sometimes we got food, sometimes we got money, we even got the odd blanket or two. We had street collections in which we would go round with a cart. We went round to market places. We went to Ridley Road market where the stallholders were extremely sympathetic. There were a lot of Jewish people in that street. I honestly believe that the Aid Spain Movement was probably the most popular and one which aroused more feeling than perhaps any other single issue in this country before or since … I had first felt that I should go without any romanticism. I felt I was not able to sit back and content myself with collecting tins of food and money, or speaking at meetings, that was not enough.

The situation in Spain became terribly serious very quickly. In November 1936 it was touch and go whether Madrid would be captured by the fascists. If they captured Madrid, I should imagine it would have had a tremendous effect on the whole outcome of the war, despite the fact that the government had gone down to Valencia. I felt that what I was doing was not enough and the situation in Spain was reaching a dreadful state, and I simply wanted to be in on whatever could be done to combat fascism.

I was not then and never have been anything of a hero. I think on balance I have always been a timid soul in fact. I didn't go out of my way to pick fights. On the other hand, it is equally impossible for anyone to knowingly put himself into a position where his life is threatened or where mutilation is threatened. Until you are in that situation it is utterly impossible to imagine it, no matter what vivid descriptions others might give.[10]

Albert Charlesworth

Volunteer from Manchester, England. Served as a runner and postman with the British Battalion, 15th International Brigade, December 1936– September 1937 and December 1937–October 1938.

My name is Albert Charlesworth and I was born in 1915 in Delph near Oldham, Lancashire. Soon after I was born my father was killed in World War I. I was too young to know what politics was about in those days, I was only about two and a half, but I can distinctly remember while I was still a toddler, before I started going to school even, my mother went to Labour Party dances held at the Mechanic's Hall, and afterwards taking us to supper at the Labour Club, and as I became older I went to the Labour Club every day without fail. Whenever elections came up I was involved in any work that I could do. Addressing envelopes, canvassing, anything whatsoever, so as time went by I became more and more involved with the Labour Party.

I left school and went to work at Measurements Ltd to serve an apprenticeship in engineering. I was still serving that apprenticeship when the war in Spain started, and as I had been indoctrinated from childbirth almost into the Labour movement, I was naturally very interested in the war in Spain.

I was at that time and still am inclined to side with any little party or any little thing where I think an injustice is being done. This, I think, is what took me to Spain, it is just something in my nature I think that compels me to go to the help of anyone who is of just cause and who is in distress. The German and the Italian involvement made me feel strongly. I knew of that before I went to Spain and that is what made it so unjust. Not just the Italian and the German involvement, the whole thing was unjust in the first place, the whole thing was absolutely unjust for a military man to try and overthrow the legal government, and especially when that legal government was a government of the people. Even at that early age I knew that.

There were no other recruits from Delph. It's only a small village. I volunteered alone and went alone. It was discussed down at the Labour Club, but I didn't discuss it with my mother. My mother only found out from the Labour Club members. I never told her. It wasn't until the day before I left that she knew. I thought she would have tried to have stopped me. I was only 19 at the time and naturally I was a minor, and she could have stopped me if she had wanted to. I discussed it with members of the Labour Club, and at that time a lot of them had been involved in World War I and they were mainly elderly people, and their attitude was good, go. So I went. There was no opposition.[11]

Bernard McKenna

Volunteer from Manchester, England. Served as a signaller and infantryman with the British Battalion, 15th International Brigade, February 1937– March 1938. Prisoner of war, March 1938–October 1938.

I was an active member of the YCL [Young Communist League] and had been for a number of years. I think I was idealistic, but what particularly got me, and probably others as well, was that we were repressed by the spread of fascism and things were getting worse. When the war broke out in Spain I thought, well, this is another step to fascism in Europe. We did all the usual things that were going on in Manchester. We were pretty active in getting medical supplies, food supplies and going to political meetings, but personally it didn't seem enough to me, and one or two of the YCL members agreed and also went. I said to the party secretary that I would like to go. He asked if I had any military experience. I said none at all. I had served in the local unit of the Territorial Army as a cadet when I was 15 or 16. I said that's all the experience I have got. A few days later they said yes, and off I went.

I had no personal commitments and nothing to stand in my way. I think the decision sort of arose naturally out of the situation. I was working at the time. I was a warehouse clerk in a small textile firm in Manchester. It wasn't really an important job, not even well paid. I didn't think I was sacrificing anything by going. I was 21 when I went.

I didn't expect it to be a picnic. I didn't expect to gain anything out of it. I think you see it through idealistic spectacles. You do it not for the future cost, you do it on impulse. For me it was something that developed over six months. In the meantime people had gone as early as September and October [1936], when the earlier brigades were formed. I felt so helpless at doing hardly anything here that would be effective. I thought it would be more effective going. Looking back it is somewhat naive, but that is how I felt. I dared not say I was going to my family. I compromised, I didn't even tell my friends ... As far as my parents were concerned, I got as far as London and posted a letter from there announcing that I was going and not to worry about me. Even in those days we were approached by reporters from the *Daily Mail* who were chasing up the families of volunteers. They tried to make out that it was a wicked conspiracy in which innocent young youths were talked into going. I don't think they got much satisfaction, but I remember when I came back seeing a very bad picture of myself in the *Daily Mail* with a very prejudiced report calling us deluded youths.[12]

Arthur Nicoll

Volunteer from Dundee, Scotland. Member of the Communist Party. Served as a political commissar with the Anti-Tank Battery, 15th International Brigade, February–October 1937.

Before I went to Spain I knew plenty of what was happening. I didn't know much about Spain and the Spanish people, but by reading I knew about the early people that were in Spain at the time when the uprising had started, such as Ralph Fox. I had read about that and the role the party was playing in Spain. I was very interested. I thought, what is the use of talking about it unless you are prepared to do something about it? This is what drove me to Spain, this question of you have to do something about it. I believe that it has been a great help to the British working class, this struggle in Spain. I know that there was a terrific amount of activity in Dundee on Spain. We had an Aid Spain Committee which was really marvellous. I've got a pamphlet at home, a programme of early February–March 1939 of a memorial service in Dundee for the people that were killed in Spain.[13]

Joe Norman

Volunteer from Manchester and Bolton, England. Served as the Communist Party organizer with the British Battalion, 15th International Brigade, July 1937–March 1938.

At the Lenin School [in Moscow] I learned political economics. How to debate, how to plan a speech. All useful stuff. After six months there I came back and did some political meetings up and down Lancashire. I became a *Daily Worker* organizer in Wigan but I wasn't happy. I wanted to go to Spain. I was a trained sailor and I wanted to use my skills there. Eventually we had a man called George Brown, the leader of the Lancashire party. He went to Spain and he was killed at Jarama. He represented the Lancashire district in Spain. I said it looks as if we have to send someone else from the Lancashire district. They chose me to go after a bit of prompting from me. I had no opposition from my family. In fact they were rather proud.

We had been receiving news about what was going on in Spain constantly, in the *Morning Star* and the *Daily Worker*. Most of the news outside the *Morning Star* and the *Daily Worker* was confusing, they covered it up with religious issues and atrocities on the Republican side and so on, but they didn't mention the atrocities on the fascist side.

I was a keen anti-fascist, very keen. Not political, just anti-fascist, from a Trade Union point of view mostly. Although I was in the party I was mainly a militant trade unionist with a keen anti-fascist outlook, and I would do anything to combat fascism in Britain and anywhere else. I would do today.[14]

Fred Copeman

Volunteer from London, England. Served with the Machine Gun-Company and as commander of the British Battalion, 15th International Brigade, October 1936–December 1937.

I was living with Kath and Sandy Duncan. He was an ex-officer in World War I where he got wounded. He was a school teacher, a really good lad, and Kath Duncan was someone like La Pasionaria [Dolores Ibárruri Gómez] in England in those early days, a great speaker. I lived with them and their mother, a Scottish middle-class family. Of course when the Spanish Civil

War started, I was doing public meetings almost every night for the [communist] party and I had a talk with Harry Pollitt. There were no communists involved, they were all students who went on their own, they were called the International Column. Some decision was made somewhere that they would be accepted but they kind of drifted in. There was no real control and anybody who wanted to help just went and helped out.

I read in the *Daily Worker* every day about what was happening. This column became more and more important and it started to get headlines. International volunteers were coming from all over the world and I thought, I ought to go. I didn't want to go because I was seeing this good-looking Scottish girl. I think I was 24 then and she was 17. She had everything in the right places. She was lovely, with red hair and lovely skin. Not having much to do with women all my life, I can only remember a couple. She was one and my wife was the other. She was a student and I admire educated people in a kind of private way. If a woman has good looks and is intelligent and clean, three things that very few women have all of, if you meet one, well, you grab it. Well we were up at Telegraph Hill, it was a little park really, and she said to me: 'Why don't you go to Spain?' I said: 'Well, why don't you go to bloody Spain? I'll go if you will go.' Anyway the next day I thought, I am not having a woman tell me what to do, so I went up to King Street [Communist Party of Great Britain headquarters in London] and said to Harry Pollitt I ought to go out. He said, 'Don't go out on your bloody own. Do a job first. Go around the country and get recruits. Try and get 500 and you will have a whole bloody battalion'. So away I went.

I went all over the country, to Scotland and Wales, to all the big halls, they were packed out to see the International Column. I was aiming at 500 and got 470. I said we are waiting too bloody long, Harry, it will be all over by the time we get there. So away we went. It was a simple method. They got us passports, we all met at Waterloo Station [London] and then away we went on a boat over to France. [15]

Notes

1 http://www.geocities.com/roav1945/osheroff.html.
2 Ibid.
3 *Socialist Worker* interview, 22 July 2006.
4 *Guardian* interview, 10 November 2000.
5 Ibid.
6 Ibid.
7 http://www.english.uiuc.edu/maps/scw/letters.htm.
8 *Socialist Worker* interview, 22 July 2006.
9 http://www.alba-valb.org/resources/document-library/document-of-the-month-september-2007/at_download/albita-file.
10 Thomas, Frederick Arthur, Imperial War Museum Sound Archive (IWMSA), London, Ref 9396/8, Reel 3.
11 Charlesworth, Albert, IWMSA, London, Ref 9427/4, Reel 1.
12 McKenna, Bernard, IWMSA, London, Ref 847/5, Reel 1.
13 Nicoll, Arthur, IWMSA, London, Ref 817/3, Reel 1.
14 Norman, Joe, IWMSA, London, Ref 818/4, Reel 2.
15 Copeman, Fred, IWMSA, London, Ref 794/13, Reel 1.

Enlistment

Due to the Non-Intervention Agreement and the fact that many political parties in the Western democracies sympathized with Franco's Nationalists, enlisting in the International Brigades was far from straightforward for individuals, especially in Britain and the United States, where it was actually illegal to enlist in a foreign army. There were no recruitment offices where volunteers could visit and sign on the dotted line.

Under the direction of the Comintern, Communist Parties organized the recruitment of volunteers. The recruitment process itself involved local Communist Party organizers making approaches to volunteers, who would then be interviewed and warned of the dangers involved in going to Spain. If volunteers were not members of the party, then they would be checked up on by trusted party members to vet their suitability. However, not all those in the International Brigades were communists. Danish Trotskyist Åge Kjelsø, for example, was not welcomed by the Communist Party. Indeed, he had been thrown off a ship taking him to Spain because he had made 'anti-Stalinist statements'.

It is important to stress that not all foreign volunteers fighting for the Republic were communists. There were also liberals, social democrats, socialists, anarchists and, of course, Trotskyists. And the clash between Trotsky and Stalin was continued among their respective supporters in Spain. Leon Trotsky advocated 'permanent revolution', a doctrine rejected by Stalin and which resulted in Trotsky's exile from the Soviet Union in 1929. But he continued to agitate and intrigue while in exile, resulting in his being sentenced to death in absentia by the

Soviets. The Moscow-backed Comintern was obviously aghast at Trotskyists fighting for the Spanish Republic, and it was also suspicious of any who weren't communists. And this included the anarchists.

On the eve of the civil war the anarcho-syndicalist Confederación Nacional del Trabajo (CNT) had around 1 million members and had as its stated aim the overthrow of capitalism. When war broke out the CNT was in control of much of Republican Spain, and was particularly strong in Barcelona. But the CNT was not the Bolsheviks; it had no economic plan, no experience of state apparatus, and no programme for exercising power. However, the Comintern-backed communists did, and when they had successfully organized the defence of Madrid in 1936, with the aid of the communist-controlled International Brigades and the support of the Soviet Union, they took advantage of their new-found prestige. The communists began to withhold weapons and ammunition from the workers' militias of the CNT and the Partido Obrero de Unificación Marxista (POUM), a small anti-Stalinist party based mainly in Catalonia. The communists eventually destroyed the power of the CNT and POUM in the summer of 1937, resulting in thousands of revolutionaries being killed or imprisoned. This in-fighting undoubtedly fatally weakened the Republican cause.

Åge Kjelsø

Danish volunteer. Served with the anarchists in the Durruti Column (Buenaventura Durruti was an anarchist leader who was killed fighting at Madrid in November 1936), August–December 1936, and in the POUM, December 1936–July 1937. Eventually forced to flee from Spain to escape the vengeance of the Soviet-backed Communist Party.

I was a member of the 'Anti-Fascist Struggle League', which had been built by expelled DSUers [DSU, Danish social democratic youth organization], who wanted a degree of joint struggle with the communists against the Nazis, and which broke up a number of the Nazi meetings in Copenhagen during their first manifestations in those years. Before I left Copenhagen in the summer of 1936, the Leninist Work Group gave me a statement to present to foreign comrades, and it was amusing for me to see the confusion the mere name of the group caused among those Stalinists who got to see it.

After being thrown off the ship in Marseilles, I again contacted the anarchists, who gave me an introductory letter to the Spanish comrades and a train ticket to the Spanish frontier, where I received an excellent reception from the Spanish anarchists, who also took care of my further transport to Barcelona.[1]

Bernard Knox

Volunteer from England. Served as an infantryman with the 11th International Brigade, October 1936–February 1937.

I left a few days later for Paris, with a group of a dozen or so volunteers that John [Cornford] had assembled. There were three Cambridge graduates and one from Oxford (a statistic I have always been proud of), as well as one from London University. There was a German refugee artist who had been living in London, two veterans of the British Army and one of the navy, an actor, a proletarian novelist and two unemployed workmen. Before we left, I had gone with John to visit his father in Cambridge; he was the distinguished Greek scholar Francis MacDonald Cornford, author of brilliant books on Attic comedy, Thucydides and Greek philosophy and Plato. He had served as an officer in the Great War and still had the pistol he had had to buy when he equipped himself for France. He gave it to John, and I had to smuggle it through French Customs at Dieppe, for John's passport showed entry and exit stamps from Portbou and his bags were likely to be given a thorough going-over.[2]

Bill Wood

Canadian volunteer and member of the revolutionary union, the Industrial Workers of the World (IWW). Served in the International section of the anarchist Durruti Column, May 1937–November 1937. His problems began when he got to Spain. He found that those who were not wholly supportive of the Communist Party were viewed suspiciously.

Letter dated November 1937.

I am out of Spain. The reasons are numerous. I was not wanted by the government as I was in the Durruti International Shock Battalion. The government sabotaged us since we were formed in May and made it impossible for us to stay at the front. All of the time I was in the militia I received no money. I had to beg money for postage stamps, etc. I was sent back from the front slightly shell-shocked and put in a hospital in Barcelona. When we registered at the hospital I told them I was from the Durruti International Battalion and they wouldn't register me. In fact they told me to go and ask my friends for money for a place to sleep. I explained to them that I was from Canada and had no friends in Barcelona, then they tried to make me a prisoner in the hospital. I called them all the lousy names I could think of.

The Stalinists did not hesitate to kill any of those who do not blindly accept Stalin as a second Christ. One of the refugees who came over with me from Spain was a member of the OGPU [Soviet security police] in Spain, which, by the way, is controlled by Russia. Every volunteer in the Communist International Brigade is considered a potential enemy of Stalin. He is checked and double-checked, every damn one. If he utters a word other than commy phrases he is taken 'for a ride'. This chap (ex-OGPU) is like all the other commies coming out of Spain, absolutely anti-Stalin and anti-communist. He skipped the country by flashing his OGPU badge on the trains.[3]

Sam Russell

Volunteer from London. Served with No 1 Company, 14th International Brigade, and with the British Battalion, 15th International Brigade, and as a broadcaster and correspondent with the Daily Worker *and as the Communist Party representative in Spain, November 1936–January 1939.*

We were told [by the Communist Party] to go to the Gare de Lyon [station in Paris] and that it was all very secretive. But when I got there it seemed to be full of people going to Spain. As for being a secret, everyone was going around with a clenched fist, chanting, '*Des avions pour l'Espagne*' – 'planes for Spain'.[4]

Stafford Cottman

Volunteer from London and Bristol, England. Served with the Independent Labour Party contingent in Spain, January 1937–June 1937.

It did not matter which of these organizations you belonged to in reality, you were concerned with the fact that the Spanish government, which had been democratically elected, was being threatened by military means. This was something which registered in most universities throughout Europe.

The Independent Labour Party (ILP) replied to me promptly. I was asked to go along to their headquarters and I met Bob Edwards, who was interviewing people for their suitability for the Brigade. The ILP unit was called the ILP Contingent. Bob Edwards was its leader. This was January 1937. At headquarters we were all interviewed by Bob and a couple of others. They asked you simple things like why you wanted to go to Spain. The idea was to find out whether you did have a sort of principle or whether it was pure adventure ... I think they were interested in finding out people's backgrounds so that they could decide if someone was purely an adventurer ... Membership of the ILP was not a qualification required for the contingent. I told them I was a member of the ILP. They were happy about that.

They enquired about whether I had any military experience. I think they asked the question with their tongue in their cheek, because what sort of chap were they going to get who had had military experience? The only experience of guns I'd ever had was a rifle at fairgrounds! They did say it was not going to be a joy ride. They didn't use the phrase 'blood, toil, sweat and tears' but that was the sense of it … They did not emphasize the danger that we could be killed. I think it was taken for granted because the Spanish people themselves were in that position, and if you weren't prepared to accept that as part of the everyday fact of life you would not be going. In my case, as I was quite young, they emphasized the fact that I was young to be going into this sort of thing.

Regarding arrangements to go, they simply said I would need a British passport. We had to get a ticket to Paris, an ordinary ticket as though on holiday, because in a way we were deceiving the authorities. But had you made such a declaration, because of the Non-Intervention Committee which was operating at the time, it was almost certain that the suspicion created would have resulted in you being unable to go. By merely visiting Paris it was then a matter of internal organization: to organize a train to take you from Paris to Perpignan, and then from Perpignan over the Pyrenees into Spain.[5]

Frederick Arthur Thomas

Volunteer from London, England. Served with the Anti-Tank Battery, 15th International Brigade, May 1937–October 1938.

I tried first of all in January 1937, and the only way then that one could hope to get to Spain was through the Communist Party. Not one person in 10,000 owned a passport in those days. The

British Communist Party wasn't terribly impressed by my offer. In the first place I proved that I was a complete idiot. I phoned them at King Street and said, 'Can you help me? I want to go to Spain'. They said, 'For Christ's sake get off the bloody line. Do you think that such things are discussed on the telephone?', and slam went the receiver. I suppose they had a point.

A few weeks later I summoned up the courage and went to King Street, in February, and I did manage to see somebody, a fellow called [Robbie] Robson, a well-known leader of the Communist Party. He made it clear to me that only trained men were being sent to Spain (I noted in my book after I had been in Spain for some time and mixed with these so-called trained men, what ways some of them had been trained in, i.e. none).

I was a formalist in those days. I did things by the book. If somebody said to me have you had military experience, it would not occur to me to lie and say yes. So I said no, I had no military experience. So that was it. Later, I heard through the grapevine that by now they were willing to take untrained chaps, so I went along again in the middle of April. They wanted unmarried chaps. They didn't want too many who had dependents. I had no commitments. I wasn't married and I was working so they accepted me. I was told to keep quiet about it and not tell anyone at all. It wasn't possible because I was living with friends, and I just had to tell them that I was going off. I did not tell my family. I have still got a letter that I wrote to my mother and father.[6]

Albert Charlesworth

Volunteer from Oldham, England. Served as a runner and postman with the British Battalion, 15th International Brigade, December 1936–September 1937 and December 1937–October 1938.

When I saw an advert advertising for volunteers in Spain, I took a day off work, went to Manchester to see George Brown and was accepted as a volunteer. This was in December 1936. I left Manchester on a bus for London the following week in a party in which was Sam Wild (*see plate 2*) and a fellow called Parkes, I can't remember his first name off hand. He was killed later on, along with two or three other comrades.

In London we were joined into a larger party led by Fred Copeman and off we went to Paris for registration. After that we went over the border in buses to Spain for more sorting out, and then off I went to Albacete.

I didn't join the Communist Party until a long, long time, until I came back from Spain. I am in trade unions but not actively. I am a very quiet person until I get aroused, and my main activities really are writing letters to the papers in reply to letters that they put in the papers, which I think are not true.

There were other people from Oldham. I did meet Oldham people out there, in particular Joe Lees and Cliff Walsingcroft. We became very good friends. There were other Oldham people as well, Glen Becket for instance. I didn't even know he was there until I saw him dead. There was a fellow called Shaw from Oldham and there was another fellow from Saddleworth. The other fellow was Joe Buckley, who came from Upper Mill, and he went during the early part of 1938. Not on my recommendation. He came to see me about going and I tried to put him off, but he insisted and I gave him the address to go to. The next time I saw him was in Spain.[7]

Notes
1   http://www.whatnextjournal.co.uk/pages/Back/Wnext29/Spanciv.html.
2   http://www.english.uiuc.edu/maps/scw/knox.htm.
3   http://libcom.org/library/soldier-returns-letter-durruti-column-american-fighter.
4   *Guardian* interview, 10 November 2000.
5   Cottman, Stafford, Imperial War Museum Sound Archive (IWMSA), London, Ref 9278/7, Reel 3.
6   Thomas, Frederick Arthur, IWMSA, London, Ref 9396/8, Reel 3.
7   Charlesworth, Albert, IWMSA, London, Ref 9427/4, Reel 3.

Getting to Spain

Getting to Spain was relatively easy for volunteers. However, in Britain one easy way for the authorities to stop people going to fight for the Republic was to deny them a passport. Therefore British volunteers travelled on special weekend return tickets to France, which required no passport. Curiously, at Victoria Station in London those buying weekend return tickets were often confronted by Special Branch officers, who attempted to dissuade them from going but did not arrest them. The Popular Front government in Paris was naturally sympathetic to its counterpart in Madrid. This meant that once on French soil volunteers usually made it to the Spanish border without hindrance (though occasionally the French authorities had a clampdown). Indeed, the recruitment of the International Brigades was coordinated by the Communist Party in France. The commander of the International Brigades' training base at Albacete, the Frenchman André Marty, was also a member of the executive committee of the Comintern.

In Paris volunteers would be met by a Communist Party representative, after which they would be given a medical and their political commitment further evaluated. From Paris they went by train to the Spanish border. There they would be divided into groups and smuggled over the Pyrenees into Spain. Once over the border they would be transported by truck to Figueras, the processing centre for foreign volunteers entering Spain from the north. The last part of the journey was a train ride to Albacete, located roughly halfway between Madrid and Valencia. Once at Albacete volunteers would be divided up into national groupings. They had made it, and their training could now begin.

Bernard Knox

Volunteer from England. Served as an infantryman with the 11th International Brigade, October 1936–February 1937.

Once in Paris, we went to the Comité d'Entraide au Peuple Espagnol and that was where John's scheme for a small British unit on the Aragon front was abandoned. We were sent to a hotel in Belleville, a working-class section of Paris, where we found ourselves a tiny English drop in a sea of large national groups – French, Polish, Belgian, German, Italian – all of them bound for Spain.

We left next morning by train for Marseilles where, at night, we boarded a Spanish vessel that left at midnight and, once clear of the harbour, turned off all its lights – there were reports of Italian submarines on the prowl. But we reached our destination, Alicante ... only to find it full of foreign naval vessels, all there, presumably, to enforce the Non-Intervention Agreement (which did not, however, apply to human imports).

As we moved in, a British destroyer crossed our bows, its signal lamp flashing a message in Morse code. 'They're telling us to show our colours', said one of our navy men, and sure enough, a few minutes later, two members of the crew, black-bearded and wearing brightly coloured scarves, came on deck with a flag they proceeded to run up. It consisted of two triangles, one black, one red. The captain of the destroyer must have searched his flag book in vain; they were the colours of the Confederación Nacional del Trabajo and the Federación Anarquista Ibérica. From Alicante we went by rail, crowds at all the stations shaking clenched fists at us and shouting UHP [Unión de Hermanos Proletarios – Unite Proletarian Brothers], to Albacete.[1]

Michael O'Riordan

Volunteer from Cork, Republic of Ireland. Founder member of the Communist Party of Ireland. Served with the Abraham Lincoln Battalion, 15th International Brigade, December 1937–September 1938.

I was due to go earlier with a small group of people (Irish International Brigade volunteers) to Spain but I got an attack of appendicitis. Soon as I got better, I was able to go, I went ... I was in contact with the Communist Party in Dublin and they told me how to get there, to go first from Dublin to Liverpool, I stayed in Liverpool overnight with a Spanish family. Then I travelled by train the next day to London. There I was given an address of the port to go to in (France). The whole thing was underground, at that time it was illegal to fight for Spain.

And I got the ticket to go to Paris. But I actually arrived in Paris on the eve of May Day and Paris at that time was bubbling over with aid for Spain, the Popular Front government was there, the Trade Unions and the people in the street were agitating for arms for Spain. And I saw the first big demonstration of May Day in Paris and from there I went to a place called the Place du Combat. It was an appropriate name for the place we had to go to! And this was the final check-off point. You were brought in (the office) and I saw a man passing through and I discovered later on that it was Tito [Josip Broz Tito, later leader of Yugoslavia] himself, he was in charge of that, of the organization, for the recruits of the International Brigade. We were interviewed by three French comrades and you were asked why do you want to go to Spain, you give your reasons and I had another reason because in Ireland they had already organized a group to form an Irish Brigade to go to fight for Franco. And I said – to at least redeem the good name of our country – that's why I wanted to go to Spain. Another one and it's not a patriotic reason, but they seemed to understand if your country does send people singing hymns, going off to Spain to fight for Franco, you must have a reaction to it. And they weren't bad fellows by the way, (the Irish volunteers for Franco), they weren't fascists, although they were remnants of the old fascist movement that had been beaten off the streets in Ireland, the Blueshirts, at that time, and then when the Spanish War broke out and it gave them (the Blueshirts) an opportunity for their leader (to reorganize the movement), whose name was General (Eoin) O'Duffy, a rather peculiar type of individual.[2]

Dave Goodman

Volunteer from Middlesbrough, England. Young Communist League member. Served with the British Battalion, 15th International Brigade, January–March 1938. Prisoner of war, March 1938–February 1939.

Fifty or sixty of us set off to cross into Spain from the foothills of the Pyrenees. We had to avoid French frontier guards and their dogs, whose barking we heard, and our guide led us, I believe, over smugglers' tracks. It was both strenuous and hazardous and we climbed all night until dawn broke next morning. It was quite unforgettable to look down at the blue Mediterranean in front and the snow-capped mountains behind. I was no mountain climber and our journey was made in the dark (me wearing a Burton overcoat). The fort at Figueras was our first stop – and there we were bombed, our first taste of war.[3]

Jack Edwards

Volunteer from Liverpool. Served with the British Battalion, 15th International Brigade, and the Special Machine-Gun Company, Republican Army, January 1937–October 1938.

We went on the Imperial bus from Liverpool overnight to London. There were four of us. We were picked up in London and stayed one night there. The weekend ticket to Paris cost £3 15s. I'd never seen that amount before.

In Paris we were picked up by a French party member and taken on the train to Portbou. There were eight of us by this time. We were formed into groups and went over the Pyrenees and met Spanish people on top of the mountains or on the other side. I walked down into Spain. I took the train to Barcelona, to Valencia, then Albacete and Madrigueras.[4]

William Kelly

Volunteer from Scotland. Served with the British Battalion, 15th International Brigade, January–March 1938. Prisoner of war, April 1938–February 1939.

On Friday night I stayed overnight in London. I went to Victoria Station, then to the coast and over to France, then down to Perpignan. A French and Spanish comrade contacted us on a horrible January 1938 night.

There were 10 of us, some English, Scots and 1 Irish. During the journey over the border one lad collapsed, but we carried on. Our first sight of Spain was a rising sun as we went down off the mountain. We went down to a granary and stayed there until 10.00 hours. Then army trucks picked us up, and then we got a train to Barcelona where we were equipped with everything but a rifle.[5]

Tony McLean

Student from England. Served as a research clerk and military censor with the International Brigades, May 1937–December 1938.

We got to Figueras but I hardly remember it. I was so tired, I just went to sleep. At Figueras we had a meal and then we were put on trains to Albacete and that was a very dreary journey. We weren't allowed to get out, particularly in Barcelona. However, when we got from Barcelona to Valencia the atmosphere changed and as we went to Valencia, through the orange groves, children would come up with little baskets of oranges and pass them through the windows. We were very well treated in Valencia. The only reason the journey was uncomfortable was because there was nowhere to sleep. Some people tried to sleep in the racks. I decided it was dangerous and that would not do, and the other thing was that the lavatory habits of our East European comrades left very much to be desired! The lavatories were absolutely disgusting. After a three-day journey we arrived at Albacete ... very early in the morning, feeling very tired, and we were taken to the headquarters of the International Brigade.[6]

Thomas Walter Gregory

Volunteer from England. Served as a rifleman and messenger with the British Battalion, 15th International Brigade, December 1936–September 1938. Prisoner of war, September 1938–February 1939.

So I wandered around London all day on my own and at the appointed hour I went to Victoria Station, it was quite late. All six of us were there and the plan was for us to keep within sight of one another but not to travel together and pretend we didn't know one another. We caught the Dover train and then the midnight boat to Dunkirk. We crossed over to Dunkirk and came off the boat, again pretending not to know one another. We changed trains a few times and it was very obvious that the French police were following us. We got to Paris. I didn't speak a word of French myself. As I came out of the station in Paris the taxi driver said, 'Englishman, Englishman', and he packed a load of us in this taxi. He didn't ask me where I wanted to go, he knew and took me to a recruiting office. They gave me a ticket for the railway and at night I caught a train to Figueras and got there on 24 December. My five companions were from all over the country. They definitely were not all communists. They were mainly unemployed and were well versed in hunger marches and demonstrations and so forth.

The Paris office was illegal, the French were constantly moving it around. It was the recruiting office for all the International Brigades. Later on it was so well organized people even got a medical check there, but there were none when I went there – too many people going through. There were hundreds and hundreds streaming through, just as the taxi driver knew where I wanted to go, so did other people. Here I was, a foreigner with vests and socks in a carrier bag with no luggage and obviously with no money, either. They knew where I was going. In fact, a dear old lady on the train sat knitting and she was looking at me and said, 'You Spain?', and even the dear old lady knew where I was going. I suppose it was obvious.

There are a lot of horrible tales about crossing the border, about the French shooting people. It didn't happen to me. The French were shutting their eyes at that particular moment. They packed us, all foreigners from all over Europe, into a darkened bus and we went up to the French border. The French border guards said something to the driver and waved us on and we were in Spain. We arrived at the Old Fortress at Figueras on Christmas Day 1936. We bedded down and I had my Christmas dinner there, a plateful of beans. After no more than two nights people were streaming in and by that time the fortress was full. A train load of us were taken down to the station and on a special train went to Barcelona. We demonstrated through the streets of Barcelona, were given another meal and put on another train and then went to Valencia. Again another demonstration, a meal and put on another train and we went for a long, long journey south to Albacete. From Albacete they sent me to a wretched little village called Madrigueras.

In Spain there were posters, streamers and flags everywhere. It was a wonderful experience. The food was atrocious: beans and beans, Spanish bread and a great big mug of vino [wine] which I was not used to drinking. But the excitement swept away all the snags and ironed out all the faults and at that stage I could not see anything wrong. All I wanted to do was to get to some sort of base, be equipped, organized and get to the front.[7]

Stafford Cottman

Volunteer from London and Bristol, England. Served with the Independent Labour Party Contingent in Spain, January 1937–June 1937.

My journey from England to Spain was very uneventful. We went on a boat from Newhaven to Dieppe, and from Dieppe a train journey to Paris. We were met by very enthusiastic and sympathetic French socialists who took us for a meal, and we stayed at a nice, clean hotel in Paris. I was only there one night. We went on the train and then we got the coach over the Pyrenees ... There was no trouble from the French authorities. We went over from Perpignan to Figueras by coach and at Figueras we had our first meal. I remember it was made up of little sardines, green artichokes and long French bread. That was quite good food, really. It gradually got worse after that.

There wasn't much at Figueras, just a few people that met us and took us for a meal and so on. Then we got to Barcelona. At the railway station it was quite festive, there was a band and we marched from the station to the POUM Headquarters in Ramblas, which is a well-known spot in Barcelona. There was a reception committee at the headquarters and everyone shook our hands, said how pleased they were to see us and how wonderful it was that Britain should respond by sending people over.[8]

Frederick Arthur Thomas

Volunteer from London, England. Served with the Anti-Tank Battery, 15th International Brigade, May 1937–October 1938.

I was met at Victoria and the only two names I remember are Tony McLean and George Baker. Tony McLean was a lecturer, a history student. He was the only one in the group with instructions. He knew what to do and where to go. George Baker was a miner and we became buddies all the way through the Spanish Civil War, and remained friends until his death.

We caught the boat train to Dover and landed at Dunkirk the next morning. I think we gave up pretending we didn't know each other because all of us were so damn scared of getting lost. We had been given money to buy a weekend return to Paris. We hung on to Tony and we got on this train at Dunkirk and went to Paris. We were really clinging on to Tony then. He knew where to go and took us straight down to the Metro. He took us to a cafe. Charlotte Haldane [British Feminist and wife of British geneticist and physiologist, J. B. S. Haldane] was in charge of this cafe. I remember it was very large, being given over for the business of recruiting, receiving recruits for Spain. There were dozens sitting around eating and drinking, and Tony marched us straight up to Charlotte Haldane to report our arrival.[9]

David 'Tony' Gilbert

Volunteer from London. Served as a runner with the British Battalion, 15th International Brigade, March 1937–April 1938. Prisoner of war, March 1938–January 1939.

My journey was full of incident. Two were lads who had no desire to go to Spain, who were seeking an adventure and maybe some cash before they got there. When we arrived in Paris it was obvious that the French Communist Party was playing a big part in seeing that we got to our destination. We were interviewed in a place called the Place de Combat and the man in charge of organizing the volunteers was Marshal Tito. I met him at the Place de Combat and told him of what had occurred on the train and that these two men should not go, they were obviously bad characters and had no intention of engaging into such a battle, but they went. Meanwhile I palled up with a young Scottish lad named Jamie, and we became very firm friends.

When we got to Nimes, Jamie and I were being housed in what might be called safe houses. In this hotel we had all the problems of not knowing the language, not knowing how to order a breakfast or anything else. Jamie said to me there was something peculiar about the set-up. There were so many beautiful girls in the cafe below the rooms, and these girls seemed to pick up all sorts. We didn't know that we were in a brothel! We didn't know in our hotel bedroom what a bidet was, we had never seen one before. Here we were, stuck in a brothel, two young innocents and then there was panic. Panic with Frenchmen coming round to the hotel, not being able to speak English, probably members of the French Communist Party and rushing us all out. We had very little baggage and were told not to bring much, just a clean shirt or two and underwear. These two characters that I had warned Tito about were determined that they weren't going any further, so they went out and got drunk.

We were given a bit of money, a few francs, but enough for them to get sozzled on. They became so aggressive in the streets that they were arrested, which is what they wanted. The officials were alerted that there were people in Nimes ready to go to Spain. So we were gathered together in panic and rushed to the foot of the Pyrenees, and there started a long and very arduous climb to the other side ... Fortunately I was fit and managed it quite well. We came down the other side, the Spanish side, to a place called Fort Figueras. It was built by Napoleon with very thick walls, a very solid effort. When we gathered there it was not just British people. The Germans had come by different routes over the Pyrenees, as well as Frenchmen and Dutchmen.

We had our first meal. Revolutionary songs of the various countries were ringing out as we had our terrible food and drank the strong wine. Then the war began for me as we had an air raid, and as the bombs began to drop we were all rushed out of the room that we were in and told to disperse in the open fields alongside the fort. It was the best thing to do, as my experience in war has taught me that when you are out in the open you have more chance of surviving a bombing raid. Jamie and I ran across the fields together. We began to move away from the railway track, which ran alongside the fort, because that could be a target. Then we stopped and looked at each other and burst out laughing. We were holding hands like two kids. Here we were, two soldiers about to enter into what was a very fierce war, clasping hands and running hand-in-hand together, wanting to gain some courage from each other.[10]

Bernard McKenna

Volunteer from Manchester, England. Served as a signaller and infantryman with the British Battalion, 15th International Brigade, February 1937 –March 1938. Prisoner of war, March 1938–October 1938.

I wasn't the only one who went and I wasn't the first who went. When I went I was the only one from Manchester, I think. I went out with a chap from Leeds and another from Liverpool. At that time you simply contacted the CP [Communist Party], went to London and got the night train on a weekend excursion through to Paris ... I arrived in Paris about 05.00 hours in the morning and the same evening I was on the train to Figueras with several hundred others. We arrived, stayed at the barracks there for two or three days and then travelled with other volunteers to Albacete.

When we arrived there we were free to walk out and never come back. This was one of the things that held one there: the fact that we were free to come back. In fact George Brown's brother had come back just before I went. He had been out and came back and George Brown [company commissar at Brunete, killed at Villanueva de la Cañada in July 1937] himself later went out about a month after me and replaced him. I felt very annoyed about it. I felt he was a somebody, he was more use in Manchester in the movement, where he was honoured and respected above any local comrade and that is with no disrespect to him. He had something about him. I think he felt compelled to go because of his brother going out and returning.[11]

Arthur Nicoll

Volunteer from Dundee, Scotland. Served as a political commissar with the Anti-Tank Battery, 15th International Brigade, February–October 1937

A bus came in the evening, took us to the Pyrenees and we hiked over the Pyrenees during the night. You had to be fit because you are climbing at 4–5,000 feet. That's only the passes, the mountains were towering above us at 14,000 feet. I remember I got my instructions from Charlotte Haldane, Professor Haldane's wife, who was in Paris. She said when you get over the border don't let them take you to any place other than Figueras, always remember the name Figueras, because there had been some attempts earlier to take volunteers to other places, in fascist territory. Spanish guides were taking us over. Most of the guides were experienced, politically mature men and they took us over in groups of about 30 at a time ... No one was allowed to smoke, to drop any paper ... to leave a mark anywhere to show that we had passed over that way because of the guards on the French side. A few chaps had been picked up and put in jail. Anyway we got to Figueras and I will never forget it, never. We got a meal and when I looked at it I thought I will never eat that. And I didn't eat it, but believe me I was eating a whole lot worse in a week's time. You had to get broken into it, you see.

It wasn't bad food. It was because it had garlic and olive oil in it ... There were really good meats, though. That was my first experience in Spain and I must say it was a major experience. I thought I was a good communist before I went to Spain, but I reckon I was 10 times a better one after I came back.[12]

Peter Kerrigan

Volunteer from Scotland. Served as a political commissar with the British Battalion, 15th International Brigade, and as a war correspondent for the Daily Worker *in Spain, December 1936–December 1938.*

So we sung 'Tipperary' marching through Barcelona. I did notice it was rather striking that the tram cars were painted diagonally red and black, anarchist colours I was told. I didn't verify it myself that they were taking fares and paying it to the anarchists' trade union at that time. At that time in Barcelona the anarchists, the CNT, were very powerful. They were not in complete control. Remember we only had a short visit through and we could only see superficially what was happening. I wouldn't give a political estimation of the situation. I only mentioned the thing about the tram cars because it was rather strange for somebody like me, and I suppose the other lads as well, having half of the car diagonally black and the other half diagonally red.

We were then put on the train again and ended up at Albacete, which was the headquarters of the International Brigades. From there we were taken to a bullring which was used as a kind of parade ground and there was a short welcome. Uniforms were then given out, a greenish khaki-coloured uniform. The British lads were sent to a village a few miles from Albacete, Madrigueras, which was the headquarters of the British Battalion. And there they did all their training. The commander in charge at that time was Wilfred McCartney, a former British officer. The political commissar was D. F. ['Dave'] Springhall, who had served in the Royal Navy and was also an active Communist Party member. They had both been appointed by the International Brigades Military Command. The man in charge at Albacete at the time when I was there was André Marty. He was assisted by a Frenchman called Videl.[13]

Joe Norman

Volunteer from Manchester and Bolton, England. Served as the Communist Party organizer with the British Battalion, 15th International Brigade, July 1937–March 1938.

In France we were met by the leaders of the anti-fascist movement, communists, anti-fascists, all sorts. In the early days it was mostly the Communist Party that provided the troops and the leadership, but later on the trade union movement came in after a change of opinions in the Labour Party. I led nine people across France and across the Pyrenees. I couldn't speak French, I don't think I even spoke English properly! But I wasn't on my own. There were people meeting us. The word was sent on that we would be at a certain place at a certain time and they were there. If they weren't there, there was trouble – you would have probably been picked up by the police. It was really a cast iron organization and they took us to places, fed us and took us around Paris until it was time to move. Then they bundled us onto a bus ...

We never clashed [with the French police]. We even had comrades in the police so if anything happened they would say, 'Don't go there, don't leave tonight, they'll be waiting for you'. Eventually we climbed the Pyrenees and met the guide. When I say I led, I had my party which I was responsible for. We went over the Pyrenees and it took us six hours in the pitch dark, and just as the sun rose we landed in Figueras and from Figueras we went to the training base.[14]

Fred Copeman

Volunteer from London, England. Served with the Machine-Gun Company and as commander of the British Battalion, 15th International Brigade, October 1936–December 1937.

I was told to report to a cafe in Paris. We had no trouble getting out of England. You could go for the weekend. We got to this huge cafe, they gave us a meal and that night we were put on a train down to Portbou. There were crowds waiting to greet you going through. In an office there we met Tito; a big lad, not too tall. We arrived at Portbou at the foot of the Pyrenees. This would be September or October 1936. Wally Tapsell was there and most of the lads that got well known were in that first bunch. By now the recruitment of the brigade had become pretty open and the French had accepted it. The customs people were down on the main road. We went to within 500 yards of them and then we went behind a row of houses to the border. All the gardens had been turned into a road where thousands of people had walked, so we just marched behind and then up the bloody hill. Everybody was already organized into sections and companies and they had their own commanders. We had a meeting along the way and I was elected commander.

I still had my 470 men with me. They took a dim view of too many coming all at once. I said: 'It's too bloody late now.' We had already been rigged out (I had been kitted out by the union). My unit had bought my uniform, binoculars and compasses, everything short of a gun and a beret. I wore a navy jersey which I had kept from the navy and away we went, which I thought was just over the hill. We went on bloody climbing right through the night, and every time a bloke would rattle his tin can with a knife and fork and somebody would bawl out, 'Keep quiet'. And I would bawl out, 'You're making more bloody noise than he is. Keep quiet'. We all thought that when we got over the top the war would be there, but actually it was miles away. We went up and up and every bloody top we reached there was another one, until very early in the morning we reached the top … you could just see the sun coming up behind us, with pitch dark on the other side. It was an amazing experience to see the sun come up over the Pyrenees and you could see for miles. When we got to the other side we were picked up by the Spanish people who were organizing it and led down to a little old town with a fort. We stayed there for about two days and then we were taken on to Barcelona. From then on it was a long parade of flags and crowds because it was all part of the publicity. We marched down the Ramblas at Barcelona and there must have been about half a million people there. The English, carrying a Union Jack, marched through the Ramblas and then it was back on the lorries and on to the next big town. We felt very important.[15]

Notes
1   http://www.english.uiuc.edu/maps/scw/knox.htm.
2   http://www.indymedia.ie/article/76157.
3   Goodman, Dave, Imperial War Museum Sound Archive (IWMSA), London, Ref 16621/5, Reel 3.
4   Edwards, Jack, IWMSA, London, Ref 808/3, Reel 1.
5   Kelly, William, IWMSA, London, Ref 819/1, Reel 1.
6   McLean, Tony, IWMSA, London, Ref 838/5, Reel 2.
7   Gregory, Thomas Walter, IWMSA, London, Ref 8851/9, Reel 2.
8   Cottman, Stafford, IWMSA, London, Ref 9278/7, Reel 3.
9   Thomas, Frederick Arthur, IWMSA, London, Ref 9396/8, Reel 3.
10 Gilbert, David 'Tony', IWMSA, London, Ref 9157/10, Reel 4.
11 McKenna, Bernard, IWMSA, London, Ref 847/5, Reel 1.
12 Nicoll, Arthur, IWMSA, London, Ref 817/3, Reel 2.
13 Kerrigan, Peter, IWMSA, London, Ref 810/6, Reel 2.
14 Norman, Joe, IWMSA, London, Ref 818/4, Reel 2.
15 Copeman, Fred, IWMSA, London, Ref 794/13, Reel 1.

Turning Volunteers into Fighters

Most volunteers had a fervent desire to fight fascists, and having arrived in Spain they seemingly were about to be granted their wish. However, not quite. They first had to be turned into soldiers, or at least be given a semblance of military training. It usually takes a few months to turn a raw recruit into a trained soldier, and most of those who volunteered to serve in the International Brigades were very raw recruits, indeed.

Taking the British volunteers as an example, around 80 percent of those who arrived in Spain had never handled a weapon before. The percentage was probably higher for American and East European recruits. The problem was made worse by the fact that the Republicans had a shortage of weapons and ammunition. Indeed, there was a wide variety of weapons, mostly aged, and an even more diverse variety of ammunition types. Many Brigaders found that the ammunition they did have could not be fired from the weapons they carried. On the whole it was a nightmare situation. It got better with regular supplies of Russian weapons and equipment, but it was never totally resolved.

Bernard Knox

Volunteer from England. Served as an infantryman with the 11th International Brigade, October 1936–February 1937.

Our British section was assigned (mainly, I suppose, because I could serve as interpreter) to the French Battalion, where we ended up in the *compagnie mitrailleuse*, the Machine-Gun Company. But for the rest of September and all through October [1936] we had no machine guns, not even rifles; the only weapon around was John's pistol, which he kept well under wraps.

Since we couldn't train with weapons, our days were spent practising close-order drill (French, English, or sometimes Spanish) and going on route marches along the dusty roads of the province of Murcia. No one knew when or where we would be sent to fight and when (if ever) the weapons would arrive, though the scuttlebutt rumours had us held in reserve for a flanking movement via Ciudad Real that would take Franco, now moving steadily towards Madrid, in the rear.

As the calendar moved through October and into November, events suddenly developed so fast that we could hardly grasp what was happening. Late one evening, we were suddenly alerted and marched to the railroad yards, where huge wooden crates were being unloaded. We were given tools to open them up; our weapons had arrived at last.

There were stamps and bills of lading and brand marks on the cases that showed they had made the rounds of the international arms markets; some were in Arabic and one case was branded with the letters 'IRA' [Irish Republican Army]. They contained rifles, American 1903 Springfields, the ones carried by the Doughboys [slang for US infantrymen] in the Great War and, at last, our machine guns. They were a sad disappointment: antique models that sported a bicycle seat for the gunner high up in the air, real suicide traps; no one, not even the French, knew what they were (though the cases had French stamps on them) until our oldest French volunteer, a patriarch known as *grand-père*, identified them as St Etiennes, a gun that was declared obsolete in the first weeks of the 1914 war. They must have been relics from the [Franco-Prussian] war of 1870.[1]

Dave Smith

Volunteer from Malden, Massachusetts, United States. Served in the Abraham Lincoln Battalion, February 1937–December 1938.

The US volunteers formed the Lincoln Battalion and later it became the 15th Brigade when more volunteers arrived. You must remember the majority of the Americans had not received any military training at home and I was at the frontline on 24 February, quite a fast trip, after receiving a rifle and three bullets to shoot, which completed my military training!

The Republican government didn't have an army and had to develop one as the war took place, and many of the young men from the agricultural areas in Spain couldn't even read – but they did a remarkable job. Later on, a training base at Albacete was set up where all English-speaking volunteers received training.

For a while I was in charge of training new volunteers at the US base in Tarazona [de la Mancha]. My last action was at the Ebro front in Catalonia where I was wounded in my left shoulder, which developed into an osteo infection, and my left shoulder is now one solid piece. I left Spain on 29 December 1938.[2]

Eugene Downing

Volunteer from Dublin, Republic of Ireland. Member of the Communist Party of Ireland. Served in the 15th International Brigade, March–December 1938.

I was one of a small group of Irishmen who, with some 20 or so British recruits, crossed the Pyrenees at the end of March 1938 to join the 15th International Brigade. Our first step on Spanish soil was an old fort on the outskirts of Figueras in Catalonia, near the French frontier. While waiting for arrangements to be made to send us on to the British Battalion further south, we spent our time on the parade ground, where we were taught the military commands in Spanish and also took it in turn to drill the group and practise issuing the words of command in that language.

On leaving to go to Barcelona, the first leg of our journey to the battalion, the group was informed by our instructor that I was in charge. Since there were older and more experienced people in the group than myself, I felt rather apprehensive at this unwelcome responsibility that had been thrust upon me. There were ex-British Army types in the group, one of whom, a Scot, told me he had served in the Black Watch. For some reason which I can't explain, this impressed me tremendously.

It transpired that the instructor had chosen me because I was the tallest and also because I had been quite good at picking up the bit of Spanish and issuing the commands at precisely the right moment when drilling the group. This piece of irrelevant flattery didn't reassure me one bit and the phrase that flashed through my mind was 'uneasy lies the head that wears a crown' – particularly if you don't want it. However, since we would be taken in hand by the authorities wherever we happened to be and told where to go and what to do, I decided that 'being in charge' didn't really mean anything and that it didn't entail any great responsibility or call for outstanding qualities of leadership.

The main hardship during this training period was the continual feeling of hunger and, for most, the scarcity of cigarettes. We were well aware, of course, that plenty of people in Ireland and Britain were familiar with those sensations without having to go to Spain. On the other hand, the hardship may have been largely imaginary since the general feeling among the members of the battalion was that they had never been so healthy in all their lives. Never having been used to high living, I had no complaint to make about the simplicity of the fare but rather the scarcity. I was quite happy with coffee and dry bread for breakfast, I just wanted more bread.[3]

Frank Lesser

Volunteer from London. Served as a training officer, adjutant and liaison officer with the 15th International Brigade, August 1937–October 1938.

Our training was directed by Captain Ramon who didn't speak any Spanish. Our instruction was given in Russian. The interpreter was an American of Ukrainian descent, and Ramon himself was Ukrainian. Ramon was formal but friendly, very accessible. We got on with him very well. He said you should always take action. He said it's like sitting in a room with an attractive woman. Would you sit there and do nothing? He said he hoped you would put your hand up her skirt and take action that was appropriate to the situation. He was saying this to a group that had no great experience in sexual activities. It was a rather doubtful illustration of what our duties of officers were to be.

Our day started at 06.00 hours with an early breakfast. Then it was drill for three to four hours, a midday meal followed by a siesta (it was much too hot), then drill until the evening meal. A long, hard day. We were given training in the use and care of arms. Standard operating procedure included being able to take the bolts of our weapons to pieces, blindfolded and in the dark, to clean them and put them back together again. The bolts of the weapons were interchangeable between the Russian rifles and machine guns. They were the main weapons of the Republican Army. But at base not everyone had a weapon with which to train.

Training was of a general nature that could be useful to a junior officer of infantry: map reading, taking advantage of terrain, where to dig in, liaison with flank units and directing fire. The idea was that in two months we would be able to replace casualties at the front. The course was the first opportunity to provide people who went to the front with training, rather than gaining experience in battle on the frontline. We were the first to benefit from this. Many cadets at the school had already seen service at the front, especially at Brunete and Jarama. A number had been sent back from the battalion to be officers. A number, though, found this irksome, absconded and went back to their units. There was no punishment for this. Others were not up to the academic aspect of training. They only wanted to fight.

I don't think anyone thought that there shouldn't be officers in the Republican Army. The main influence was the Spanish Communist Party, which was working in a country where anarchists and socialists also had influence. The communists had to contest the anti-authority attitude of the anarchists, who were an important political force, especially in Catalonia. This issue of should there be a military hierarchy had been raised and settled, probably in the first six months of the war. By the time I got there, in August 1937, there were no questions about this, it wasn't a problem.

When I graduated I was made a lieutenant, a training officer at the base. When I went to the front, to the battalion, what rank I had there would be decided by the commander of the brigade. Thus when I went to the front I was interviewed by the brigade commander and was appointed a sergeant, which actually was never confirmed (I was still officially a private). We knew that we had to earn rank.

At cadet school I got jaundice. They thought at first it might be typhus until I started going yellow. There was little they could do. They put me on a diet with no fats or olive oil. The treatment was good. I missed two weeks of officer training because of this. When I got back to base I was appointed a training lieutenant and began training new infantry volunteers.

One of my duties was to maintain the spirits of people in training. Most of them were anxious to get to the front as soon as possible to fight the fascists. I explained to them that training wasn't as long or as thorough as in other armies, but that they would be more useful at the front if they tried to make the most of it. I had a combined instructor/political commissar role.

I gave no political lectures. At the end of a morning's training, by the side of the road, I would simply chat and make little speeches. One important feature of officers' training school was that we were taught Spanish by a very good Spanish teacher. As a result I felt I could give commands in Spanish. It was the policy, down to company level, that there should be in the International Brigades a complement of Spaniards, usually a third. This meant a command of the Spanish language was important. The physical condition of the recruits was reasonably good. Some English volunteers who were unemployed were undernourished, but this wasn't a great problem.

Later we set up a month-long course for non-commissioned officers (NCOs). An American, Eugene Loveman, was the commander and I was the adjutant. It worked out quite well. Most of the NCOs were Spaniards. One was a butcher by trade who killed a goat and cooked it for us. The battalion had been at Teruel and had suffered considerable losses, as had other 15th Brigade battalions. To make good these losses, those that had been training at Tarazona de la Mancha went to the Teruel region to reinforce the battalion, which was out of the line to the rear, waiting for reinforcements. We arrived in winter, with snow on the ground. The men were living in dugouts in the hillsides, with straw on the floor. Others were in the open air. We went back into line shortly before the Aragon offensive, which was unleashed at Belchite in March 1938.[4]

Jack Edwards

Volunteer from Liverpool. Served with the British Battalion, 15th International Brigade, and Special Machine-Gun Company, Republican Army, January 1937–October 1938.

We did our training with the old Colt machine gun, which had a big brass tripod. They fired about two rounds every bloody hour! There was a little part on the trigger, a little pin. It lasted about half an hour when you were firing the gun.

I'd done no military training but I thought it was effective enough. If you have the will to be trained that is the top and bottom of it. Such things as how to stay alive, how to keep close to the floor. You had to survive. We were there to win a war, to break fascism. We were serious. We were there because we wanted another kind of life, in fairness, not scraping for pennies. No battles on the streets, no means test. A life in which everybody would have a decent standard of living. This was a socialist principle. And I thought when you saw the unity in Spain, this was the answer to it.[5]

Tony McLean

Student from England. Served as a research clerk and military censor with the International Brigades, May 1937–December 1938.

When we were at the barracks there were troops of every nationality, and the next day the English section came to see us, including a fellow called Bill Rowe who was ex-RAF [Royal Air Force]. He asked if any of us knew languages and I said I knew French. They despatched us after a day to the International Training Battalion at Madrigueras, where we had a French commandant. There were French, Greeks, Germans and us British. The training at the British Battalion was sketchy in the extreme. There was a certain amount of bullying and a certain amount of resentment. There was much more bullying of recruits in the British Army but, on the other hand, you go into the British Army with different expectations. You know the sergeant-major is going to chase you. In Spain you had the strength of your comrades and you were not so pleased when someone tried to bully you and push you around, so it was a slightly different psychological atmosphere.

I cannot prove this, but there was not allowed to be too much fraternization between officers, NCOs and other ranks. They [slept] in different messes, you were not allowed to be on Christian name terms with the boys, ... you had to treat each other in accordance with the rank that you held. I think it is almost certain that they got these instructions from the Russians. Tom Wintringham was always terribly matey. Bill Alexander was a private at that time like myself, but later when he became captain he had a very good relationship with the people under him. Both the officers in Madrigueras attended public school. They were Malcolm Dunbar (see plate 13), who rose to be a staff major in the International Brigade; he was incredibly brave but made it clear that he did not regard the rank and file as the same order of being. The other one was Hugh Slater. He was very brave but extremely arrogant. Both of them were extremely arrogant, good-looking intellectuals and there was some resentment among the working-class types.

I had a Cambridge background, but as long as you were not conceited, as long as you were not arrogant, soldiers took you very much as they found you. They did not give you a bad time if you were in another rank. Working-class chaps in Spain were very untypical. They were so full of left-wing enthusiasm and very different from the rank and file of the British Army.[6]

Thomas Walter Gregory

Volunteer from England. Served as a rifleman and messenger with the British Battalion, 15th International Brigade, December 1936–September 1938. Prisoner of war, September 1938–February 1939.

Madrigueras was a dreadful little place. The poverty was breathtaking. I had come from Nottingham where there were miners, where they hadn't worked in years, but I had seen nothing like this. There were no pavements, just a dirt track down the middle of a street. There was one water supply: a stone column with a lead pipe. It could have been there for centuries. People had to queue up for water. First there were 100, 200 and 600 British in this village, including Irish, Scots, Welsh and even some from Australia and New Zealand. The water situation was so desperate that somebody had to queue day and night to get drinking water and cooking water. The people were very good to us but they had nothing to give us, nothing to sell us either. They could not sell us a chicken, an egg, a bit of fruit or anything.

There was no tension with the villagers. I am proud to say it was wonderful all the time. One thing I have to admit, we did far too much drinking. We didn't have our own canteen; we shared the village canteen, the bar. We staggered back to our billets in the dark and singing 'Bandera Rosa, Bandera Rosa'. We must have been a nuisance to the villagers who were trying to get children to sleep but they never, never once complained. I am told to this day that the people still proudly boast that the British stayed with them during the civil war ...

We worked hard at training and it was remarkable how soon they knocked us into a unit. The commander of the British base at Madrigueras had been Wilf McCartney. We had been there a week or two when we were issued with rifles and a nice warm uniform. It was cold, bitterly cold, though we didn't see any snow. There were mornings where the puddles had frozen over and we even had fog. The warm uniform was very welcome and we were issued with Soviet rifles straight out of the packing cases. What a day that was when I took hold of that rifle. I was going to conquer the world with it, there was just no holding me back. The excitement was enormous ...

I was put in No 3 Company and our company commander was a London colleague, Bill Briskey. He had been an active trade unionist in the Transport and General Workers' Union and he was a bus-man. I was very proud to serve under him. There was a problem throughout Spain, a shortage of good soldiers, and the higher up you got the worse the shortage got. He made me his messenger, because there was no radio communications. I took verbal messages to headquarters and vice versa.

Briskey had no rank at that time. You would be in charge of this and that or whatever, but no one was designated corporal, sergeant, lieutenant. The Republic was starting from scratch. They had a lot of lessons to learn and they hadn't learned them at that stage (1936 and early 1937). The chain of command was dreadfully weak and in some of the anarchist units it didn't exist at all. At least the British went to Spain with a tradition that somebody is put in charge of you, you obey his orders and that person in charge of you has got someone in charge of him and he would obey his orders. They did it out of tradition not because of any badges or because somebody got more money in pay. We had no badges at all at this time. We all wore the same uniforms. We knew who was in charge of each platoon and each company and so forth. It was a poor system but that's the way it was.

My company was part of the British Battalion of the 15th International Brigade. We were all English speaking at Madrigueras. We should have been mixed from the very start but we weren't. There were ambitions of making us into two battalions. When we had the awful losses of February [at Jarama] when they were not made up by recruits from Great

Britain, then the Spanish Republic gave us a Spanish company. But again we hadn't learnt our lesson, the Spanish company remained a separate Spanish unit and I think it ought to have been mixed in with us.

Training consisted of a lot of marching to harden our feet, that was very essential. We learnt the Spanish formation of marching in threes. We fired 15 rounds from our rifles. It is important to record that because people are saying that we were dragged off the train and pushed to the front: 'Here you are comrade, here's your rifle, you put the bullet in here and it shoots that way.' That didn't happen to me. I fired 15 rounds with my Soviet rifle. I oiled it and learned to strip it and so forth. I pulled the pin out of a hand grenade, learnt to give it a good throw and to get down out of the way. We had a go at learning a few simple Spanish words and this is where our contact with the village people came in very useful.

We were quite busy, we worked a full day. Mostly 06.00 hours in the morning until 18.00 hours at night. Occasionally we would have a night manoeuvre to learn how to cross the Spanish countryside without getting lost, to be able to manoeuvre in formation in the dark. It was chaos at first so it was a jolly good thing that we did train in this. We reached quite a nice standard.

We had political commissars. Their duty was to look after our welfare, our political instruction, to see that everybody wrote home or wrote to organizations, and to see that everyone was satisfied with the way that things were going. A couple of people wanted to go home so the political commissar arranged that they should go back home. I don't know why they lost heart in the struggle, but they did. It was the political commissar's job to organize meetings, to get people to ask questions and to get up and speak, to state opinions. If people complained about the food then it would be explained. There was an awful lot of dried fish called *bacalao* and it needed soaking to take the salt out of it. It was English lads who volunteered for the cookhouse and they didn't understand Spanish food. They were short of fuel and short of water. The food was atrocious, so people were complaining about it. He [the commissar] put the problem to these comrades and said if you really feel you can do better I will put you down for the next vacancy in the cookhouse, and so forth.

Of course we could not buy tobacco. I don't smoke, but soon the smokers realized they could not get tobacco because Franco had all the tobacco, it was made in tobacco factories in the fascist areas. The only way they got any tobacco was through parcels coming through the Spanish Aid Committee and it meant days and days without a cigarette. The smokers were going up the wall and all that had to be explained to them. These were some of the hardships of the war. I would not have liked to have been a commissar. He had a tough job to satisfy everybody.

Morale was very, very good. There was too much drinking but people sobered up and it was a huge joke in the morning. There was no falling out, no fights. Generally speaking the morale was extremely high and after a fortnight we wanted to get to the front. We hadn't come to drill, we hadn't come to do night manoeuvres. We were chafing to be off.[7]

David 'Tony' Gilbert

Volunteer from London, England. Served as a runner with the British Battalion, 15th International Brigade, March 1937–April 1938. Prisoner of war, March 1938–January 1939.

We were taken to the place where we were to be equipped. Albacete was the main camp where you were kitted out in your common uniform. You just wore what fitted you best and you were equipped in that way. We had no weapons there, but what we did have were some discussions with political leaders trying to discern who could make officers, who could make political leaders. It was crude but absolutely necessary.

Albacete was very primitive. It was a big camp, thriving. When I say primitive I mean the fashion in which the clothes were distributed, the fashion in which you were housed in barracks. I found it all very primitive and with no real knowledge of what was going to come. The only thing I can remember were these political discussions.

There were three-tier bunks in the barracks, one on top of another. I had never slept like that, ever. They were bare and I suppose the discipline in the barracks was something new to me: lights out at 21.00 hours or 22.00 hours and waking up at 06.00 hours in the morning and doing some physical exercises. Then off to breakfast, which was the poorest food I ever saw. I was brought up in the East End of London and the food was not plentiful and not of high nutrition, but nevertheless what I was eating in Spain was something that I was not used to. The meat, for example, you would have to hold it and tear pieces off. It was very tough. This is what I mean when I say it was primitive.

There were people in charge of all nationalities. They were British that were responsible for us, and of course like everything else in the world lots of things depended on who you know, and who knows you. I was from Bethnal Green, working class. We had to fill in questionnaires. What was your schooling, either elementary or university, and from these questionnaires people were chosen to be given jobs of some importance. This man was from Bethnal Green, he was born there and when he saw my questionnaire he saw I was from Bethnal Green and a member of the Communist Party. The fact that I was only a recent recruit to the party didn't seem to have much influence. He interviewed me and asked if I wanted to go to officer training. I told him that I had never held a gun in my life and knew nothing of military warfare, so how could I be put in a position of authority, and he accepted it. I never went off to any special school. I went off with the rest to Tarazona where we had our military training …

It was very short, not much more than two weeks at the most, but I had begun to get a knowledge of how fierce that war was. Jamie and I became friends with a Spanish lad named Martin who taught me how to roll cigarettes. They took me to the local church and this was my first insight into both the horrors and necessities of warfare. In Tarazona a group of fascists supporting Franco had installed a machine gun in the church tower, and of course that tower controlled every single street. Nobody could move. The only way they could get them out was to burn it down. They crept out at night and set fire to it. Many religious buildings suffered and sometimes suffered complete destruction because in every Spanish village the church dominated the whole area. One capable machine-gunner could hold the whole village to ransom.

There were some Soviet instructors. I can only remember one at Tarazona and he didn't talk to us about military manoeuvres, how to fight, how to use the weapons. The rifles that we carried were Soviet models. World War I efforts in the main and on the barrels there would be an engraved hammer and sickle. We used to call them Mexicanists [Mexicanskis] because they came from the Soviet Union via Mexico, as it was difficult for convoys carrying weapons from the Soviet Union to get through the Mediterranean and then to Spain. But going back to this Soviet instructor, if there was one thing wrong with us, we weren't really soldiers, we were a political symbol. We had come from Britain where there had been no tradition of militarism, particularly among people where I came from. There were such organizations as the Boy Scouts (I boxed for the Boy Scouts when I was a schoolboy). We had no military training, nor did we have the military tradition which the German Brigade had, i.e. some rifle training. In the main, we knew nothing.

The men and women who went with such enthusiasm to fight fascism believed that to cower in a trench was cowardice. We were the worst type of soldiers. I remember this Russian talking to us about it. He said you could become a liability to the Republic because if you were wounded somebody had to tend to you, and you were no longer able to carry on. He said we must learn and listen to our instructors and take care of ourselves, protect ourselves and use cover. That lesson remained with me, not only there but later throughout World War II.[8]

Peter Kerrigan

Volunteer from Scotland. Served as a political commissar with the British Battalion, 15th International Brigade, and as a war correspondent for the Daily Worker *in Spain, December 1936–December 1938.*

The early Britishers had passed through the Thaelmann and other battalions, the French at least. I know that there were Slavs as well, because I came across and got very friendly with a little Bulgarian representative who was a base commissar for the Bulgarians. So there were Eastern Europeans and Polish there. Later, among the British, there were Cypriots and others. Among the Americans were Cubans. The battalion at this time was about 600 [men], with my group, No 1 Company, and the other volunteers that were trickling in. In January a big thing happened: a packing case arrived with new Russian rifles. You fired these rifles with the bayonet on and they made a very big difference. There was also the old Maxim, an old-fashioned heavy machine gun, but rather deadly when it was being used, especially if at not too long a range.

The command structure in the British Battalion at this point was that each company had a company commander with NCOs below them. Above them all was the battalion commander (Wilfred McCartney), the deputy commander

(Tom Wintringham), the second-in-command and the battalion political commissar. I was the base commissar. It was at about this time that [George] Nathan was taken away to divisional headquarters. He became Chief of Staff at division and he was killed at Brunete. He was a very brave man. He worked by example as well as being disciplined.

I think I should mention here what happened in connection with McCartney, who had to go back to England. He didn't ask to go back but he had to go back. I understand that he had done 9 years of his 12-year sentence for espionage. He wrote a book afterwards called *Walls Have Mouths*, which was about his experiences in prison. I don't know if he was guilty or not but he was found guilty. Anyway, he was going back and I visited him in his room before he went back to have a talk with him about the situation with the battalion and so on. It was the intention that he would come back. This was about mid-January but he had a big, heavy revolver and I had a rather small Belgian revolver, and he said: 'Look Peter, how about you giving me your revolver. I am going through France I don't want to lump this thing about'. I said all right. He asked to show me how to operate it. I took the revolver in my hand but I can't say for sure whether or not I touched the safety catch, or whether it was off or not, or whether I touched the trigger, but suddenly there was a shot and I had hit him in the arm with a bullet from the small Belgian revolver. We rushed him to hospital, got him an anti-tetanus injection and he was patched up and off he went.

Why did he go back? I am certain it was not to get him out of the command position although he was, how shall I put it, a British military officer type. He was not terribly popular in the battalion but I think he was respected for his ability. He was a capable military officer. He had a rather arrogant style. I was not given the job of getting rid of him. I have nothing to hide about it. It was an accident.[9]

Joe Norman

Volunteer from Manchester and Bolton, England. Served as the Communist Party organizer with the British Battalion, 15th International Brigade, July 1937–March 1938.

The training was first class but we had no proper rifles, very few rifles, and the few that we had were very old. Old Lee Enfields from War World I. They were good rifles but there weren't enough of them. Eventually the Russians, after losing four to five ships in the Mediterranean, managed to get us some new Russian rifles. They didn't compare with the Lee Enfields for quality but they were pretty good. We then got a few anti-tank guns and some tanks at one time but there weren't enough of them. When we got to the battalion there was an election and I was elected battalion party organizer to explain our objectives in the Spanish struggle.

It was different to being a battalion political commissar. The party organizer was there to get the contributions from the lads to pay their party dues. The commissar was a different kettle of fish. He was really a personnel officer. He had to understand the politics, but if anything went wrong in action he held an inquest with the top brass asking, 'Why did this go wrong?' He would tell us what he had found out. The Spanish Army was like any other army. The International Brigades became part of the Spanish Army so we were subservient to it. Whatever they decided, we had to do. Whatever action they decided, we had to go in. And believe me, they pushed us in some awful places. The political commissar was for all of the men. It didn't matter what party you were in. He looked after your needs – medical, clothing and food needs.

There was always a battalion of Spaniards as well as British [in the brigade]. In the early days, of course, they were separate because they weren't organized into the International

Brigades. There were Yugoslavs, Bulgarians and Italians. After the Republican government decided to synchronize the leadership and incorporate everybody in the country into the Spanish Republican Army, then we came under the command of the Spanish hierarchy. They were a mixed-up crowd, some were good and some weren't so good.

The International Brigades were often put into worse positions than the Spanish. There is no doubt about it, in 1937 and the beginning of 1938 we got some awful hammerings. My company at Teruel lost 30 men in one action and we were sent into rearguard actions without any proper information. In fact, after Teruel we went into the Aragon where there was a big breakthrough by the fascists and we were left isolated in some olive groves. We were lying in the olive groves waiting for dawn, that is when I got captured. The next morning we lost our battalion observer. No one knew where he had got to, so Sam Wild said to me: 'Joe, you take three men and go out in front and observe what you can.' We thought we were going into a position to relieve someone and then all hell broke loose. We just turned the corner and [the fascists] swarmed all over us. We had just captured two fascist patrols and handed them back, and then I looked round and I am looking at a tank. On either side of the olive groves it was swarming, with machine guns and rifles going off and there were 100 of us snaffled. It was a terrific slaughter.[10]

Frank Ryan to all Irish Comrades.

Albacete, 1 January 1937.

As most of you will have read in the newspapers before leaving home, an Irish unit of the International Brigades is being formed. It may be necessary to make clear to some why all Irish comrades are not just now together. The fact is that the military situation does not allow the war to be held up so that all Irishmen can be collected and formed into a unit.

This unit will be part of the English-speaking battalion which is to be formed. Irish, English, Scots and Welsh comrades will fight side by side against the common enemy – fascism. It must also be made clear that in the International Brigades in which we serve there are no national differences. We are all comrades. We have come out here as soldiers of liberty to demonstrate Republican Ireland's solidarity with the gallant Spanish workers and peasants in their fight against fascism.[11]

Notes

1   http://www.english.uiuc.edu/maps/scw/knox.htm.
2   http://www.geocities.com/roav1945/dsmith.html.
3   http://www.geocities.com/irelandscw/ibvol-EDInCharge.htm.
4   Lesser, Frank, Imperial War Museum Sound Archive (IWMSA), London, Ref 9408/7, Reel 4.
5   Edwards, Jack, IWMSA, London, Ref 808/3, Reel 1.
6   McLean, Tony, IWMSA, London, Ref 838/5, Reel 2.
7   Gregory, Thomas Walter, IWMSA, London, Ref 8851/9, Reel 2.
8   Gilbert, David 'Tony', IWMSA, London, Ref 9157/10, Reel 4.
9   Kerrigan, Peter, IWMSA, London, Ref 810/6, Reel 2.
10 Norman, Joe, IWMSA, London, Ref 818/4, Reel 2.
11 Marx Memorial Library, Box C, 8/6, copyright unknown.

Battle for Madrid

By early November 1936, the Nationalists were poised to make an all-out attack on Madrid in the hope of capturing the Spanish capital. If they did they would win the war. The forces at their disposal were led by General Emilio Mola and the majority of them were units of the Army of Africa. Mola ordered Colonel Jose Varela to attack the northwest flank of Madrid's defences, and by 16 November Varela's troops had forced a bridgehead over the River Manzanares.

During the following week almost three-quarters of the 'University City' fell to the Nationalists, but the poorly armed militia units that comprised the Popular Army, led by General José Miaja and aided by Russian tanks and aircraft, stemmed the Nationalist advance. Further assistance to the Republicans came from the first International Brigade units to reach the frontline.

It is worth noting that the 11th Brigade, comprising mostly German, Polish and French volunteers, actually arrived after the frontline had stabilized. By 23 November both sides were exhausted by the fighting and began digging in. Varela had failed to achieve the desired breakthrough. Although the Nationalists held the areas to the north and west of the city, it was obvious that all further frontal attacks upon Madrid would be costly and likely to fail.

Bill Scott

Volunteer from the Republic of Ireland. Member of the Irish Republican Army. Served in the Thaelmann Battalion, 12th International Brigade, November–December 1936.

We saw Alex, our German commander, talking to Arnold Jeans at the end of the road. We knew something was in the air. They pointed across the valley to the hill occupied by German fascists and Moorish troops. The valley of death, as we used to call it, lay between our lines and theirs. The Thaelmann Battalion [made up of Germans] must hold it at all costs for the price of its capture was enormous, and it was the key to the hill dominating University City [Ciudad Universitaria]. Arnold Jeans, a man of amazing courage, was our section leader. He could speak eight languages. He and the German commander came walking down the road, talking in German. Over to the left and beyond our lines stood a big red house. It was towards this house they were pointing as they walked down the bullet-swept road. The German fascists were very soon to surrender the hill to men from their own country.

Arnold Jeans approached us. He said he wanted six volunteers: it always meant five and himself. We were to creep over to the red house and see if it was still occupied by the enemy. I can't remember how many times La Casa Rojo Grande was captured and recaptured by our men. It had been shelled all during the earlier part of the day by our artillery.

Over we went, with Raymond Cox singing 'The Rose of Tralee'. I often cursed the day I taught him the words of that song. Cox and I were pals. I met him first at Portbou station in September 1936. He had run away from home, purchased a weekend ticket to Paris, made his way to the Pyrenees and, under cover of darkness, crossed the frontier into Spain. He was arrested by the Catalan police and taken to Portbou station for interrogation. He said he wanted to fight fascism. On account of his youth they sent him back across the border. A second attempt ended in his being arrested by the French police. Finally, he was picked up in a semi-exhausted state by a patrol. The four militia men listened sympathetically to the story of this Southampton youth. They gave him food and drink and a lift to Barcelona, where I met him a second time. We became great pals and always went out together.

At Sarria Barracks, where we were in training for a few weeks prior to going to Madrid, sleep was impossible after 06.00 hours. Cox would be one of the first to rise and with him 'the pale moon was rising above the green mountain'. Usually at night when we wanted to sleep, 'the cool shades of evening their mantles were spreading'. As we passed through our lines we were greeted here and there by an inquisitive comrade as to where we were going. We didn't know. Are you going to give yourselves up, somebody would ask? We left our frontlines behind us.

As we reached La Casa Rojo the weird singing of a shell, terminating in a terrific explosion, made us dive for cover. Alex gave an order. We followed him up a slope leading to the house. Three of us were posted outside to keep watch while Alex led the way into the deserted red house. The brick wall behind us was crumbling fast before the fascist machine-gun bullets. Now and then a shell would burst a few yards away. Over to the left we could see hundreds of Moors running around in a disorderly manner. Obviously they had abandoned the house when it came in range of our artillery. We didn't fire on them; that would betray our already precarious position. But they got it that night.

A shell whistled overhead. It struck La Casa Rojo. With our faces buried in the ground we knew the wall behind us had crashed. We knew the four men inside must all be dead. To us that meant disaster, for good leaders have a way of inspiring confidence, and how could we get back without Arnold Jeans? How could our company exist without him? Fate had often tricked us before. This time it had presented us with a miracle, for the four men came walking out of the house carrying some war material with them. We started on the journey back to report to our battalion. Again we passed our comrades in the frontlines. We passed the lads who a short time before had thought we had embarked on journey's end.

The Thaelmann Battalion attacked that evening. All through that night a battle raged for possession of the hill, held by the fascists. Next day it was in the hands of the army of the Spanish Republic.

Today a pile of shattered ruins stands as a memorial to German comrades who routed German fascists and Moors in the vicinity of La Casa Rojo. Arnold Jeans and Raymond Cox are dead. With five other British comrades they fell in an engagement with a Moorish column on 19 December [1936]. The young lad who wanted to fight fascism was buried with military honours, along with six of his countrymen, at Fuencarral, a northern suburb of the city they died to save.[1]

Geoffrey Cox

British war correspondent writing for the News Chronicle *in Madrid, October 1936.*

These militia men were often just sitting around the place, cutting a slice off a loaf of bread, opening a tin of sardines, a tin of herrings or rolling themselves cigarettes and lounging around in a state of what struck me, as one of complete disarray. I had some military training myself, because in New Zealand where I grew up we had a form of limited, compulsory military service which we had to do, a certain number of drills at night, also at an annual camp. We were all drafted members of the Territorial Army so the basic principles of military discipline and warfare were known to me, and there was very little of that about at that time, and these chaps were all very aware and frightened of any sound in the air. They had been quite heavily bombed and machine gunned in their trenches further south towards Toledo, and it took only the slightest sound of an aircraft to give them considerable alarm. At the time I thought this was a sign of them being untrained troops. But, of course, I found in World War II that even trained troops, until they got accustomed to aircraft attack, were liable to get very nervy and very scared.

The Republican people and the Republican government were so absolutely convinced of the rightness of their cause that they were very eager to have the international press around. The knowledge that a journalist was there opened doors to you rather than closed them. Also, the organization on the Republican side was sufficiently slack for there to be no effective policing of the areas near the front. I went forward near Madrid with a German photographer, because I wanted him to get a photograph of me in the trenches. We found some chaps digging a trench on the outskirts of Madrid, and there was no sign that this was anything other than a reserve trench. So I duly got into position and the cameraman went a bit ahead to get a picture of me and crouched beside these militia men. All of a sudden a shell burst almost on him – we were in fact on the frontline and we didn't even realize it, so chaotic was the place.

On the outskirts of Madrid, if you went forward to the barricades or to University City, they were very pleased to see you, very confident of the rightness of their cause. Therefore I never had any problem getting to the front in Madrid, other than the logistical one. Once the fighting got established in and around University City it then became difficult, because the lines of communication were quite often heavily shelled and it was very often difficult to persuade anybody to show you where to go forward, let alone go forward with you.

In Madrid there was very little opposition to the Republic. The police said that in the fashionable suburbs of Madrid, government trucks and cars were fired on regularly at night by snipers placed in wealthy flats. They had cars in which a chap with a light machine gun sat in the back seat and the car drove slowly down the street in the hope of attracting fire, the idea being that you then spotted where the fire came from and you moved in. But in fact we spent a night patrolling up and down these streets and found nothing at all of any excitement ...

In the initial stages of the siege of Madrid the spirits of the civilians were surprisingly good. I was astonished the cinemas were kept open. You had a sense very much of life as usual. It was only after 7 November, when we all thought that Franco's troops would break in, that the streets were deserted and a real sense of apprehension was in the air.

By the 7th there was no doubt that it was a city at war, a dangerous city to move about in. At night in the dark there were rifle shots going off all the time. I think these were often as not nervy guards shooting at shadows, but that was when we moved out of the hotel that we were in, on the Grande Vere, and moved into the British Embassy to sleep because we were of the view (the British press) that once the Moors came through, there would not be much time to explain to them that we were decent self-respecting journalists and not Republicans going to put a bullet through them.

We went back to the Hotel Grande Vere by day but we continued to sleep at the embassy right up until the time I left. The only other sign I had of people who were at risk from the Republicans was this extraordinary site of a model prison being evacuated as the fighting got near to it. This was three or four days after the attack was fully joined. We went down there in the evening and the whole courtyard was filled with people with this terrible prison pallor and unshaven faces and I recollect them each having a blanket around their necks, but it may not have been all of them, and they were standing in lines apathetically waiting to get onto buses. It must have been nerve-racking for them because here were their liberators, as they would have seen it, within a rifle shot away because you could hear the battle going off in the background very clearly, and of course these were the chaps who were massacred, taken out of their buses and shot by the anarchists on the road outside Madrid...

You had everywhere these requisitioned cars and lorries with the initials of the unions on them. The Ritz, I think, was a workers' kitchen or a hospital. I know that one great hotel had been turned into a hospital. I think the Ritz at that time was one of these great public restaurants where you got a cheap meal. Everybody was dressed in what passed in those days for proletarian style, that is there was nobody wearing any clothes of any smartness at all. We rapidly did away with our own collars and ties and wore an open shirt or jacket. There were guards on all corners and really there was a mixture of a city at war and a city in revolution.

The regular life of the community went on. The bootblacks were busy in the Puerta del Sol. The cinemas were open. There was quite clearly very little private property that had been appropriated at that stage. The outward signs of power were those of the unions and of the Left. Whether or not factories had been taken over and to what degree, I didn't know because, of course, I was so busy covering the war that I had no time at that stage to investigate it.

The only contact I had with the British Embassy was Forbes, Ogalby Forbes, who was the chargé d'affaires. I thought he was a very sensible chap indeed. He was too busy to see us often, but strangely enough I don't recollect any British journalist consistently going to the embassy for information. We slept in the ballroom. We were very glad to have a cup of coffee and a bit of bread for our breakfast and we went out and did our work.

There was no evidence in my time about British diplomats in Spain hampering the Republican cause ... The only argument that you could possibly make was the embassy did not open its doors to any member of the International Brigades or was not prepared to do anything to help anybody in the International Brigades. Similarly, they were also not prepared to take refugees. Franco had refugees inside the embassy and there was, of course, a great hullabaloo when we discovered that one of the Romilly brothers [Giles and Esmond, nephews of Winston Churchill], I think it was the older brother Giles, had spent a night in the embassy as a guest of Sefton Delmer [head of the *Daily Express* Paris Bureau]. And also among the journalists who slept in the embassy was a man whose name escapes me for the moment, who was a deserter from the International Brigade who had managed to get himself taken on as Delmer's assistant – Scott Watson, one of the many eccentric figures that gather around civil wars. Delmer made him his assistant and there was some anger when the British Embassy discovered that they had on the premises a man who could have been thought of by the Republic as a deserter from their forces.

I had no contact with the British platoon in the Thaelmann Battalion on the line because on the two occasions that I went forward to see them they were out of the line, so my contacts with them were mainly when they came back off leave, which, of course, was very easy to do in Madrid. People came back from the line by tram, had a bath, went to the pictures and went back to the battle again. This is when I saw on several occasions Sam Russell, Esmond Romilly and others who were members of the British platoon. This was shortly before they had very heavy losses …

On the whole the British lads were truly admirable. Particularly the earlier people, they were all sincere people. There was no doubt the occasional adventurer among them. They were genuine, responsible chaps who wanted to stand up against what they felt was a force that was wrong. I think at this stage the danger in Britain was not uppermost in their minds, these were the bulk of the early volunteers. The International

Brigades were either communists or people who were close to the communists in their ideas and they were very strongly anti-fascist, and it is difficult now over these many years to explain why fascism appeared a very real danger to us then, but it did. We felt that we were fighting to keep our own country from ultimately going authoritarian, and that in the case of Spain this was allied to a feeling that the Spanish people were being made the victims of the power of the Nazis and Mussolini.

Suddenly people in Britain felt here was the International League of Nations standing up for their rights and this was quite different to the old nationalist wars. This was a chance for a real new order based upon peace and there was a surge of idealism and a very real sense that we might have to go and fight. I remember in the *News Chronicle* newsroom that we would discuss with great earnestness if we would go into the infantry or the air force. We looked the possibility of war in the face and found that we had to face it. Now some of that idealism was, of course, completely blunted and smashed within weeks by the realization that while the British government had been calling for a stand against tyranny, in the name of international order, it had been busy doing a deal behind the scenes. I don't say necessarily if we would have been better off. It was the hypocrisy of it that shocked people. That same idealism I think animated the people that fought in Spain, and no doubt as the numbers grew much larger you got a wider range of people who were cynical or out for adventure, but it took a lot of guts and a lot of genuine idealism to put yourself into the hands of a foreign army that shot its deserters and was very tough in its discipline. For the early International Brigaders I have the most profound respect as they were people who put their lives on the line for an ideal, and voluntarily, and that takes quite a bit of doing.

I think Esmond Romilly was one of those. I think there was the streak of the maverick [in him] as I think there was in the whole of the Romilly family. I think they are an almost exhibitionist family and there was a touch of that in Esmond, but basically he had volunteered and took the risks that came his way. I knew his brother Giles much better and Giles did a longer stint than Esmond. I remember talking to him after he left Spain about the question of courage and he said, 'I can honestly say that I have not ever taken a decision based upon fear. I have never gone out of the way to prove whether I had courage or not. But in all honesty I can say that I think I did the right thing at the time'. These were very sincere people.

A number of them, of course, were party members who had been drafted in. Quite a lot of the early members of the International Brigades had simply been rung up by their local party secretary and said your duty to the party is to go off and enlist. They did so at a time when it was a sincere faith in communism because, after all, by 1936 the show trials [in the Soviet Union] had not got under way. You had the appalling example of the mass collectiveness but that was very rigorously brushed under the carpet by the bulk of the British press.[2]

Sam Russell

Volunteer from London. Served with No 1 Company, 14th International Brigade, with the British Battalion, 15th International Brigade, as correspondent with the Daily Worker *and as Communist Party representative in Spain, November 1936–January 1939.*

While I was still in hospital a number of our chaps told me that there was somebody in town who had let it be known that if they wanted to leave Spain they could arrange it. We enquired a bit more and discovered that it was this Honorary British Consul, who was trying to organize desertion from the International Brigades. I decided to go down to his office (I was still on crutches). At first he refused to see me, but then I said that I would stay until he did. This man had a picture of Mussolini in his office! Anyway, I let him know that I was aware of what he was trying to do and we had a real row about it. He denied that he was organizing desertion, but said that as the Honorary British Consul if a British citizen came to him and asked for assistance to go home and they had no means of going home, then it was his duty to assist him ...

I didn't have more than about three weeks' training near Albacete. That was in early November 1936, when we were told that we were going to Madrid. We were taken down in trucks to Albacete, put on trains there and went up to the front with the French Battalion. We didn't see really anything of Madrid right away, we arrived there during the night. We actually went into action on 6 or 7 November 1936. By the time we got out it was light and we marched through the streets. People gathered around and at first thought we were Russians, but they soon realized that we were not. There was a tremendous reception because the word went round. While we were getting out of the trains and forming up, the crowd gathered and cheered us. We didn't realize immediately how serious the military situation was and how close to Madrid the fascists had got. We were taken into University City, that was the first encounter ...

University City was a brand new university campus. It was modern and really up-to-date in every way. A luxurious installation, including something that puzzled the British for quite a bit – the bidet – which most of the British had never come across before. It took quite a while to get them to appreciate that it was not a loo. This became quite academic because with the fighting the whole of the sewage system was destroyed, and so one could not use the toilets in University City anyway. So this was at the edge of Casa de Campo, and we were the British unit in the Philosophy [Filosofia y Letras] building. The rest of the battalion was in nearby buildings – the clinical hospital and other buildings. We made ourselves as comfortable as we could in the lecture halls.

We were equipped with Russian Maxim machine guns. Most of us were only familiar with Maxim machine guns from Russian films that we'd seen, but I was one of the few that had done training on the Vickers machine gun. I soon found that the Maxim was very similar to the Vickers gun except the big difference was that the Vickers was on a tripod. The Maxim was mounted on wheels, which we soon found made it a damn awful thing to have to carry around. You could take the gun off the two-wheeled carriage that it was on, but you would have to have one man carry the gun and another to carry the carriage. The carriage with the two wheels was much heavier and much more difficult to carry around than a tripod. It was also less manoeuvrable when firing compared to a tripod.

Those that had rifles had these Austrian models, although they were soon changed for Remingtons. Where these Remington rifles came from I can't remember, and the Lewis guns. In the first couple of days, when we were getting installed, John Cornford and John Sommerfield had come across a great store of English books. Mostly Everyman editions, so we brought these along. They had also come across two sorts of tourist posters. One had a picture of the fountains of the Alhambra [at Granada] and said, 'The sun is waiting for you in Spain', and the other had a sort of bull and bullock cart and said, 'Spain, the charm of the East with the comfort of the West'. They stuck these up in the lecture hall on a blackboard. John thought this was a great joke. We had just sat down when suddenly there was an almighty explosion. The place was full of smoke. When the smoke cleared there was John Cornford with blood pouring down his face and head. We later discovered that it was one of our own anti-aircraft shells that had fallen short and had come through the side of a wall. They took John off and that afternoon he came back with his head bandaged, looking very heroic and romantic.

Well the fighting then got pretty intense. At one stage we got out of the building and were fighting across the Rio

Manzanares. Most of the time the Rio Manzanares was a ditch, not much in the way of a river, but there was some very savage fighting to and fro across it. It was there that we also first encountered the problem of the anarchists. One day when we were in the Philosophy building, we knew that there was an anarchist unit nearby. We sent a patrol over to see what was happening with them. I was with the patrol and went over and found that there were only two or three people there. We asked what had happened. They said the rest had gone to the pictures. We thought this was a pretty poor show. It was one of the problems with the anarchists, you couldn't get more courageous people, but they had a very strange idea of military business. There was nothing happening, so off they went. This was one of the problems that was very serious – the problem of forming a disciplined army.

The fighting carried on and we had quite a number of casualties, including from accidents that happen in war. We were moving position one night. We were going along the road and we noticed the flashing of lights behind us. It was a lorry coming. We hadn't been told about this. We were crossing a small bridge over a railway line and there were a lot of telephone wires. The lorry behind us accelerated (it later turned out that they had thought we were fascist troops). It drove right through us. We were scattered. We were mostly to the right and left of the road but some people were in the middle and knocked down. This lorry broke one of the wires and got it stuck in the front mud guard, pulled it and it got lashed around poor old Freddie Jones' neck. It ripped his head off his shoulders from his neck. We found his body in the morning, along with a number of others who had been killed. We knew the driver but it wasn't his fault. He hadn't been told: he thought we were fascists. He had a load of ammunition on board. It was just a stupid accident.

The first time we met the Moors we quickly discovered the accuracy of their snipers – if anybody showed their head they'd had it. You had to be very careful, you had some really crack shots amongst the Moors.

There wasn't much exchange of territory. It was just in and out of the buildings. But what we did do was stop the advance of the fascist troops, because until that time they had been advancing pretty rapidly.

I remember before we went into position in the University City, we had arrived at the north station and then, after marching a short distance, were put into lorries and drove during the night. We were ordered to get out of the lorries and we were standing on the road. We didn't know where we were except vaguely near Madrid, and then we saw the remnants of the Spanish troops coming along the road. A most frightening sight. They were obviously defeated: people who had not slept for days, in a terrible state. While we were standing there watching this we saw a small car that came along with two lorries filled with Russian rifles and ammunition, with Spanish Army officers in these trucks. A woman and two men in civilian clothes got out of a small car. A Spanish Army officer and the woman got up on this lorry and started talking – we were about 150 yards away. Then we saw a number of Spanish Army officers trying to stop the retreat. I mean it was just a panic, people shuffling along, and after this someone said, 'Why don't we go up and have a listen'. I said to Fred we will go up and listen.

It was a Spanish communist woman, Dolores Ibárruri, La Pasionaria (The Passionflower; see plate 9). I had heard of her and this was a most amazing thing. It was the first time I had seen her in action. There were hundreds of people trying to get out, get away, and bit by bit they got people to stop and to listen, and as some stopped more and more stopped until they had hundreds of people, most of them in a most lamentable condition, mostly rags thrown over their arms. Then the officers started getting people formed up into units while she kept on speaking. She was talking about attacks on Madrid and in a very short time this sort of absolute rabble of defeated people started forming up. Rifles were distributed and they marched back in the opposite direction from where they had been fleeing to.[3]

Peter Kerrigan

Volunteer from Scotland. Served as a political commissar with the British Battalion, 15th International Brigade, and as a war correspondent for the Daily Worker *in Spain, December 1936–December 1938.*

When I got there [Albacete], there were already British volunteers there, including a British Company that had been formed and incorporated into a French volunteer [14th] Battalion commanded by a French officer called Delasalle. The political commissar of that battalion was Ralph Fox, the English writer [killed in action in December 1936], a well-known writer who was a member of the Communist Party. The company commander was George Nathan, who had been an officer in the Brigade of Guards [elite unit of British Army]. He had the rank of captain. I remember the battalion numbered 600 men. It wasn't like the old 1,100-men battalions that we had been used to in the British Army in World War I; in Spain they were in the continental style. I was appointed the political commissar at Albacete for all the English-speaking volunteers. By this time some of the Americans had already begun to arrive, and I was commissar for them as well. Later we were very strict and sent home 18 year olds when we found out their real age because they were supposed to be 21.

In about mid-December when I got there, [Wilfred] McCartney was the commander of the British Battalion and Tom Wintringham was his second-in-command. Frank Ryan, a well-known Irish revolutionary, Springhall and myself were taken on a trip to Madrid, where we visited the front and met among others General Kleber, and there I made my first acquaintance with Hans Karl, a commander in the International Brigades who later came to Britain. He ended up as the military correspondent of the *Daily Worker*, and I think that after the war he went back to East Germany and became the Chief of Police. He died in about 1947. He was a very fine person and an expert at this kind of thing. During our visit to the front we were at a hospital in the University City and came across a firing party for a funeral for a member of the Thaelmann Battalion that had been killed.

Just before Christmas, Delasalle's battalion moved off to the southern front, near Córdoba, and I remember Springhall and myself spending some time with Ralph Fox having coffee and a talk. A few days later, after they had gone south, I was called to Brigade headquarters and sent off to the southern front. They were asking for some responsible people to go down to inspect the situation and to report back. It was quite a long car journey and we arrived at a small village not very far from Córdoba called Lopera, and as we approached the front we were coming through trees. I was a bit worried because my interpreter was a young chap, aged 18 or 19, who spoke French very fluently. He was the son of Professor Haldane, or rather he was the son of the wife of Professor Haldane (Charlotte Haldane). Ronnie Burgess was his name and the bullets were coming thick and fast and I thought, what would happen if this young boy gets hurt? As we approached the front through these trees we saw General Walter. That was my first dealings with him. He was a little man and a very capable, likeable person. I saw him talking to some of the French soldiers, members of the brigade who were obviously coming back from the front, and I soon realized he was trying to convince them to go back into the line. I spoke to his Chief of Staff, an Italian called Marande, and he explained that there had been heavy fighting and that the fascists were occupying a high ridge and our troops were below them. Anyway we never saw Delasalle. I learned latter that his battalion headquarters was behind the line, further back from the front. When we got up to the frontline we discovered it was an olive grove. They were dug in small, shallow holes behind rather thin little trees. There we had the company headquarters of the British Company; Nathan was in charge and everything was under control. He told us there had been very heavy fighting and that unfortunately they had to launch attacks over open ground, with the fascists and their machine guns pinning them down. There had been quite a few casualties and Ralph Fox had been killed. He had given me some papers that had been taken off his body, but they hadn't been able to retrieve the body. Nathan promised me that during the night they would get the body back …

The British had been trying to take the hill. They had been pinned down and the French companies that were on each side of them pulled back. All the members of No 1 Company were already in action and they suffered heavy casualties; we had lost people in the British section. Delasalle disappeared for a period, but I never saw his headquarters so I can't verify where exactly he was, but I can tell you what happened to him. I stayed the night at a place in the line, in a house. The machine-gunners, Polish anti-fascists, were in pretty good shape. I think they all had military service before they had been there. Anyway we decided to come back the next day to rejoin the British. When we got back they weren't in the line, they had been pulled out during the night. I was told they were sent to Madrid.

The battalion had been regrouped and had been replaced by another battalion. It was obvious they were trying to get them sorted out and they were taken away the next day to Madrid. Shortly after they were back in action in Madrid. I then learned that Delasalle had been arrested, court-martialled and shot. I understood at the time he had been shot for cowardice. Later there were stories that he had been a fascist agent. Personally, I thought it was the only thing that could be done with the man because in my opinion the soldiers had been demoralized by the actions of their commander.

I returned to Albacete and spent my time between there and Madrigueras in connection with the battalion. I advocated very strongly we should get a British Battalion established as quickly as possible. People kept coming out and I had got 120 [men]. In mid-January the British No 1 Company came back from the Madrid front. It had been bloodied both at the Córdoba front as well as the Madrid front.[4]

Notes

1   http://www.geocities.com/irelandscw/part-IrDem3709-10.htm#371016Six.
2   Cox, Geoffrey, Imperial War Museum Sound Archive (IWMSA), London, Ref 10059/4, Reel 2.
3   Russell, Sam, IWMSA, London, Ref 9484/6, Reel 3.
4   Kerrigan, Peter, IWMSA, London, Ref 810/6, Reel 2.

6

The Battle of Jarama

In February 1937, having failed to take Madrid by frontal assault, Franco gave orders for the main road that linked the city to the rest of Republican Spain to be cut. A Nationalist force of 40,000 men therefore crossed the Jarama River on 11 February 1937. In the Battle of Jarama alone, 7,000 Republican soldiers died, with another 13,000 wounded. The Nationalists succeeded in creating a salient in Republican lines, at a cost of 25,000 casualties, but did not achieve their objective to cut off Madrid. The British Battalion fought in the newly formed 15th International Brigade, but unfortunately had no maps of the Jarama area. For many foreign volunteers, Jarama was their first time in battle.

Tom Clarke

Volunteer from Dundee, Scotland. Member of the Communist Party. Served as a stretcher bearer with the British Battalion, 15th International Brigade, January 1937–July 1938.

> I remember there was a bit of a retreat [at Jarama]. There was a rumour went round ... and they started retreating. We'd gone back a bit, and some of them were actually running. And here we came across three women who were sitting behind a machine gun just past where we were, Spanish women. I saw them looking at us. I don't know whether it shamed us or what. But these women – they sat there. We sort of stabilized the line.[1]

Richard White

Volunteer from Dorset, England. Served with the British Battalion, 15th International Brigade, December 1936–September 1938.

I dropped down behind a tree with my rifle in front, and just as I dropped down getting into position I felt as though a locomotive had run over me and put a bullet through both legs. It was such a shock and then a numbness set in, but while I was trying to think, a few seconds later another one hit me through my left shoulder. I just lay there and one of my comrades from behind another tree knew I was hit. He made a run over to join me to see what he could do and laid down beside me. I almost immediately then got another bullet through my left hip. It exploded on a metal case I had in my pocket and tore a lump of flesh out of my hip. I said to him, as far as I was able to talk, to get the hell out, get away, which he did. There was nothing anybody could do. I was obviously under observation. I was being sniped at and I just stayed there, stayed still …

I waited about four hours. It was winter in February and not very hot in the daytime. In fact it was cold in the evenings. I had an overcoat on and I went into action with it on. I must have passed out a number of times. I became unconscious, semi-conscious, just waiting. I thought I had had it. When I received that bullet in the hip I thought it must have gone through my bowels and everything, and I thought that was it. They were firing at me all the time. There were bullets whizzing over all the time from our side in the early part of that period, and of course from where the fascists were firing.

I realized I was being observed because of the nature of those single wounds, the way they picked me off like that. It was a sniper and therefore I was under observation. I thought that if I lay dumb he would think that I was finished, and he would no longer waste his ammunition on me … I was frightened, especially when we went into the attack. I don't think anyone cannot be frightened, but it is the unknown and it's the fear of being afraid and the fear of this and that. That gives you fear but you have to overcome it.

I ran about 60 or 80 yards before I was hit. I could not see the enemy, that is why I kept running as far as I did, because I could not see any targets and therefore I did not think that they were close enough to be able to snipe at me as they did. I was dodging them and I thought I was lucky, but as I lay down I was hit. I was armed with an old .303 rifle, an Enfield, but I never had a chance to fire it. You could not fire on the run. The main thing was to get as far forward as I could safely, to be able then to fire. They [stretcher bearers] came back at dusk, picked me up and laid me on the stretcher face down and took me back to the trench. I was given a cigarette and a cup of tea and I think I had an injection. I was carried back some distance to an ambulance, put in it and taken to the field hospital. They didn't attempt to do anything about my right ankle. The bullet had gone through the right ankle, shattered it. They didn't even take my boot off at the dressing station, but they put my [left] arm in a rough cradle and gave me some injections.

After a while I was loaded onto another ambulance which took me to another hospital. I was then put on a train in the morning and finished up in Huete. There I went into hospital and I was the only English person there. All the staff were either Spanish, French or American. There they gave me a thorough examination. They took the boot off my foot. I believe they took out the loose fragments of bone and closed the jagged part from the foot and the leg together, which shortened the leg by a couple of inches. Then they reset the shoulder and from there the only thing they could do was try and heal the infection in my ankle. I was not in a fit state to move around. In all I spent from February until September before I was able to get on crutches and make my way with assistance from the hospital to Albacete.

I had to go before a medical commission, which assessed me 90 percent disabled. From there I had to make my way to Barcelona. I stayed in a hotel in Barcelona for nearly a week with a wounded American while we were trying to get passports, because I had lost my British passport.

I had to replace my lost passport with a temporary one from the British Consul in Barcelona to get back and he had to do the same, to get an American passport. Finally we set off and I linked up in Barcelona with Jack Brent, who was Canadian-English and who had been wounded. He got shot in the spine and was paralysed from the waist down. He was in Huete hospital while I was there but in another ward, and we communicated via the nurses where we could. We were both released at the same time, and Jack and I made our way by train from Barcelona down to Portbou. This was in September 1938.

I think the hospital treatment was marvellous under the circumstances, because the circumstances were dreadful. There was a lack of medical supplies of all kinds, therefore there were high incidents of infections of one kind or another because it was very hot. They hadn't the facilities. They were overcrowded and then there was the food question. We knew that a lot of Spaniards were having to go without necessary rations so that we could be fed and nursed. We felt that we were a burden, although the Spanish people never gave any impression of that, and they willingly gave everything they had to the International Brigaders in the line and those in hospital. We got enough food. Eggs were in good supply. There was no limit to bread and wine. The doctors said we could drink the wine, said it was good for our blood and helped our healing, so we drank plenty of red wine!

One doctor was Dakin. I think he was French and he was the one who introduced a method for attempting to deal with infection, they called it the 'Dakin Treatment'. He used it on me but it was not successful in getting rid of this infection in my foot. We had discussed, on my insistence, whether my leg should come off. I could not see any point in retaining it. I could not see how they were going to get over this infection. Then what would I have: a useless foot in the long run. They were loathe to do that because of the lack of facilities and thought it would be better to hang on until I was well enough to make my way back to England and have the amputation there, if required. This is what happened.[2]

Albert Charlesworth

Volunteer from Manchester, England. Served as a runner and postman with the British Battalion, 15th International Brigade, December 1936– September 1937 and December 1937–October 1938.

I was in Albacete. The story at Albacete has probably been told by other comrades. My story is no different from theirs. I do remember that when we left the farmhouse on that morning, 12 or 13 February, the whole battalion left and started to go up the hills (the first morning of Jarama). We dropped down into the first gully and there we were told to leave all our packs. More or less over the top of us there were aircraft and one [German] plane was brought down. Since the war I can verify that plane was piloted by a German called [Adolf] Galland. He became very famous in World War II. We continued to advance.

There was still no fighting going on, at least not with us. We could hear artillery and the like but there was no fire of any kind coming towards us, and we were not firing. We continued the advance through the olive groves and then my platoon of No 4 Company was directed over to the right, down a gully right into the front. We went along there until we came to a tiny hillock, and the platoon took up position on top of this little hillock, which was flat on top. We could not see the rest of the battalion. It was a glorious day, the sun got up and it was very warm. The birds were singing very nicely to me and firing seemed to be taking place. It was not until 11.00 in the morning that I had realized that the birds that I thought were singing were bullets whistling past and there was a fierce battle going on. We were out of sight and not being fired on, and all this terrific fire was going on behind us where the battalion must have been.

Over to our left on top of the hillock was a white house, and as the battle progressed we could all see bodies rolling down this hillock from this white house position, 16 or 20 I must have seen roll down there. I knew then that casualties were being suffered but still there was no firing coming our way. It was peaceful as far as we were concerned. It was obvious we were out of sight or had not been seen at any rate.

It must have been late afternoon when, over to the right, about half a mile away, I could see a battalion, the enemy, advancing up the road led by a tank. They advanced to a position approximately level with us and after a few minutes the tank must have spotted us, and opened fire on our position on this little hillock. We were dead ducks there, because they were actually looking down on us. We had to evacuate it and scramble back up the hill as best we could. I got over the hill and found that there weren't many comrades left. There were a lot of dead bodies, which were being used as sand bags. I went 10 yards behind the actual frontline where there was a little dip, where an ambulance and first aid men were. I took up my position with the others in the firing line and stayed there until the order came to fall back to the sunken road.

We fell back down this shallow valley and then back up to the sunken road. There were not many left to go back and I can distinctly remember when I got to the road one comrade was standing with what I thought was a bullet wound in each shoulder. He had blood on each shoulder and his arms folded in front of him.

Then a wagon came along the road and the wounded were loaded into it. There were three wagons that went away along the sunken road. It was now dusk. The average fellow couldn't possibly know what was going on all around, but I assumed the Machine-Gun Company was being placed approximately 100 yards in front of the sunken road, in some trees. It wasn't many minutes after that when either an artillery shell or a mortar exploded near me and I went through the air. I picked myself up and didn't appear to be wounded, but my left arm refused to move. I reported to the medical section and I was bundled into a lorry and sent down to Morata, where there was a proper first aid station. I had to stay there overnight and the following morning I was put into an ambulance and sent to Madrid.

In hospital it was found that there were no wounds but my arm was paralysed. There was nothing broken, nothing severed, it was probably just a result of shock. I was put under medical treatment and in a few days the use started to come back into my fingers, and slowly the use came back into the whole arm. In a fortnight I was able to return back to the battalion, which at that time was having a short rest down in Morata village.

Within a day or two the battalion marched back up towards the front. We went into reserve. We were there for perhaps two days and we went forward down the valley, up a hill on the other side and came into a communications trench, which led into a line of trenches. This was the frontline. The line was quiet then and there were already entrenchments in the trench for firing positions and I took one up. That was my home for the next three months. During this time it was quiet. Most of the time there were shells and intense firing, but there were no attacks or counterattacks.[3]

John 'Bosco' Jones

Volunteer from London. Served as a runner and infantryman with the British Battalion, 15th International Brigade, November 1936–October 1938.

After about the third day at Jarama when we went into action, there was very little defence. We were out in the open and people were standing up when they should have been taking cover. They were being shot down and we were losing quite a number of men and right to the front of us, about 500 yards away, there was a big white house. We were hoping to capture that white house but we never got near it. Our commander, [Bert] Overton, came over to me and said: 'I have forgotten my binoculars.' I was a runner then, a messenger, and I said I would go back for them. He said, 'No, I will go'. I said you can't go and leave the company, but before I said anything else he walked off and he was gone. I didn't think too much more about it. I thought that maybe he had been killed. So many people got killed, especially officers, at that time.

It was about six months later, at Mondéjar, that I met Peter Kerrigan, the commissar, who was a very stern and severe but good commissar. He did things for everyone's good. He says to me, 'There is a battalion trial, go and get the prisoner'. So I went in and there was this bloke sitting there. It was Overton. I looked at him, sort of remembered his face, told him to come along and marched him in. I remember Kerrigan and a fellow called [George] Aitken were sitting there. Overton was asked about this and he told them the same story as he had to me: that he had left his binoculars and he went back to fetch them. He was accused of cowardice, taken in front of the battalion, stripped of his officer epaulettes and was dishonoured. That was the last I saw of him. I was told he went off to another front and died there. After the trial I did say to Peter Kerrigan that because Overton had given my name as a witness I should have been allowed to step forward. I couldn't have made any difference. I would have told the same story, but it seemed a bit unfair to me. Kerrigan said he was a coward and that men had died.[4]

Joe Norman

Volunteer from Manchester and Bolton, England. Served as the Communist Party organizer with the British Battalion, 15th International Brigade, July 1937–March 1938.

After Jarama the discipline began to slip a bit. That was one of the reasons why the party sent the cream of its leadership to try and lift the morale of the troops. Because at Jarama they got such a hammering and they had no leave. The morale began to slip a bit and like any army getting a hammering and not having any relief, we had to have a fresh influx to build up the battalion because it was practically decimated.

The symptoms of this lack of discipline after Jarama were disinterest and no enthusiasm to fight. They never refused an order but they didn't fight with enthusiasm like they did in the early days, there was a sort of apathy. There were a number of desertions. Some got away and some didn't. Some were snaffled and put in prison for a time. But it was like any other army, if you deserted and got caught you were punished.

Joining the Spanish Army affected discipline. For the first time we had to salute officers. Before when you saw an officer you just said, 'How do you do'. I think that helped a bit to lift morale, plus the constant explanations as to why this was and so on. I didn't have much to do with the officers, although I was battalion party organizer. I could go to Battalion headquarters and discuss things with the battalion commissars and occasionally I went to brigade as the battalion representative. We didn't see much of the apparent difference between anarchists, communists, Labour, what have you. The main idea was that we were there to fight fascism and how we fought it didn't matter a great deal as long as we got enough ammunition, enough to eat and were being led properly.

In the International Brigades I would say 50 percent had a working-class background or trade union background, and 50 percent were middle class, from Oxford and Cambridge. They were equally effective, first class because they had a political outlook ... Most of the people who went out to Spain had political thinking behind their decision, but in any war there were people who went along who were adventurers. This is where morale comes in if you have a number of these people in the group after a battle. It didn't help if they were grumbling all the time, so that is why they were there, the commissars. They did their job and the party organizer did his job. He would stiffen the morale of the troops and would talk down the adventurer types.

I never met any women fighting. They were there, of course. We saw photographs in the newspaper *The Volunteer for Liberty*, which was published every month. There were pictures of other fronts, other leaders, what they thought and so on, the usual morale-boosting stuff that you get in any army. Felicia Browne was killed before they formed the International Brigades [on 28 August 1936]. Quite frankly, apart from propaganda, which intends to paint an optimistic picture, we didn't know what was going on ... Apart from our own front where we could see our own successes and our own defeats, we were taking a lot for granted when we accepted all the propaganda. We know better now it wasn't so. In some places they were telling lies about what was happening on fronts, probably to boost morale.

We had various visits of Labour leaders from Britain. Noel Baker, who was Secretary to Clement Attlee, the Labour leader, and Alan Wilkinson came to our battalion. I was in No 1 Company and we were named in honour of the Labour leader because his visit was a stimulus to recruitment and the morale of the troops: the feeling that the Labour movement in Britain was behind us. So we named the No 1 Company the Major Attlee Company and I was there at the presentation of the flag. It is now in the London Museum. They told us that they realized that their support for non-intervention was a mistake, which was a big thing, and that they were prepared to fight and arouse the Labour trade union movement in support of the International Brigades. They chatted among us and went to a dinner which I didn't attend because I wasn't 'big' enough, being just one of the lads.[5]

Fred Copeman

Volunteer from London, England. Served with the Machine-Gun Company and as commander of the British Battalion, 15th International Brigade, October 1936–December 1937.

Then we went up the line in lorries with the 12 big Maxim guns and a Russian who couldn't speak a word of English. I was given the job of going from lorry to lorry, with a gun in each one, teaching the crew how to use it. We got up to Morata Valley with a little river running through it, just north of Jarama. You have to go over hills and then you come to Jarama Bridge, towards Toledo. Franco had advanced and was going to cut the Madrid–Valencia road, so a number of brigades were brought up: 15th, 14th, 11th and 12th.

In our brigade we had the Dimitrov Battalion and the French Battalion. We went over the top and had breakfast in lovely sunshine in a beautiful farmhouse, which was our headquarters. There were huge wine vats underground. You could live in them, huge things. The ground was very rough with huge rocks, and by the time we got moving we were all mixed up.

Before the Battle of Madrid in December 1936, Major Delasalle was accused of spying for the Nationalists and was shot. I wasn't there, that was No 1 Company with Jock Cunningham and Nathan and the other poet fellows who got killed there, Ralph Fox and John Cornford. Jock's attitude was that he thought it was wrong. The fellow was nothing of the kind. André Marty was the head behind all that. He was a bloody mad man if ever there was one. He just got an idea and carried it out and he dabbled in everything. His idea of discipline was court martial and to shoot you if you deserted. If they had done that, there would have been a few thousand shot. My attitude was that desertion wasn't an issue at all. I couldn't see how, if it was a voluntary army. These lads came straight from their homes or college and with their own will went to Spain to fight. Well, surely the same fellow can say, I have done my bit, I want to go back. The spirit of the brigade was completely voluntary, with no pay, just go and die. Who has the right to say when a fellow has done his whack? My attitude was: if they did anything at all that was more than anybody else did.

The English find it very hard to shoot their own, even in the Guards, nobody likes it. If you are in a war and there is a court martial and a lad is shot, it seems other people take it for granted. That's it and it is done. Not our fellows. I didn't find many people who stood for that. None of the commissars in the British Battalion agreed with shooting people. They did finally shoot two and I thought that was bloody awful. Historically it smudged the record. There is a French way of doing things, an English way, a German way and a Russian way.[6]

Notes

1   http://flag.blackened.net/revolt/spain/women_afa.html.
2   White, Richard, Imperial War Museum Sound Archive (IWMSA), London, Ref 9407/5, Reel 4.
3   Charlesworth, Albert, IWMSA, London, Ref 9427/4, Reel 3.
4   Jones, John 'Bosco', IWMSA, London, Ref 9392/6, Reel 6.
5   Norman, Joe, IWMSA, London, Ref 818/4, Reel 2.
6   Copeman, Fred, IWMSA, London, Ref 794/13, Reel 1.

The Battle of Brunete

Brunete was part of a Republican offensive to relieve pressure on the capital. The offensive was launched on 6 July 1937, with the first objective being the seizure of the heights around Brunete, thereby pushing back Nationalist artillery out of range of Madrid. The Republicans mustered 50,000 men, 136 artillery pieces, 128 tanks and 150 aircraft. The 15th International Brigade was at first held in reserve, but after a Spanish unit failed to capture the village of Villanueva de la Cañada, the brigaders were ordered to attack and capture it.

The brigade now numbered six battalions, plus the newly raised Anti-Tank Battery. The infantry were grouped into two regiments: the British, Lincoln and Washington Battalions in one; the Franco-Belgian, Dimitrov and Spanish Battalions in the other. The brigaders captured the village but failed to take Mosquito Ridge, the height overlooking the River Guadarrama and the village of Romanillos and Boadilla del Monte. By 11 July the Republican offensive was at a standstill, and then came the inevitable Nationalist counterattack, which captured Brunete, signalling the failure of the Republican offensive.

Jim Prendergast

Volunteer from Dublin, Republic of Ireland. Served in the British Battalion, 15th International Brigade, December 1936–November 1937.

On my return to Barracks HQ [headquarters] I found a letter awaiting me. Inside it was addressed to all officers and non-coms of the International Brigade instructing them to immediately proceed to a military centre outside Madrid for 'battle orders'. Much as I loved and respected Frank [Ryan] I felt it was safer to obey the written instruction, and I set out on the long hitch-hiking journey. I arrived at the reporting point to learn that a great Republican offensive, known as the July Brunete Offensive, had already begun, the objective of which was to raise the fascist siege west of Madrid. For the participants on both sides this was a truly terrible battle when one realizes that in the box or salient driven into the enemy ranks by the Republicans, a mere 10 miles long by 12 miles wide, some 35,000 lives were lost. Attempting to catch up with the brigade, I had an awesome sight of the battle from the heights of Guadarrama. The only battle I can recall to compare was Tobruk [in World War II]. Through the carnage of close artillery, tank and aviation fire I eventually caught up with Frank Ryan, at that moment attached to 13th Brigade HQ. His face went as red as a beetroot when he beheld me, and I got the usual stormy ritual of abuse for having disobeyed his orders – it all seemed so bloody silly in that great bowl of destruction and sudden death, and eventually Frank reverted to his usual kindly self.

For several days I remained with Frank, whose duties kept him just in the wake of the gruelling advance. Along the road from Villanueva to Brunete we came across rows and rows of bodies, many with their names pinned on slips of paper. Many of them were British lads. I remember one, who had been a Labour councillor at home, clutching, of all things, a dead rabbit. Frank told me that Will Paynter was in the very front position with the lads. The next day Frank took me over to the 15th Brigade HQ located in a huge pantechnicon. George Aitken, the brigade commissar, was seated on an upturned box, banging grimly away at a typewriter; from time to time the pantechnicon shuddered as bombs dropped nearby. Frank told George to give me a safe conduct back to Albacete, explaining his reasons. After much grumbling George gave me the precious slip of paper with the brigade stamp. Again the emotional farewell, and shortly afterwards I found myself alone on a raised road trying in vain to flag down the madly speeding vehicles and in a veritable criss-cross of shellfire. At last a quaint box-like little ambulance car slowed down and stopped and, of all people, out jumped Will Paynter! He was covered with grime and dust. At that moment I think he was hardly conscious of my presence. On the road he started arguing with his fellow passenger, a British chap whose name I cannot remember now. It became horribly clear to me from the argument that just a few miles up the road men were going through a veritable inferno so bad that some had even committed suicide. The British chap was telling Will that his job was to take him back to the base HQ and that instructions should be carried out. Will wanted to return, fiercely arguing that he had just seen Wally Tapsell trudging back to the front with a machine gun over his shoulder and that was what we should all do now. At that moment he seemed to become aware of my presence, and turning his back on the other chap he asked me outright if I was prepared to come back with him. I cannot honestly say that I felt very brave at that moment but I did say to him that I would go back to the front if he agreed to continue his journey to Albacete where he had work to do. Will looked at me for a moment then suddenly said: 'Let's all get in the bloody box', which we did and continued, on what was to be the most hair-raising journey of my life, back to the base town.[1]

Sydney Quinn

Volunteer from Lisburn, Northern Ireland. Served with the Royal Artillery 1935–36, No 1 Company, 14th International Brigade, and the British Battalion, 15th International Brigade, November 1936–October 1937.

We were getting reinforcements. I remember one, a Canadian called Dick who couldn't wait to get to the front. The Moors used to imitate boys crying in pain. We decided it was a ruse by the Nationalists, but Dick just rushed over the top and was killed. We couldn't restrain him. It was a trick by Moorish soldiers. A tragic loss of life for nothing.

A lot of Irish Guardsmen lost their lives there [at Brunete]. The decision was taken to bring us back, but we lost a lot of men just getting back. The Nationalists chased us. I put one [a bullet] through a man's stomach. We had to leave our wounded behind, and tanks rolled over many of them. But we couldn't carry them – we were spent. We buried a friend, Nathan, in a makeshift coffin. There were entrails all over the place. I'm convinced that the war was lost at Brunete. The stupid insistence of taking a village [Villanueva de la Cañada]. It was touch and go, but we didn't have the strength to get into it. I always remembered the courage of the men.

I remember a Republican officer saying to me: 'You should take the road back to Madrid. This thing is hopeless.' There were only seven of us left of the original party – a lot of new fellas. Fred Copeman was taken away after Brunete because of an argument with fellow commanders. Joe Hinks took over. He was an unassuming character, didn't like to put men in positions where they were going to get killed. We were put in reserve, and three or four weeks later I and a few others went on leave. We weren't running away, but we thought that we had done our share.[2]

Tom Murphy

Volunteer from County Monaghan and Belfast, Northern Ireland. Served with the Machine-Gun Company, British Battalion, 15th International Brigade, March 1937–October 1938.

In Spain the uniforms came from different countries, i.e. we had Swiss trousers. Everybody had different clothing. The weapons were very bad: a lot wouldn't work properly. At Brunete I went to give a fella a hand with a heavy Russian machine gun and got a bullet through my left arm. I got five days' leave in Madrid afterwards. The people in the city wouldn't take any money off me when I was travelling in the tram cars. Madrid was '16 foot high'. They had covered all the monuments and taken all the carpets up.

Rations were poor: a lump of bread, three-quarter pound of rice and three-quarter pound of flour. That would do you for a week. A slice of bread a day. My right weight was 12 stone and I went down to 8 stone.

Day-to-day life consisted of being in the trenches. The miners were the best at making dugouts. There was a sap leading out into no-man's-land, towards the fascists. Guard duty lasted an hour, trying to see if there was anything rattling at the barbed wire (where there were tin cans filled with stones). There was a grenade attached to a wooden stick, with string attached to the pull ring going back to our trench. The fascist trenches were 300 yards away. Frank Ryan used to talk on the speakers, 'Irishmen, go home, your fathers would turn in their graves if they knew you were fighting for imperialism. This is the real Republican Army, the real men of Ireland'. He was talking to the Irish Blueshirts.[3]

Alun Menai Williams

Volunteer from South Wales. Served as a nurse and first aider with the Thaelmann and George Washington Battalions, March 1937– December 1938.

There was no water at Brunete to clean wounds, and no organization to bring up water either. The only water we had was in our water bottles. There were no water carts, nothing.

The Americans at Brunete were under fire for one whole month, but the main phase of the battle lasted three to four days. We took the village of Brunete then dug in. The counterattack came after four or five days; it was trench warfare from then on. We were counterattacked by a lot of Moorish troops. The Washington Battalion captured some Moors and Spaniards; I saw the prisoners. They were treated as normal prisoners; they were frightened but no harm was done to them. They got the same medical treatment as us. I was with the Americans for the whole of Brunete. After Brunete I had a bullet wound in my leg. I went to hospital in Madrid for three or four days. By that time the battalion had been pulled out of the line to Tarazona. Morale was very good but subdued after the battle.

The dressing station was 100 yards from the top of Mosquito Hill, at the bottom in a river bed. There were 40–50 fellas, badly wounded, laid out. The cry was 'water'. A lot died and there was nowhere to bury them and no one to bury them. They had no ID [identity] tags, nothing. You had to go through their pockets, but even if you did find any identification, who were you going to report it to? To this day no one knows where those who were killed were buried and who was killed.

We were at Tarazona for two weeks and then we went back to relieve other troops on the Madrid front. There were no major battles; it was trench warfare and it went on for months.[4]

Albert Charlesworth

Volunteer from Manchester, England. Served as a runner and postman with the British Battalion, 15th International Brigade, December 1936– September 1937 and December 1937–October 1938.

We were eventually withdrawn from the trenches. Then we were assembled again for the Brunete Offensive. We marched and then we carried on in the trucks up the mountains, up the road for hours and hours until we came to another road. We went through a couple of villages, disembarked and bedded down beside the road. The following morning I was able to observe that we were on some low-lying hills and they were in the form of a horseshoe. You could see for miles down into the valley, although you could not recognize anything there. We were there for several days and we could hear wagons rumbling by at night, and we found out that there was artillery and all sorts going up the road, so we knew there was going to be a big offensive. When the time came to move, we marched from there towards the front, and that night we went off the road and down the side of the river and into some trees to bed down. It was there that night that I met George Brown.

The following morning we went back to the road and marched on and came to moorland. We were met by an officer on a horse wearing a cloak who spoke English and who asked how we were. From that point we were led off onto the moorland, across it and right to its edge. From there we could see deep down below us a flat plain with a village, which was probably two or three miles distant. This village was Villanueva de la Cañada and it was being shelled by two pieces of artillery, just slightly to our right, and cavalry was charging round on the flat ground outside the village. The British Battalion advanced down the slope and into the valley, along the dry bed of the valley, along a gully until we came to a ridge which was probably six miles away from the village, and there we were pinned down. It was a very hot day and during the afternoon most of the water supplies had run out. So I collected three water bottles and said I would try and get near to the village to get some water. I crept along the top of the ridge over to the right of the battalion and eventually came to a dike by the side of a road. This road ran into the village.

I crept down the dike, towards the village, and eventually came to a small bend in the dike and in the road, but as soon as I went round this small bend I was fired on from the village, so I went back round the bend and waited there for several hours because I could not go forward and I could not go back. At dusk

I could not see anything down in the dike. I then heard a terrible hullabaloo, firing bursting out from all directions, shouting and screaming. After a few minutes I could hear the voice of Fred Copeman shouting 'Stop firing, stop firing'. Very shortly the firing did stop and everything went deadly quiet. I kept my head down because it was close to me and I didn't know what was happening. I stayed there a little while longer and then three people appeared above me with bayonets pointing at me. I didn't know who they were because I didn't know what had gone on. They beckoned me out of the dike, so out I got. They were Spaniards and they questioned me as to my identity and what battalion I belonged to, and who was the battalion commander's name. Not knowing who they were, I gave them the name of the battalion, my own name and the name of the battalion commander: Jock Cunningham. Upon giving this information they stuck the bayonets in my back and marched me off towards Cañada. I thought I had been captured.

When we went through the gate which led into the village of Cañada, I recognized several men of my battalion refreshing themselves at a water trough, and I immediately ran to them and said how pleased I was to see them. I then produced my identity card to these three Spaniards who patted me on the back and went on their way. The battalion stayed that night in Cañada and the following morning we were told to get out because the place was going to be bombed. We marched along the road to Brunete, which was about three and a half miles distant, but before we got to Brunete we could see the American Battalion, perhaps 200–300 yards in front of us in another field.

The battalion was at its further-most point of advance, a place known as Mosquito Ridge. Not the Mosquito Ridge you will see marked on the maps in all the books because they got it on the wrong side of the road on the maps. I was going down to fetch the mail from the river, which was about a mile back. Jock Cunningham [the battalion commissar] had a little dugout in this square of trenches and again he was liaising for the brigade and as I was going by I heard him shout from the dugout. I popped my head in and said I am just going down to the river for the mail. Straight away he shouted 'Never mind the mail come here, I want you to take a message'. It was as if God himself was speaking. The brigade was at the riverbank, I was going there for the mail. It meant nothing to me to take the message, it was the same place I was going to get the mail. I didn't argue about it but I never seemed to get on well with him. Anyway I went down and got the mail and the cookhouse wagon was there at the same time, so I got a couple of great big dixies [cooking pots] of grub, soup, meat and potatoes, all mixed up. I delivered this message to the brigade and stood outside this little dugout expecting a reply. I had been there for 30 seconds and the commanding officer came out and he was fuming, saying 'Get away from here, get away from here, you will have us bombed, you will have us bombed'. They had been bombed a couple of times so I just went off and sat under a tree. I waited there half an hour and nobody bothered about a reply so I went and I got my letters.

I walked along the riverbed and came to a group of Yanks, 20 or 25 of them. They begged me to let them have some food but I wouldn't let them have any because it was for the British Battalion. I walked on another 100 yards and I turned to go up the hillside. Suddenly there were bullets flying all around. The first thing I did was drop to the ground, put the cans down and dart behind a big tree. Anyway it died down and after half an hour I crawled back and picked up my dixies and made my way back to the dried-up riverbed. When I got back the Yanks told me I had been wandering around in no-man's land.

Later we were advancing when the battalion got shelled. Charlie Goodfellow was killed, he was hit by a shell splinter and his head was chopped off. It wasn't five yards away from me. They had a little ammunition dump which was set on fire by a shell, and two or three of the lads from the Anti-Tank [Battery] were dragging all these boxes away and one of them exploded and killed one of the blokes that was a few yards the other side of us. We then went up this square trench and advanced along it, slightly downhill to a little shallow road, a cart track it was, really. I don't know if it was a bullet or a stone chipped by a bullet that caught me across the nose and little bits went into my eye. I felt a burning pain across my nose. My eye felt like it had bits in it. It didn't seem bad, there was no blood. Anyway two days later I could not open it, it had gone solid with pus and the like, so I had to go into hospital. The doctor I saw was a Spaniard, an eye specialist who had been trained at Cambridge so he spoke perfect English. He operated and eventually it cleared up and he told me I would need glasses from then on.

I went back to the battalion. A truck took me to the riverbank and it dropped me there. I was the only one left on the truck, the only one to get off there, not a soul in sight anywhere. So I set off down the road and drew level with this square of trenches. I could see a fire with one of those big frying pans on it, so I walked towards this frying pan and almost got there when bullets started splattering around my feet. I about turned and dived into the dike. I crawled along it for about 300 yards. They could not see me there so the firing stopped. While I had been in hospital the enemy had occupied the battalion's positions.[5]

Walter Greenhalgh

Volunteer from Manchester. Served in No 1 Company, Marsellaise Battalion, 14th International Brigade, and the British Battalion, 15th International Brigade, December 1936–October 1938.

I didn't realize that what the lads were facing were the Blitzkrieg tactics of the Germans. This was the first time that it was ever used. We didn't realize then that this would be the end. Okay, we had been in battles, the same as we were in at Brunete, when you were within 500 yards of achieving your objective but it does not happen, so you fall back again.

Every member of our Young Communist League group went to Spain. Even old Randy Garrett who was an ex-seaman and who must have been in his forties, he went. Hughie Barker was another one who was wounded on the second day of every offensive. He went to Jarama and was wounded; at Brunete he was wounded and he went back again every time. How many from Manchester that fought came back? Not many. Tommy Freeman, myself and Hughie Barker came back. One of the things that I always regretted was the night before the Brunete Offensive. George Brown came to me and gave me a songbook, an international workers' songbook which was circulating there. He had all the signatures of the Manchester men on the fly leaf and he gave it to me for safekeeping, which I did for quite a long time. One day a Polish woman who was a writer asked me if she could borrow it for a day, to take a copy of the songs in it. I foolishly lent it to her and that same day I had to leave and go off on a journey; I never saw it again. Every man from Manchester who was in the battalion at the time signed it, including George Brown.

In the Lopera battle, after we had retreated, [George] Nathan ordered me, Pete and somebody else to make a reconnaissance into the next valley to see how close the enemy was. We crawled on our bellies in Indian style up this hill, down the other side and still could not see anything. Then, in the distance, we saw three horsemen so I said to Pete to stay behind and I would go further on. They could cover me while I found out who they were. Halfway down the hill I put a foot wrong, fell down a gully and made a terrific noise. I don't know how far I fell, but by the time I pulled myself up I was so scared that the horsemen had either seen or heard me that I just made off as fast as I could. By the time I stopped and got my breath back I hadn't the faintest idea where I was. I didn't know which direction I had run or where the other two were or anything, and for the rest of the day I wandered around and eventually went into a big farmyard. It was deserted and had been set on fire. The place had been wrecked and so I got out of there. As night fell I was getting more and more despondent and more tired, and then I saw some lights. It took me about an hour, approaching these lights very slowly on my stomach, thinking, well, if it's the fascists, it's the fascists, there is nothing I can do about it. But it was our own unit. I just walked in and Nathan said, 'Where the hell have you been?'

Nathan was a remarkable person. He joined us through the Jewish anti-fascist movement. The strange thing about Nathan was he was a Jew and a member of the Guards. He was very proud of his membership of the Guards. I liked him. Hugh Thomas suggested he was a homosexual. I was close enough to him and as far as I was concerned he was nothing like that. I never saw any suggestion of it and if there had been Tony would have told me anyway, as Tony was very close to Nathan. He went over to the 14th Brigade with him as his interpreter because Tony was bilingual. Nathan died on the eve of the Battle of Brunete. It was in an air raid, not in the actual battle itself. George Aitken was heartbroken because Nathan was the one man who could have become the military leader of the English-speaking brigade. The English-speaking brigade broke up after that because there was no one of Nathan's capability, although we had Jock Cunningham ... a brigade officer at Brunete but he wasn't a military leader of that nature. He was a very good inspiration within a small unit like a battalion, but when they put him in charge of larger units it didn't work out. The story goes that after the battle, when the brigade staff presented him with a cigarette case as a mark of appreciation, engraved on it was a map of Spain. Someone remarked: 'This is his first lesson in map reading.'

The people who were there [in Spain] representing the communist leadership in my view made a hash of things. Tapsell definitely made a hash of things. I know for a fact that he caused a tremendous amount of despair among those who survived the Battle of Brunete. I was present at the meeting and I told George lots of these lads had arrived after the main part of the battle was over and so we suffered a defeat. In fact we hadn't achieved our objective, we had to fall back and things had been bad, but it wasn't any different from anything that had ever happened before. We always got so far but we never had that little extra which enabled us to make anything out of it, because we didn't have the weapons and so on. Their [fascists'] aeroplanes used to come over and just stand out of range, our anti-aircraft would fire at them perhaps for an hour and then we would run out of shells. So then planes would come, they would bomb and they would strafe. It was nobody's fault that we weren't an organized army, we couldn't possibly be and therefore we were bound to have defeats.

After the battle we were exhausted. A lot of the men were new and just arrived and there was Tapsell telling them that the reason for the whole of this is because the military command was useless; that they weren't revolutionary enough and what we must do is demand that there should be full cooperation between all ranks so that there was full discussion of all tactics, rather than having orders given to you from above, and so on. And that if we had this revolutionary strategy running right through all the forces in the army then these defeats would not occur. I went to George and said the way things are going on, every lad in the battalion will go home because he was telling them that their officers were useless and that they are being driven to the slaughter like cattle. So Tapsell was arrested and of course the next thing there was a political struggle, because Tapsell was representing the Communist Party.

At base we had Peter Kerrigan, who was a similar thing to Tapsell, and it would have been too politically dangerous for Tapsell to have been put on a proper charge for disaffecting the troops, although there was a 30 percent desertion after his speech and the morale in the unit went right down to zero. What happened was that Tapsell and George Aitken went back to England.

After that I was with the battalion and was then an old timer. I was one of the few remaining from the first English company. Aitken lost his battle in England so Tapsell came back and I was asked to make a speech of welcome, to welcome Tapsell back into the battalion. Of course, I couldn't, and at the same time not only could I not do that but I couldn't say why because then I would be just as bad as Tapsell. So for the first time in my life I went out and got drunk. I just sat in a cafe and drank a bottle of rum (I have never touched rum since). So I avoided that. It could be that Tapsell was a different person later on, because instead of being an observer he became a company commander in the battalion and was killed on the Ebro front.

There were national intrigues in the International Brigades. The Americans were very brash and wanted to run the show (this was the time that the Americans were saying that communism was 20th-century Americanism). They did everything in this big, brash American way. During the time I was attached to them in their village, their military police had long white sticks and used them on any of their troops who got drunk, threw them into jail and all sorts of things. They had the raising of the flag and bringing the flag down at dusk with everyone standing and singing and so on, real old-time stuff. At the same time I got on with the men themselves. They were traditionalists, law abiding and all believed in it.

Before Brunete there was the demand for the ending of the militia [system] and the creation of an army. Of course, at the spearhead of this creation of an army and the end of the militia units the International Brigades had to play their major role. They were to be the first to accept complete integration into a unified command, so there was an attempt in creating this English-speaking brigade with the Canadians, Americans,

British and two Spanish brigades, making this one big brigade. But we didn't have the military people once Nathan had gone. [6]

Bernard McKenna

Volunteer from Manchester, England. Served as a signaller and infantryman with the British Battalion, 15th International Brigade, February 1937– March 1938. Prisoner of war, March 1938–October 1938.

On the first day of the offensive we were being attacked, with planes going over and tanks going forward, and the British were moving up. I was on the right trying to organize telephone lines from where we started from, and we ran right into it and I got a bullet in the foot. Fortunately it wasn't permanently damaged. We were moving in this group and we could see the British Battalion moving into the streets of the village. Some Spanish first aid men grabbed hold of me, stuck me on a mule and started walking me backwards. I don't know which was worse, the pain of the bloody wound or being jolted up and down on that mule. I must have gone for bloody miles before I got to a field ambulance where they gave me a dose of anti-tetanus and bandaged me up. I sat there for two or three hours and in the evening they took me to Madrid. It did not take long. We got into the hospital in Vilaseca and the same night it was bloody bombed. I only had a slight wound: a machine-gun bullet through the foot which sliced through and barely bruised the bone. Within a week I was all right, I could limp and had a stick to get round in Madrid. As soon as I was all right I got out.

There was hardly any food in Madrid. I remember having this watery vegetable soup and some mutton. I had the money and could have stayed there, but I got so fed up I decided to get back to the front. I more or less hitch-hiked back to the front. The only things I owned were a pair of black trousers which were blood stained, a white shirt and a pair of black pants. I was hoping to get re-equipped, but by the time I got there the battalion was in the line. I remember going back in the middle of the day with a food wagon, going right across this plain that had been shelled to blazes. The truck darted this way and that, the shells were falling and it was a bit grim. I got back to base. We left at dawn and started to withdraw. We were on a wide road when the fascist aviation came over and bombed us to hell. We scattered as we heard them coming over. So the trucks got out quick and drove off and we were all scattered among the rocks and they bombed us, bang, bang, bang, and that was when [George] Nathan was killed.[7]

Bill Alexander

Volunteer from England. Served as political commissar with the Anti-Tank Battery and as the commander of the British Battalion, 15th International Brigade, March 1937–October 1938.

There was no strafing because we still had anti-aircraft guns and a few of our own planes, so it was all high-level bombing. But the fascists dominated the air. Our fighters came over from time to time and when they came over the fascists cleared off, but the domination of the air was perhaps 90 percent fascist. This certainly played a part during the early stage, not so much in the frontline but in preventing our forces being reinforced with men, supplies and materials ...

When the Nationalist counteroffensive started, what caused a retreat by the Republic? First of all our forces were very tired. The Republic undoubtedly had insufficient reserves. For example, the British Battalion had been involved in active fighting all the way from Villanueva right up to Mosquito Ridge, and it suffered casualties both in the battle and from the dysentery that was having a really devastating effect at the time. We were pushed back by overwhelming weight of numbers, and the fact that a sector of the front had cracked meant that the other battalions would have to pull back to prevent them being encircled or caught by flanking fire.

When the Nationalists were advancing towards me I was deafened. I was standing with this gun crew, slightly in front, and saying 'over there, to the left', or 'over there, to the right', as we saw a group of men, platoon strength (30 strong), get up and run forward. The gunners were doing an extremely good job: rapidly swivelling and adjusting the sights. With one shell we could actually see bodies flying apart. But we just could not do enough to keep all the fascists from breaking through. So we were ordered to pull back …

Brunete was a very costly battle. The 15th Brigade was withdrawn to the mountain behind and we were in a state of exhaustion. We finally laid down to sleep and the whole world was rocking round me as I went to sleep. But it was a nightmarish sleep. Then there was an order that, because the front was breaking, what was left of the 15th Brigade should go back to the line. There were some sharp exchanges as to whether this was possible or not. As far as the Anti-Tank Battery was concerned, we were prepared to go back, what was left of us. We had suffered heavy casualties. Malcolm Dunbar was wounded and a number of Spanish comrades had been killed – we probably lost about a third of our 26 or 28 men. We were not sent back into the line again, though. The situation had stabilized.

We were sent back [to the rear] and for the Anti-Tank Battery it was an idyllic period. We were on a little island in a river where there was a mill house, an island surrounded by cool rushing streams. It was cool and pleasant. It was heaven. Miles Tomalin took over the two-room mill house and began to issue *Assault and Battery News*, a war paper that he wrote twice a week. It was of a very high level (he was an extremely capable writer). The whole battery relaxed and grew happy in the surroundings …

I was then approached and asked if I would go to the battalion, so I went to be the adjutant (Fred Copeman was still in command at the time). When we left Ambite we then went up to the Aragon front where we attacked Purburrel Hill and later Belchite. In Belchite the anti-tank guns really came into their own. The fascists had been completely surrounded and were holding the church as a strongpoint. It was in the centre of a whole system of interconnected houses, with holes battered between the walls so they could retreat down the street towards the church. We took our guns right into Belchite, pushing them up behind the sand bag barricades which the fascists had left behind, poked our muzzles through and fired either armour-piercing or high-explosive shells directly at the church. This undoubtedly played a part in the final fascist surrender.

After the retreat from Belchite we were in a state of complete exhaustion and a certain sense of defeat, in the sense that a big offensive had not achieved its objective. There certainly was some people who were demoralized, but in the Anti-Tank Battery, which was a small and rather elite unit, there was certainly no demoralization.

In places like Brunete the Republicans had to retreat. The main reason was the overwhelming artillery and bombing they had to face, and the fact that they still had insufficient reserves to consolidate and then expand their initial victory. This was still in the early days when many of the Spanish battalions were still badly led and not yet consolidated into a serious army.[8]

Fred Copeman

Volunteer from London, England. Served with the Machine-Gun Company and as commander of the British Battalion, 15th International Brigade, October 1936–December 1937.

Jock Cunningham was a bit of a problem. He didn't get on with

Harry Pollitt [British Communist Party leader]. Harry Pollitt worshipped Fred Copeman, he was the boy for Harry. I could not do anything wrong as far as Harry was concerned, and when I took over the battalion he came out and said, 'Fred, this is the most wonderful thing from a party point of view'. I said, 'I can't think why it should be because I am not in the bloody party'. I hadn't joined the party. I had always worked with them but I didn't hold a party card, but Harry thought I was the bee's knees and he was quite happy about that. I have a feeling that Harry was so anxious to build me up for the future that the danger he saw was Jock Cunningham, who was already more important than I was. He was a good lad and I accepted that. I thought Jock was the best. Anyway the end product was Harry said that the only people who had expressed a point of view as to what was happening to the battalion at that moment had been Fred Copeman and Wally Tapsell. His proposal was that we return to Spain and everybody else remained where they were. Jock just broke down. I have never seen anything like it. I tried to help him out but it was no good. I said, 'Jock, it will be all right'.

The next thing we were on our way back. I insisted on getting a proper political document to establish my authority, which I got. It made me a big shot that piece of paper, you would be surprised, even in the communist movement internationally among the top people. We arrived back and we took another crowd with us, about another 400. This was the last lot.

At Brunete it seemed the energy of the battalion, and the whole brigade, was diffused among the villages. There weren't any other villages once we passed Villanueva de la Cañada, though, it was all open country up to the hill. You could see places in the distance but they weren't in our sector. It was all open country. We had to take the top of that bloody hill. That was the thing. The only thing that stood out for miles around. It was to the west of Madrid and was an important military objective. Everybody else was spreading to the front to give that hill support once it was taken. That was the whole idea. Other brigades would have villages to take and places like that, but certainly not in our sector. Not a bloody building between Madrid and Villanueva where we were and we couldn't see anybody within sight either, except the peasant battalion of Spaniards.

Ammunition, that was the key thing. When our ammunition dump blew up the 15th Brigade had had it. They only had the ammunition that they were carrying. We were in the same boat as everybody else. There was a time when we didn't have any rifles or ammunition. We had to depend on the anti-tank guns, which were well behind us, to fire a few rounds every so often to let them know we were around. We kept Villanueva and lost Brunete. Franco simply blew the bloody place up when he got it, for punishment because they gave up without a fight. Some of the destruction in Brunete is still there today, deliberately left there by Franco as an example of what happens to people who [did not] fight for him.[9]

Notes
1   http://www.geocities.com/irelandscw/ibvol-Prendergast.htm.
2   Quinn, Sydney, Imperial War Museum Sound Archive (IWMSA), London, Ref 801/3, Reel 3.
3   Murphy, Tom, IWMSA, London, Ref 805/2, Reel 2.
4   Williams, Alun Menai, IWMSA, London, Ref 10181/5, Reel 4.
5   Charlesworth, Albert, IWMSA, London, Ref 9427/4, Reel 3.
6   Greenhalgh, Walter, IWMSA, London, Ref 11187/9, Reel 6.
7   McKenna, Bernard, IWMSA, London, Ref 847/5, Reel 1.
8   Alexander, Bill, IWMSA, London, Ref 802/5, Reel 2.
9   Copeman, Fred, IWMSA, London, Ref 794/13, Reel 8.

The Battle of Teruel

Having completed the conquest of northern Spain, Franco turned his attention towards Madrid and Republican-held territory to the south and east. The Republican government, though, having moved from Madrid to Valencia, struck first. The Republican armies of the East (General Hernández Sarabia) and the Levante (General Leopoldo Menéndez) launched a joint attack on 15 December 1937 against the city of Teruel, 138 miles east of Madrid. At first they were successful, with the garrison surrendering on 8 January 1938. However, Franco then launched the forces of Generals José Varela and Antonio Aranda on a counteroffensive to retake the city.

On 17 January the International Brigades were committed to the battle to stem the Nationalist advance. In the days that followed the British Battalion lost one-third of its strength. On 7 February a Nationalist cavalry attack drove back the Republicans north of the city, taking 7,000 prisoners and inflicting 15,000 other casualties. By 20 February the city was encircled by the Nationalists except for the Valencia Road to the south-east. The Republicans withdrew, leaving behind 10,000 dead and 14,500 prisoners. The Republican offensive had ended in total failure.

For those who took part, Teruel was a battle of utter misery. It was fought in one of the bitterest winters Spain had seen. The only compensation was that the blizzard conditions prevented the Nationalists from using their mechanized forces and aircraft. Nevertheless, the losses suffered by the Republicans meant that the government was forced to call up younger and younger recruits, who were a poor replacement for seasoned troops. And the International Brigades were also suffering from a drying-up of volunteers. The truth was that the Republican Army was slowly being bled dry.

Alun Menai Williams

Volunteer from South Wales. Served as a nurse and first aider with the Thaelmann and George Washington Battalions. March 1937–October 1938.

The casualties in the Lincoln and Washington Battalions had been so bad that they amalgamated both battalions. They became known as the Lincoln-Washington Battalion. I was with them at Teruel. They were all Americans together and they were happy to be with their own countrymen. In my battalion there were a lot of negroes, including a battalion commander. With the Yanks was Steve Nelson, a battalion commissar and a super fella. Nelson looked after the troops and made sure I was all right. I thought the commissar system was good, a great morale booster. The commissar was the link between the military world and the civilian world. Everybody liked their attitude.

As far as I was concerned the Battle of Teruel happened at the North Pole. It was a bitter winter. My hands were sticking to metal and frostbite was a major factor in that battle. It was a cruel battle: the cold, the weather, the short days. By this time things were getting short in the war, such as food and clothing. In this battle I didn't have any shoes, just rope sandals. My feet were killing me and I was wrapping them up in anything I could find.

The battle started as a Republican offensive but ended as a rout. There was no fuel for heat so we burned olive trees – they burned beautifully. I was in a village and I had my first aid post 200 yards from the frontline in a railway tunnel. It was cold in the tunnel, very windy but reasonably safe. That's how I remember Christmas Day in the snow at Teruel in December 1937. I was at Teruel for three weeks, always with the Americans. There was

1. *First British group to arrive to form the 1st British Battalion, 14th Brigade:
Left–Right: Maurice Levine, Eddie Swindells, Brigader Wilson, Bill Benson,
Rear: Jud Coleman, Tony Theodoupholous.*

2. *British officers of the 57th Battalion before Ebro:
Far right kneeling: Sam Wild; Centre: Bob Cooney.*

3. Soldiers from the 15th International Brigade in 1937.

*4. London's Bouverie Street in February 1939. Artists painting
hoardings around London to raise funds for Spanish Refugees.*

5. *The front line at Brunete.*

6. *Dr Reginald Saxton's clinic at Torrelodones.*

7. *Soldiers at Huete Hospital in 1937:*
Left–Right: Milton Felsen, Willie Remmel, Danny Gibbons, with two
unnamed brigaders; Sitting: Fred Thomas and an unnamed companion.

8. *International Brigades on the march*
at the Brunete front, in July 1937.

9. 'It's better to die on your feet than to live
forever on your knees.' – *Dolores Ibárruri.*

10. *The 57th Battalion training for the Ebro offensive of July 1938.*

11. *Roderick MacFarquhar at the Ebro.*

12. *The Republican Army crossing the River Ebro.*

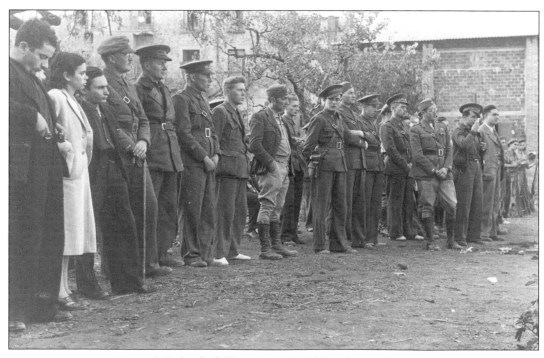

13. *12th Brigade Officers in their Disbandment Ceremony:*
Middle: Bob Cooney (without hat, white shoes); Malcolm Dunbar (3rd from left).

14. *Banquet for the 15th International Brigade Farewell in 1938.*

15. *Twelve members of the Abraham Lincoln Brigade shown on 10 May 1939, on arrival in New York, following their release from Spanish Nationalist prisons.*

16. Four hundred members of the International Brigades returning from Spain on 15 December 1938, marching out of Victoria station in London, bearing their standards.

17. Post 1939: International Brigaders including Bill Alexander (first left).

chaos, lots of casualties and we were even cut off. I was with some Americans trying to get back. We moved at night. Fortunately one of the Americans knew his way about and we got through enemy lines after five days. After the battle we went up to Catalonia for rest.[1]

Frank West

Volunteer from London, England. Served as company commissar with the British Battalion, 15th International Brigade, September 1937–October 1938. Prisoner of war, November 1938–March 1939.

One or two weeks after I got into the frontline there was this attempted fraternization between the two sides. I was the first one to open fire over their heads. It was just an automatic reaction to me. You don't sit and talk with an enemy that's done what the fascists had done to you under any circumstances. I mean, I have a tendency to go too far anyway. As a shop steward I would not talk to a governor on his own under any circumstances. If the governor wanted to talk to me I would say OK, arrange a meeting. I would have my chairman the ⌐ or if I was the chairman, I would have my secretary there. No way would I talk to them. That to me is all wrong.

I must have fired three or four shots before I was stopped. But then the battalion commander, Sam Wild, said: 'Fire.' Then we opened up over the top first until they were separated, and then the fascists got what they had coming to them when they got about halfway back.

The Republican Spaniards complained about it and there was a general discussion about it. Because if something went wrong in action, you discuss it afterwards and then elect a representative to go to each section until you got to the top.

I was a section representative. You had a company with a commissar, and the company was divided into three sections.

Each section had a man that represented it and worked alongside the commissar on the basis of doing practical things that a commissar would do, i.e. look after the food, clothes and general conditions. The commissar, of course, had to do a bit more because he was responsible for the morale of his company. He was also responsible for any publicity, for contacting parents, families, things like that. For example, one of the biggest things we had when I first went out there was that not every wife was getting the money from the compensation aid. You would have somebody who quite often would not want to worry their husbands and would not say anything. Gradually it would become known and you would have to chase around and make certain that they got their cash. This was the sort of thing the commissar had to do, but the section representative, he just made certain that the food was there. I was a commissar afterwards ...

We were most apprehensive of the Germans [fascists]. We had a long front, and my company held that front. When they started the lads had to get down in their dugouts. The shell would come along and take our parapet off and we would be standing up there, taking the mickey, and then we would get down and they would stand up and take the mickey, and we would all have to fill up the parapet again.

We had rifles and machine guns. We had the Russian Tokarev and Degtyarev light machine guns. The Degtyarev had a drum magazine, they had 47 rounds. They were all right, but of course carrying the extra ammo meant that it was much more heavy. It wasn't like carrying a load of bullets in a belt – you had them in a box.

As far as I can remember I was just told that I was commissar. You didn't think of choice, you were out there to do a job and if someone said this is this, then you did it. The job of commissar was absolutely necessary. There was so many curious rumours and things going on that unless it was brought out into the open, the whole business of morale could be really bad. It was a question of getting people to come in and to talk about what was taking place, what it meant while we were there, what we expected, to keep the talk going so the lads understood what it was all about. Then you got the other business where they think to themselves, I wonder if I am going to get wounded, am I going to get killed? Your mind goes that way, so if you get them on the positive instead of negative things then this was a necessary part, but only a part, of the commissar's job.

The discussions with the commissar took the place of the strict discipline that you had in an ordinary army, because as a result of that you had individual discipline, discipline within yourself, and the lads would do it too.

We did get individuals who wouldn't discipline themselves. We had one lad who was a leading figure in the ICL [International Communist League] and we got back across the Ebro. Our battalion was given 10 miles of the Ebro to look after, so of course as we got into position I said 'shovels out and dig in'. There was a bit of an argy bargy about being six weeks on the run and having to dig in, and I got them together and said: 'Right, you are tired and you have had enough but you've done six weeks on the trot, never knowing if you were going the right way, never knowing when you were going to get any grub, never knowing when the fascists are going to appear in front of you. You are faced with a situation where you can look forward to a further six weeks if you don't make certain that they don't cross this river. That's as far as you are concerned. The other thing is that if you don't make certain that they can't cross this river then you are letting all the Spanish people down.' Well this lad, who was district secretary of the ICL, decided to have a fight about it and refused digging in. So I told the others to dig in. He will be dealt with when we get back. Later he was sent to the Punishment Battalion, digging trenches without any arms or ammunition.

Commissars invariably led, they went over the top first. There was an argument about that because I found that one or two needed a little assistance going over. I wasn't always too keen to go over first. The trouble was, I invariably found myself going over first without the company commander. For various reasons I was a little bit short with some of them. I had a sergeant out of the British Army when we went to a forward position in Teruel. Even before we got into position he started talking about getting more support, so I got a bit annoyed and told him to go and get it, so he did. He marched off. When he came back it was a bit too late – we had all left the position.

At Teruel they [the fascists] put shrapnel shells down and we were in a diamond formation; outside each formation were fire points containing three people. There was another firing point in the centre which I took over. We were firing and up on my right was a fascist machine gun (I was standing up above the trench). I had a lad with me who was very scared. We had a box full of rifles and a box full of ammo and he was filling these rifles up. I was taking a reloaded rifle off him and firing. I saw this machine-gunner and I thought, he is a danger, he has got to change his belt at some time, and when he did I got him. I didn't know until afterwards that he had fired first and just missed me – he shot me through my hat. Anyway, I got a shout from the section commander and as I turned to find out what it was, a shrapnel shell went and cracked his head down the middle. I looked around and there were 12 of us left. I thought to myself, we can fight another day, so we got out. We came out and nothing had been said, but I imagine there was a feeling that we should have stopped there. The company commander was a soldier out of the British Army who had military training.

We had trouble right from the off because when we went up to Teruel, we had taken another position before we went into our last one. We took it over from the Americans and were told that it was fortified. Well, having known what that meant we weren't surprised when we got in the trench. There was a trench which gradually got shallower and shallower, at the end of which there was a white house. This meant that if we had that as headquarters, anybody going to it had to run above ground and take their chances if they wanted to reach it.

We got in there and the commander said this is headquarters, and I said this is not headquarters mate, headquarters is down there. No, he said, it's headquarters. I said you have got no right to ask the men to run above ground and risk getting shot to come and see you or me, and no way am I going to stand for it. So anyway he went up and took the house over, and I stopped in the trench.[2]

Reginald Saxton

British doctor. Served with medical units in Spain, August 1936– October 1938 (see plate 6: Dr Saxton's clinic at Torrelodones).

At the Battle of Teruel, Teruel was captured and then lost again, following which the fascists split the Republican forces in two. It was a very hard battle, there were heavy losses. The terrain was very difficult; mountainous and muddy and snow bound, and most of the time very cold. Our patients were treated in all sorts of odd buildings and we were subjected to air attack and to snipers even, if you got anywhere near the enemy side of the town. We did acquire a lot of medical equipment, foreign equipment, which was in Teruel the time it was taken.

When we had recovered from this battle and came out of Teruel, we had done what we could with the wounded. It was a very trying time. The situation was very unpredictable and so cold and so miserable. At that time I acquired a very large vehicle. I think it was specially built according to my specifications. The body was a laboratory with benches on two sides with a refrigerator in one corner and a sterilizer in another, and across the width of this wide vehicle were a couple of bunks for me and my assistant (between the driving part of the front of the vehicle and the laboratory part at the back). So we were more or less a self-sufficient organization. We had cupboards and a refrigerator where we could store blood. I never intended to get down to actually drawing blood for storage because this required rather more facilities and sterile conditions, and required donors being examined beforehand, and actually taking blood for storage. This was done in Barcelona and Madrid.

So this was my laboratory and blood transfusion vehicle which I took with me and a driver. There was one other permanent assistant, who slept on the front seat. Anyway myself, my driver and assistant were always with this vehicle, and occasionally when we stopped for a length of time we did accumulate three other laboratory assistants, one Italian and two Americans. This laboratory when we were stationed long enough took on jobs of ordinary laboratory work.

We went to a town called Valls, not far from Tarazona, which was on the sea and there was quite a big station, a civilian hospital, which was being used for military purposes. We opened up our laboratory there and we would do all sorts of fairly complicated tests. At one stage people were afraid they were being poisoned by arsenic. We had to test various foodstuffs. We had to rig up apparatus and use laboratory equipment to test it out. We satisfied ourselves that the salt was not contaminated with arsenic. We then had to test the local farmers' milk. The goatherds were selling goat's milk to the hospital and they suspected that the milk was being watered down and that the hospital funds were being swindled. We were set this problem to determine whether the milk was watered down. In the end we hit on a brilliant, simple idea. We went out and found a goatherdsman and demanded that he give us a pint of milk, straight out of the goat. We took the milk out of the goat and compared it in various ways with the milk that the hospital had. We came to the conclusion that the milk that the hospital was getting was about one-third water, so no drastic action was taken. I was always afraid, though, because I am not a pathologist, and here I was having to do certain pathological tests of which I had no previous experience. We worked it out from books; fortunately those two laboratory workers from the States and one from Italy were very good.

In this laboratory we had blood donors and I used to do blood grouping. We gathered quite a lot of volunteers to be blood donors. We were a medical unit working for the army and were insulated very much from the civilian troubles that existed. Just occasionally, civilian difficulties would overflow into our work. Getting together volunteer blood donors meant contact with the various civilian organizations that might help or provide us with these donors. There was a little bit of antagonism between them. The Socialist Party would be a bit edgy about the Communist Party or the Republican Party, i.e. who is really going to organize it, who is the more important of these three organizations? Feelings of resentment between these groups interfered to a large extent with the welfare side of the hospital.[3]

Morien Morgan

Volunteer from Ynysybwl, Wales. Served with No 2 Company, British Battalion, 15th International Brigade, September 1937–January 1938. Prisoner of war, January 1938–January 1939.

We got up one morning very early before dawn. We were to march to the front to replace a division that was returning. This was near a place called Calaceite. We marched forward, the infantry in two single lines on the edge of the road. No 1 and No 2 Companies and the Machine-Gun Company marched for an hour or two. No 1 Company had gone up and around a bend in the hill and then we heard some shots. The next thing we knew the shots were being directed at us. So we got off the road and into the terraced vineyards. It was only later we discovered what had happened. No 1 Company had gone around the corner and coming towards them were armoured cars, armoured tanks – we knew that our division was returning from the front and that we were to relieve them. No 1 Company thought they were the returning troops. It was only when they were in the middle of them that they realized that the uniforms were different. The uniform of the Spanish Regular Army was the same uniform worn by both sides. They both had a star but one star had one point more than the other. It was only on close inspection that they [the fascists] realized that our No 1 Company were the enemy, who were then surrounded.

When the firing started, we got down into the terraces and set up machine guns and started firing. Normally the practice in those days was to have Molotov cocktails to burn up the tracks of the tanks and the lorries, but this was much too sudden for anything to be prepared for that sort of an attack. All we could do was use the machine guns. The fighting went on for hour after hour. We were given the job of trying to halt this convoy while all the other companies retreated backwards. We were able enough to do this, we were lucky enough to hit a tank somehow and they could not move it, but inevitably their men got up on the hillside and shot down at us with heavier fire than we had.

In the end there was very few of us left. One chap was badly wounded in his arm and in his knee and we put him on a stretcher. For safety's sake we put him in the culvert that went under the road. His name was Morgan Havard. We kept them back for some hours and then we felt that it was hopeless, there was only a few of us now. So then we decided to retreat, taking Morgan Havard with us on a stretcher.

We started retreating in broad daylight. We found it very difficult and by this time we were very thirsty and had no water. We were very hungry and then the planes started coming over to strafe us – they were coming down quite low. They looked like silver trout swimming through water, a lovely sight. We kept on all that day and gradually we picked up one or two other people, and by the evening there were about 20 of us altogether. Carrying Morgan Havard hadn't been too onerous, but then we wondered how we could continue so we held a meeting. It was pointed out to us by people more experienced than ourselves that the terrain we were going to cover was very precipitous and hilly; we could not follow the roads and would have to travel at night. If we travelled in daylight we would be caught. If we travelled at night we had a chance of escaping. It would be almost impossible to carry a stretcher at night-time. Later on I found this to be quite true. We were forever sliding down into ravines and we couldn't keep our footing half the time. So we couldn't make up our minds what we were going to do with Morgan Havard. We obviously couldn't abandon a comrade. At the same time it would be ridiculous to risk the lives of 20 men for the sake of one. So the matter was put to Morgan Havard, explaining to him what the problem was. Without hesitation he said, 'All you go on, leave me by the roadside on the stretcher, in the shade of a tree if possible, with cigarettes'. He would stay there, wounded though he was. We carried on marching.

He was found by the fascists and taken to hospital. His leg was operated on but he lost an arm and eventually he got back to Britain. He is still alive today. We continued marching at night and resting during the day. Then the tonsillitis that had plagued me earlier struck again. I found myself completely unable to keep up with the rest of them because the tonsils swell up, they fill your throat; you can't talk, you can't drink, you can't do anything. I just collapsed on the mountain side and fell fast asleep.

I woke up feeling better. Then I started marching roughly east. Very interesting things happened then. I saw a small hut in an olive grove and smoke coming out of a chimney, so I thought I could go there and get some help from a peasant. But when I got there it was empty. I then started looking around for food and eventually found a piece of bread about two inches square, dirty and rock hard. I went to a stream, dipped a corner of the bread into the water and then sucked it. It was like nectar. It was the sweetest thing I had ever tasted in my life, amazingly sweet. I snapped off little bits of the bread and let it stay in my mouth while it gradually softened and spread a delicious taste through my whole mouth. The hour or so that I spent there was absolutely delicious, like many a lovely hour I spent by a stream, just listening, looking at the scenery and reciting poetry to myself. Then I finished it and carried on.

By this time I had probably been about a week without food apart from this one little bit of bread, and I remember coming to a brow of a hill. Looking down I saw a farm, a farmyard which looked remarkably like any farm you would find in England or Wales, with a hedge round it, a fence and the sound of dogs barking. But as I walked down the hill I could hear the shoo, shoo, shoo of bullets going past me, so then I crawled down carefully. When I got near the bottom there was no farm. There was no hedge, no barking dogs, no railings. I then moved back up the hill, crawling, the bullets still coming down and I could see the farm again. By this time it was becoming clear to me I must have been mentally affected: the farm was a delusion. I was reminded of the Old Testament where the prophets of old would spend so many days in the wilderness and there they would see visions, burning bushes, conjured spirits and all sorts of sights. Well, I knew that it was a mirage or a mental aberration. So I just continued on my way, knowing I would never see this farm.

I finally came to a hill, looked down and saw an encampment with horses by a stream and soldiers. I approached in the deep evening dusk. They all seemed to be speaking a sort of Spanish, not good Spanish, but Spanish. The sort of Spanish we had in the battalion, and then I saw the uniforms like ours and the star. I went up to them with a cigarette and asked for a light and they gave me one. I sat down near the fire and had a meal with them. I went in a tent to sleep and when I woke up the next morning I was captured. They were fascists and I don't think they realized who I was until they saw this star on my uniform, which was either five or six pointed.

It was a Spanish unit. My throat was still hurting pretty bad and my Spanish was very halting and when they questioned me I found it very difficult to talk. Then they took my glasses off me. That made it very difficult for me to see. They searched me and found in my pocket a very small metal shaving kit which had been bought in Woolworths. It was neatly contrived and took up very little room but they were convinced that it was made of silver for some reason. They also found a university diary in my pocket. Now the Spaniards were so utterly poor that they knew that anyone who could afford a silver shaving kit must be very wealthy, and even more so that I was able to go to university. Anyway, they then felt that I should not be shot (up until this date all prisoners had been shot by the Francoists). I was then taken to another place. I was not treated roughly. Not kindly but not roughly. I had to sleep outdoors with no shelter at all. I can't even remember if they gave me food or not. I don't know, though if they had I could not have eaten it with tonsillitis.[4]

Notes
1   Williams, Alun Menai, Imperial War Museum Sound Archive (IWMSA), London, Ref 10181/5, Reel 4.
2   West, Frank, IWMSA, London, Ref 9315/8, Reel 4.
3   Saxton, Reginald, IWMSA, London, Ref 8735/9, Reel 8.
4   Morgan, Morien, IWMSA, London, Ref 9856/4, Reel 2.

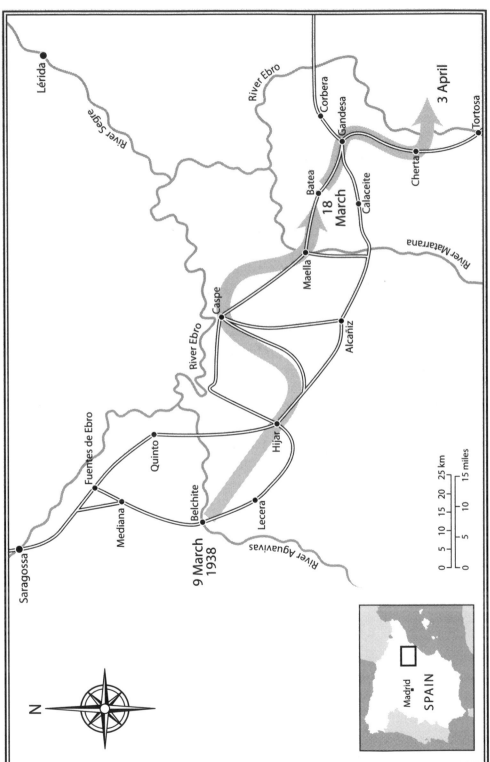

The retreat of the British Battalion through Aragon, 1938.

Fighting on the Ebro

In early March 1938 Franco launched a large attack in Aragon, causing Republican lines to collapse. The 15th International Brigade set up its headquarters at Belchite. However, Nationalist attacks forced the brigaders to retreat, with many in the British Battalion being captured (the Anti-Tank Battery was forced to leave one of its guns behind, enemy aircraft destroyed the other, resulting in the battery ceasing to exist). Belchite fell to the Nationalists on 10 March. The 15th International Brigade, along with the Republican Army, was falling back. The British Battalion abandoned Caspe on 15 March, and four days later the International Brigades' base at Albacete was closed.

At the end of March the Nationalists launched another offensive in Aragon, south of the River Ebro. The British Battalion, numbering 650 men, fell back to Calaceite, where it was attacked by Italian tanks and Nationalist aircraft. Losses were heavy and the survivors had to retreat across the River Ebro. It seemed that the Nationalists were unstoppable, yet within four months, much to the surprise of many, the Republic launched its own offensive along the Ebro to take the pressure off the Madrid and Valencia fronts. If it succeeded, communications between Catalonia and the remainder of Republican Spain would be restored.

The newly formed Army of the Ebro (100,000 troops), commanded by General Juan Modesto, began crossing the Ebro on the night of 24–25 July 1938. The opposing Nationalist Army of Morocco was taken by surprise, and was initially pushed back and lost 4,000 prisoners. The Republicans advanced into enemy territory before being stopped short of Gandesa. By the beginning of August, Republican troops began digging in to protect themselves from air attack and to await supplies. As August progressed National air attacks intensified, but the Republicans held on. However, they had lost the initiative and all they could do was prepare for the inevitable Nationalist counterattack. It came at the end of October, resulting in the Republicans being thrown back across the Ebro by 18 November.

The four-month battle had cost the Nationalists 33,000 casualties and 200 aircraft lost, but for the Army of the Ebro it was far worse: 30,000 dead, 20,000 wounded and 20,000 captured. The International Brigades had suffered a staggering 75 percent casualties. The Republic had lost its last chance on the battlefield. A Nationalist victory in the civil war was now inevitable.

Morris Miller

Volunteer from Leeds, England. Served in the British Battalion, 15th International Brigade. Arrived in Spain on 24 September 1937 and was wounded at Caspe in mid–March 1938. Miller was hospitalized and returned to the British Battalion in May 1938, where he was named assistant political commissar/political delegate, reporting to the chief commissar, Bob Cooney. Killed in action at the Ebro, August 1938.

By this time the boys were thoroughly tired. Night and day they had made Herculean efforts. To add to their difficulties water was kilometres away and very rarely could details be spared [to fetch it]. Moreover communications had not yet been established with the Intendencia [battalion supply service], though Bob Cooney, battalion commissar, had succeeded in getting up a small amount of tinned stuff that had been captured from the fascists. The fascist shells were landing in our forward positions. When battalion commander [Sam] Wild gave the order to withdraw, the last attack had ended. Among the comrades we lost in this attack was our brave comrade Lewis

Clive [a rowing gold medallist at the 1932 Los Angeles Olympics and descendant of Clive of India; killed at Gandesa in August 1938], who had returned from the hospital the previous day to take command of his old company. He was killed while directing the fire of his men.[1]

Billy Griffiths

Volunteer from Wales. Miner and member of the Rhondda Communist Party Committee. Served as the British Battalion's Communist Party Secretary in the summer and autumn of 1938.

Our food was quite monotonous. It hardly varied: bread and coffee for breakfast; carrabunces for dinner and lentils for supper. However, there was some slight advantage in being attached to HQ [headquarters]. After dinner, and sometimes after supper, Monty Sim's batman brought out the scraps for disposal into an improvised bin. All eyes were fixed on him as he scraped the plates clean and when he had gone, there was a concerted rush to delve among the scraps! It was an undignified sight. These were cultured men. Hickman, the head of the observers, had led a sheltered life: prep school, public school, Cambridge, a degree and an apprenticeship with Dunlop, then Spain. Joe Latus, a trawler captain; an American news reporter and so on. Yet the food was irresistible: a bit of liver or meat on a bone, perhaps a potato. It was a change.

One evening, while larking about, Joe Latus started to wrestle with one of his mates, an electrician from Liverpool. Joe was a big chap, about 5ft 10in. His opponent was well over 6ft and well muscled. It was a good scrap. While it was on, Sam Wild came along. He watched for a while and when it was over he challenged the winner. I think it was Latus. Sam was not very big – about 5ft 7in, wiry muscle and bone. They rolled about stripped to the waist, over stones and pebbles and rough ground until both were exhausted. It finished in a friendly atmosphere. I relate this incident to indicate what sort of a man Wild was, perhaps one most fitted for the job he had to do.

Billy Griffiths: On the advance to Corbera (25–26 July 1938)

We returned to the road (after strafing by Nationalist fighters). Sam (Wild) told us to pick two men and scout the right-hand side of the road towards Corbera. I chose Morris Miller and a fellow from Swansea. Miller, though young (about 20) was a seasoned campaigner. He had been wounded badly at Caspe. In fact he was stalked around a tree and fired at five times at close range and left for dead. An ambulance picked him up on the side of the road and now here he was in my scouting party. The other was very young, and it was his first experience.

We moved leisurely through trees laden with fruit: black, luscious figs, pomegranates, grapes. It was like the Garden of Eden! We climbed upwards until we arrived at a prominence overlooking Corbera. There was nothing to report. There seemed little movement. On the way back we took the shortest direction to the road, calculating that the battalion would have moved forward to that point. Suddenly we came across a camp! There were horse and men. Morris and I assumed them to be Moorish cavalry. Our companion became hysterical and wanted to run down and join them, insisting they were our men. This could not be. We had no cavalry! We pulled him down and Miller sat on his head until he regained his composure. We told him to take the long way back to keep out of danger. This he did. In the meantime, Miller and I crept closer to the camp. We came across a mule loaded with rifles and immediately decided to pinch it. Scarcely daring to breathe, we untied the animal and led it away.

When we reached the road at a point a few miles further down, we found ourselves under fire. We scampered off the road and lay behind a bank. To our right was a house. I hung onto the mule while Miller went to investigate. It was a temporary brigade headquarters. The British Battalion was in action, attacking some strongpoint in the hills on the other side of the road. We left the mule in the care of the officer in charge, telling him he could have the rifles, but the animal was ours. Having done this we dashed across the road to join the battalion.

Then Sam heard about our mule. We were ordered to enter Corbera and look for grub. We set off, the three of us on the back of the mule: Dobson, Miller and myself. The place was deserted. They had left in a hurry. There were masses of stores. Tinned milk, tinned food of all kinds and lots and lots of boots. We drunk a few tins of milk, and while Dobson searched for a pair of boots to fit him, Miller and I went to look for a cart. We found one, and a harness. Soon the mule was hitched up, the cart loaded and we were on our way.

After Hill 481 the battalion went into reserve returning to the front on the evening of 15 August. It was good to relax. Hot coffee in the morning and evening. Even the carrabunces and lentils seemed more appetizing. I had a parcel from home, the only one I ever received! Cigarettes from the local club, salmon and chocolate. This was indeed luxurious living! Morris Miller and I were making a dugout. Most people thought us daft, but I was always over-cautious. We had stopped work to share out the parcel. I didn't smoke, so the cigs were a free distribution. A fair crowd had gathered and we sat around eating chocs and generally gossiping. Half a dozen planes came over and dropped a few bombs. The crowd melted like magic. All went into the dugout, piled on top of each other. All that is, except me and Miller. We were the only two left outside. There was no room for any more. It was quite a joke. At least, they thought so!

That evening [15 August] I shared blankets with Lesser [Sam Russell]. The food truck came at dawn, and Lesser had gone down to the road to wait for it. The road continued in the direction of our rear in a straight line for about half a mile along a narrow valley, no more than 20 yards wide flanked by steep hills. Where Lesser waited it swung sharply to the right in the direction of Gandesa for about 200 yards, and then disappeared in another bend which seemed to block the valley completely. To the right of where I sat, the terrain took on a new and more sinister appearance. It was as if a giant's hand had cut a cleft through the mountain, revealing the rocks in all their nakedness below.

Through the jungle of boulders and projecting needle-like rocks, dwarfing a man by their size, a narrow, tortuous path wound its way from the road, skirting precipitous drops and running onto the open at a point to the right. Skirting the head of the ravine, the path got lost in a more open stretch of level ground before the hills rose again, sharply to the crest and the frontline positions of the British Battalion. One tried to avoid as much as possible the path and open ground because of the intensity of shell and mortar fire, which at times came over at the rate of 40 per minute. Yet this was the only way to the British Battalion HQ, the Canadian positions and the frontline. I got caught twice, but each time was fortunate to be near a shallow slit trench. Morris was not so lucky. He was killed outright. So also was the Chief of Fortifications for the Brigade (Egan Schmidt), who with his staff was caught in a barrage not far from the Brigade HQ. He and three of his staff were killed and a number wounded.[2]

Bob Walker

Volunteer from Edinburgh, Scotland. Served with the Machine-Gun Company, British Battalion, 15th International Brigade, March 1937–October 1938.

Tanks started to come round and our machine guns were sited in the middle of the road. They were putting bullets below the tracks. The tanks backed away, then made a second effort to come round and this time we got one below the tracks and the tank caught fire. Two of the crew baled out and made a run for it. They were shot at but I don't know what happened to them. Then the other tank backed away. By this time I was climbing up the side of the hill to the left of the road to see what the position was. I climbed to the top of the hill and saw two groups of fascists coming up, about 20 men in each – an advance guard. I wasn't carrying a weapon, so I picked up a stone and pretended it was a hand grenade. I 'pulled the pin', lobbed it and they all went down. This allowed me to race down the hill and warn the lads who were on the side of the hill, about four of them. We all moved back to just outside of Calaceite.

Malcolm Dunbar [Chief of Operations for the 15th International Brigade] came up from brigade. By this time the remainder of the brigade had gone up to Batea. Malcolm, myself and another lad climbed a hill to see what was going on. We all got hit: I got some shrapnel in my side, Dunbar got shot in the leg and the other lad got hit in the head. Malcolm hobbled down the hill, I picked up the other lad (he was unconscious), but couldn't carry him because I had been wounded in the side. So I kicked him and swore at him and he came round. I got him down to Doctor Simon, who was very calm. The ambulance had gone so he tended to my wound.

The lads said that the machine guns were out of water [they were water cooled]. I felt fear for the first time. I decided I had to get water for the guns. I got on the road but then the planes came over, strafing us. I curled up on the road and just hoped for the best. I changed my mind about going for water! Then the ambulance came up. Malcolm told the lads to just stay where they were and try to hold the enemy. Defend, don't attack.

Malcolm and I were taken in the ambulance to a hospital in a railway tunnel. There was a generator in the tunnel for the lights. The procedure was that when you arrived you were examined to see if you were an urgent case. If you weren't an urgent case they wouldn't operate on you; you waited for an ambulance to take you elsewhere. I wasn't considered an urgent case so I was taken to Tortosa.

I didn't like being there because the [fascist] bombers came over regularly. They [the nursing staff] tried to take away Malcolm's pistol but he wouldn't part with it. He said he would never see it again, and anyway the next day he was going back to the front. He said he was only there to be dressed. He made the doctor sign a receipt for the pistol. Sure enough, the next morning he presented it, got his pistol back and went back to the front. His body was riddled with shrapnel, all over his back as well.

Then they sent me to Mataró, 15 miles above Barcelona. I went into a hospital run by nuns … They took my shirt and socks away. There were big holes in my socks. They brought them back and they were beautiful, the darning was like weaving … The doctors were training the nurses and showing off a bit. When they got to me they had to get the shrapnel out. I used to bite the sheet when they were doing it.

I stayed there for five days before I was transferred up to brigade hospital. I remember this Liverpool lad who had shrapnel in his back. We got an idea that we would go back and thank the nun who had looked after us. So we each got a bunch of flowers, but didn't realize that in Spain if you give a woman a bunch of flowers it meant you were courting. We arrived on a Sunday but the other nuns said she couldn't come out, but they took the flowers. She must have been very embarrassed.

I went back to join the battalion in June 1938, in a valley near the Ebro … I was asked to move to the brigade Machine-Gun Battalion which was being created. I joined a company containing Czechs, with Germans in charge. There were four companies and I was in the English company, except there were no Englishmen in it! They were all Canadians and

Spaniards. There was an interpreter, a Canadian, who spoke German well. But I didn't feel comfortable in that battalion because of communications – I couldn't converse easily. We did a bit of training on light machine guns and prepared to cross the River Ebro.

We crossed over on barrels that had been tied together with planks on top. They bobbed up and down and one or two fell off. Our job was to go into the mountains and chase any fascists who had taken shelter there. I'm not too keen on heights. We were up on little ledges. We discovered some groups of fascists. I remember stopping at one house and asking the owner if we could have some water. He said yes and told us that the fascists had been through the area but didn't want water but had demanded wine.

We were two days up there, then we went down to Corbera. I remember the terrific bombing in which people were killed. We went to where food was being dished out but when we arrived it had all gone. There was only a little rice left. The men were complaining, especially a big Canadian lumberjack carrying a light machine gun. He said he was going to wrap the machine gun around somebody's neck.

We got into Corbera, which had been captured. When we halted I told a couple of lads to go and see if there was any food. They came back with boxes full of solidified jam – not very appetizing. Then there was a buzz and half the company disappeared. I went to find out where they had gone, which was a store where there were boxes of champagne. I stopped the lads passing cases to each other; I didn't want them drinking champagne on empty stomachs.

We took up positions in the hills on the left and supported a morning attack. There were also fascist trenches in the hills and in the valley opposite us. We occupied some of these trenches but they came back and drove us out again. A mortar round got me in the side of the head. The German commander said I had to go to hospital. I was bandaged up but I wasn't badly wounded, not a serious case.

They got me down to the bank of the Ebro where there was a bridge, but it had been badly bombed. There were caves in the cliff on the side of the river, and we were in there. They took us across the river in the morning in rowing boats. Boats were going back and forth, with stretchers laid across them. We got over without being bombed and they put us on a train.

I ended up in a clearance hospital outside Barcelona. There were fleas all over the place. I went into Barcelona where I bumped into Sam Wild [commander of the British Battalion]. He asked what I was doing. I said I was waiting to be assigned. He said he wanted me at the battalion, and so I went back to the British Battalion.[3]

Bob Cooney

Volunteer from Aberdeen, Scotland. Served as adjutant and commissar with the British Battalion, 15th International Brigade, October 1937–October 1938 (see plates 2 and 13).

I was in Belchite [August 1937]. We had to fight our way out, the line had broken. Sam Wild was the battalion commander. Every retreat was a retreat by yards. We ended up behind a low stone wall. The fascists were advancing and we were fortunate to find a drainage channel in which to fall back. I saw George Fletcher bend down. I said it was pretty hot, but what I didn't realize was that he had received another wound. But he got out.

We went to brigade and said the position we had been given was hopeless, completely flat, no cover. They agreed and told us to get to the nearest high ground. As we were moving we went through some hefty bombardments. Sam Wild discovered that we were surrounded, so we were given the last of the cognac ration then the whole battalion set off again. We were escaping one encirclement and going into another. In one trek we covered 57km, with just the occasional pause. It got worse because there were streams of refugees retreating.

In March 1938 we were in the Calaceite affair. On 31 March we got a message that the front had broken. We moved out in formation with scouts ahead and on the flanks. We were racing to get to the front. As we came round a bend in the road we were confronted by enemy tanks (our scouts had already been captured). The only thing that saved us was that they couldn't depress their guns enough because we were so near to them. George Fletcher cried: 'Get to the high ground.' We scrambled up to the high ground as best we could through a horde of Italians. But some of the lads wouldn't move and stayed where they were.

Joe Harkins and I moved along a terrace on the hill, then along the next terrace up, hoping to get to the top, as near to the woods that were on the far side. But then, above us, there was an Italian officer with some soldiers. He told us to get our hands up. Then we saw the lads who wouldn't move being escorted by the fascists and then being frisked. They forgot about Joe and I. So we made a run for the woods. About three-quarters of the way across a machine gun opened up on us. But we got into the woods. About 160 of the battalion was captured out of 600 men.[4]

Edwin Greening

Volunteer from Wales. Served as an infantryman and observer with the British Battalion, 15th International Brigade, September 1937– October 1938.

They were the ones that did the damage, not the artillery, not the aerial bombardment, but the mortars with their devilish, deadly accuracy. We were subjected to these in the blistering heat of an August summer in Catalonia, high up on those limestone ridges, the Sierra Pandols. My mother was sending me newspapers and letters, such as *The Aberdare Leader*. When there was a lull in the fighting I crawled down to where my friend Tom Howell Jones was. I said: 'Here's the *Leader*, read it, Tom. I don't want it back.' I went back up. We were all filthy, unshaven. Everywhere was the smell of urine, excreta, dead men and dead mules and all the rest of it. It was hell on earth. If that was hell, Dante didn't have to invent it, that was it. Well we had another terrific barrage and I heard a shout: 'Come quick Taff.' Tom Howell Jones had been hit. So I crawled down this precipice to where Tom Howell Jones and his three friends were in this kind of crevice. They'd had a direct hit, and they were killed. I just held him in my arms and he went. I was covered in blood and I went back up. You can imagine how I felt. The next day we got them out and buried them. You could only bury them by covering them with stones. There was no earth there. We found a crevice. We put the four men in and covered them with stones and I said a little prayer. I'm an atheist, I am not a religious person. I said: 'Tom, I will remember you if 50 years pass.' Well, 50 years have passed and I still remember him. The next night they came and said we are moving out. Tom was a cultured man: well read, kindly and humane.

We moved out and went up and down this precipitous place while the new troops came in, then we marched along this gorge for about two miles. We got on lorries and got put into the reserve. The next day I washed up, shaved and everything else and tried to pull myself together.

On 27 August 1938, we were south of the Sierra Pandols. I was resting there when the mail man came around. He handed me a letter. It was from a girlfriend. She said she was so sorry about my niece, Sheila Phillips, how sad that she had died at 12 years of age. And I never knew a word; I didn't know that she was ill. Well with Tom Howell Jones being killed and my niece who lived opposite me dying suddenly like that, you could imagine how I felt. I felt absolutely terrible. Then Harry Pollitt, leader of the Communist Party, saw me sitting by the side of the road, and he came up to me and said, 'How are you getting along, comrade?' I said I was feeling absolutely terrible, and I broke down completely. It was such a terrible situation. Anyway, an hour later I had recovered. But it was a hell of a situation, so many had been killed in the Sierra Pandols. We were fighting the magnificently equipped and trained armies of Germany and Italy, and there they were trying out their tactics and weapons for World War II. They were using the Spanish people as their testing ground, aided by that scoundrel Franco and the Catholic Church of Spain.

On about 7 or 8 September we were ordered back into the line. We got on lorries and drove to a place that I knew. It was a place called Sandesco. We arrived in a desperate flurry of lorries and took up our positions. Vants sent Paddy O'Daire to find out what was in front of us, and three observers went. Next day he was gone. Repatriated to Britain. He had been there two years. They took him out, you see. Morris Davis was wounded. We were in front and of course the enemy attacked us. And then we were relieved, we came out but not into the reserve, just back a bit. Then we were in the next day and out again.

One day they came and said to my best friend George Murray, my observer: 'You are wanted back at battalion headquarters.' He went back, then returned and told me he was being sent to another brigade and that I would have to make do with Amy Torents. Well, Amy Torents was a 19-year-old Spaniard from Barcelona and I said, 'I can't do that, I need somebody else'. So I went to the Company Commander, Arthur Nickel (Paddy O'Daire had been sent back), and I said I had lost George Murray. He has gone back to the brigade. I must have some strong, reliable people to help me. He said who do you want? I said I have two good friends, Bill Thompson and Jock

Maclean. He said, 'Right, send them to me.' So they sent for them and they agreed to become observers. While this went on, there was heavy fighting – bombing, tank attacks, artillery – all through that part of September in and around Sandesco and towards Corbera. We were suffering losses.

We four were sent forward to a position by our company commander to report. We were overlooking this village of Sandesco and could see tanks arriving. Infantry getting off lorries. So I said to Amy go back and tell them what we've seen. Off he went. As soon as he had gone there was a terrific barrage on our positions. So we had to seek shelter because we were not dug in. So we crouched and ran back, and when the barrage lifted we turned and had a look at what was happening. All we could see was dust so we continued to go back. Then the barrage started again so we crawled into a feature, which is common in those limestone areas. It is like a part of the surface of the land collapses and you get like a little basin. You can go down to the bottom and it is just earth, and all around there are trees growing out of it. Scrub and fawn trees.

So we lay there with a barrage all around us but then it turned dusk. It was now time to get back to the battalion if we could, but then we could hear the clanking of tanks and loud voices, which meant it wasn't our tanks. We didn't have any. Must be fascist tanks. So Jock Maclean pushed his head up through the scrub, came down and said there was about 50 fascist soldiers and about six tanks, and they were only about 50 yards from us. I said let's hope they go away quick and that none of them comes here and pisses over us. It was quite possible they could have a shit and throw it in the hole. So we lay there, hardly daring to breathe as it grew darker and darker. We were hungry and in exceptional danger. We could see the silhouette of the tanks and the soldiers standing or sitting around the fire, so I said to Jock Maclean and Bill quietly, 'The best thing we can do is to get out of here. Go back towards Sandesco 'cos we can't possibly break through them to get to our own lines. We will have to go back to Sandesco. Get around Sandesco and go down to the Ebro, and we can find the *barranca* [dry river bed].' If you could find a *barranca* you could go down to the Ebro and wade across. So we crawled away from the men around the fire for about 200 yards and then stood up, and then walked under the olive trees looking for a clay road. We found one and began walking back towards Sandesco. There was a danger of meeting somebody so Jock Maclean, who had the keenest eyesight, walked in front. I came 10 yards after him; Bill Thompson another 10 yards back. Then we walked and came to a building, stopped and waited. We put our hands up to feel if there were, say, apricots or peaches on the fruit trees, but there was nothing – the fascists had taken the lot. So we were getting increasingly hungry and all we could eat were grapes, there was plenty of them around.

We could see Sandesco in the moonlight, and about an hour and a quarter later we could see Fayon, which is on the right bank of the Ebro. We could see lorries passing along the little roads towards the front and sometimes we could see a fire. It was not likely to be peasants, but a battalion or a company of fascist infantry resting for the night, so we had to avoid them. Then we came to where the clay road stopped and we knew that there was a *barranca*. We had to find a path down. So we searched and at last we found one and went down. I knew that there was a railway down there on the side of the Ebro running all the way from Barcelona, a one-track railway. And there was bound to be an arch to allow the water to come down in winter along that *barranca* under the railway and into the Ebro. So we went down quietly and came to the arch. Then we went back up, searching for tomatoes and grapes, which we found. We spent all day in there while the battle raged. We couldn't come out. We could be shot by our own men across the Ebro or we could be shopped by a peasant who had seen us. If this peasant was anti-Republican he would report us to the fascists, and we would have had it.

So we stayed there until it grew completely dark, and before the moon was up we went down. We had to get moving. Once the moon was up there would be patrols each side – it was not very safe to wade across the Ebro with Republican patrols on the other side. But I knew that the Ebro was a very shallow river with shores appearing everywhere. So we walked into the warm water and used our rifles as supports all the way across. Then we climbed the other bank, fell on our faces and didn't move. We got up and walked towards the north. But before we had gone 100 yards we were challenged by a Republican patrol. They took our rifles and led us away to a big farmhouse, which was about half a mile beyond the Ebro. We were interrogated, our clothes were taken away and we were given a blanket and a hot meal. The commandant said we were very lucky.

We were there for about two days, resting. Then they gave us back our dried clothes and our rifles. We were joined by a lorry load of other soldiers, Spaniards, Americans, Canadians. We were expecting to be sent back to the [front] line, to the British Battalion. But we weren't. We had been in the line since 25 July. We had seen more action on the frontline than some of the men in World War I, in four years of fighting. I had two friends killed in Burma [in World War II] but they were not killed on the frontline, they were killed in accidents.[5]

Jim Brewer

Volunteer from Wales. Served as a gunner, range finder and quartermaster with the Anti-Tank Battery, 15th International Brigade, January 1937–October 1938.

We were blazing away when suddenly the number one on my [anti-tank] gun, Chris Smith, fell over. I took one look at him and blood was seeping around the bottom of his abdomen, and my training as a St John's ambulance man took precedence over everything else. We had no bandages, but I noticed that over to our left on the road was an ambulance. So I told the number three on the gun, Jimmy Sullivan, a lad from the Gorbals in Glasgow, to take over. I picked Chris up in my arms and carried him about 200 yards over open ground. He thought I was carrying him down the hill but it was flat ground dominated by the church tower.

I didn't know where the bullet had come from, but it had obviously been fired from our right, from the vicinity of the church, so I picked him up and shielded him with my body and walked across to the ambulance. I told them: 'Now for God's sake get busy on this chap.' It transpired that he had a bullet through the penis of all things, and I have tried to fathom out since how that bullet had missed the number three and number four on the gun, had missed me, but it had hit Chris in his vitals. I just could not work it out.

When I got back to the gun Jimmy Sullivan was in pride of place. He had perfect eyesight, he had an artist's or a safebreaker's skill with his hands and he was really marvellous at laying the gun so I was quite content. I had defective vision, it was no good at the rate of fire that we had got up to, having anybody on that gun sight with spectacles. I always ensured that the gun was loaded at the earliest possible second after the recoil. Then I would slap him on the shoulder and he could fire. We were told later on that day we had achieved a firing rate of 20 rounds a minute from three guns – 60 shells going across.

Bobby Walker, who was commanding a company of the battalion, an ex-Scots Guardsman, was lying down on this open ground and he made a reference to the fires of hell. He felt sorry for those blokes who had to face up to it in those trenches. Then there was a bit of a commotion on our left, and Tom Wintringham, Slater and Dunbar were standing there discussing what they had to do, when suddenly Wintringham was hit in the shoulder. It was evident to Dunbar where the shot had come from. They got Wintringham away to the same ambulance that had taken Chris Smith out, which returned to pick up more casualties. Dunbar said, 'Well, there is a sniper in the church tower.' So we turned our gun on it and first of all we rang the bell, there was a bell case in there so we got a shot plum on that, an armour-piercing shell. We thought that the sniper would be coming down from the bell tower and make his way out the back door of the church, so we put another armour-piercing shell through the door of the church, followed by a high explosive one. I didn't like it, I knew the building was sacred to other people and I didn't like the idea of stooping to the level of the enemy in regarding it as a fortified place, but of course that was a bit too chivalrous. I forgot how many rounds we had fired, a hell of a lot, but the people on the hill surrendered (they said they would have surrendered earlier if it had not been for their officers). So the battalion got that without any casualties. Earlier some people came up from battalion headquarters. They had caught this [fascist] man trying to get away dressed in ordinary trousers and a shirt with no identification, and they had held a drum-head court martial and sentenced him to death. They came up to our guns looking for a firing squad.

The charge was being on a battlefield dressed in civilian clothing. Obviously it was a soldier who was trying to escape. If he had been taken in his uniform, being bound by the rules of war they would have had to make him a prisoner. But the fact that he had divested himself of his uniform and identity card, well that was it. It was a very speedy proceeding in which they said they wanted a volunteer firing squad – you and you and you and you. They pointed at me and I said 'no thank you'. I said behind us is a legitimate government which has got legal institutions and that man is entitled to a trial. It was a point of honour to me because that man, if it was the sniper who could have shot me in the back, had refrained from doing so because I was in his sights for 200 yards. He could have shot me in the chest and he didn't do so, so I felt it was a matter of honour that I would not be involved in shooting a man that could have killed me. I refused steadfastly and they didn't argue with me because they could see I was determined. They blindfolded him, turned him around a few times and he ended up with his back towards us, and they shot him. I was bloody horrified and disgusted. They thought those people on the hill would see this and it might knock the stuffing out of them, but it didn't so we had to re-engage and blast them out of it, as it were.

Our final service was in second Belchite where Franco put in a counterattack and we were strung out. God we had a tremendous field of fire, but I didn't know where the battery headquarters was. We got no instructions and we were just there waiting for the enemy. These light Italian tanks came over the hill and I told the number one, Jimmy Sullivan, 'Hold your fire'. Now of course we had an ex-artillery man, Frank Proctor, in the battery, and if they had made him the drill sergeant then the one thing that we would have learned was the command to stand fast. In the Royal Artillery, whatever you were doing, when the command 'stand fast' is given you freeze. If I had shouted at him 'stand fast' he would not have fired, but he fired one armour-piercing round which missed by about 20 yards. Those damn tanks turned around, going back over the hill – they weren't going to come forward and risk coming on to our guns. We were sitting there, waiting for them to come again in greater force, when up comes Frank Proctor and he says we are to retreat because otherwise we are going to be cut off. Jimmy Sullivan, a chap brought up in the Gorbals [Glasgow] in those bloody dreadful circumstances, who owed nothing to Britain because of his miserable life (his mother had died, his father struggled to rear him and he lived in a hovel), turned round to Proctor and said, 'The British never retreat'. That was our sentiment – we were not going down, we were going to fight it out. Frank started arguing with us and off he went back to battery headquarters.

Ten minutes later he came back armed with [Malcolm] Dunbar's Mauser pistol. Frank said: 'I am ordering you now, as battery commander, to withdraw. If you refuse to withdraw I have been instructed to shoot you.' Of course we had no side arms, or anything like that to defend ourselves with. He said: 'I was trained in the Royal Artillery and in the Royal Artillery when we are given an order we bloody well obey it. So you are going to withdraw.' So we agreed. We would withdraw but we would not damn well retreat, but with all the goodwill in the world we just could not retreat because the driver of our lorry had absconded. Not one of us could drive and we were there with a truck load of ammunition, our equipment and the gun. We had locked the gun, closed the trails and put the drag ropes on – and with that down came the Messerschmitts [German fighter aircraft]. There was an olive grove there and three squadrons came in, one after the other, and I think they shot every damn leaf off those olive trees. They assumed that there was infantry there, but we didn't see any, so in the brief period between one squadron finishing and the other one coming in we inched the gun away down this central road. We got onto the tarmac, a decent road, and there was a farmhouse on our right and chickens running around. So the other four now decided to get a chicken for their dinner because the place was going to fall into enemy hands; they went off and told me they wouldn't be long. I saw them go towards this building and I thought, you silly buggers.

When we were first created as a battery we had a reception at divisional headquarters, and told the guns were of more value to the Republic than our lives – that was what registered in my mind. So I saw them go and I thought, to hell with it. They are now risking being caught: if there are enemy troops infiltrating they had had it. I got the two drag ropes over my shoulder and picked up the trail and off I went down the road on my own. It was nice and flat, I had no hills to climb. I let the gun gently down the other side and I was going along expecting them to catch me up at any moment, but there wasn't a sign of them.

I was strong so I could pull it. It had rubber wheels and was beautifully balanced, and a strong chap could move it. I had already proved that because I had saved a gun on an earlier occasion by simply leaping on it and dragging it out of the line of fire. I was going along quite happily down this road, hoping that I would run into somebody in authority or some troops. Everything was quiet and there were even one or two birds singing. There was a bend ahead of me and nosing around it was an armoured car with its guns ready to fire. I thought, oh well, if that's an enemy armoured car then I have had it ... It turned out to be one of our divisional armoured cars, one of the few that they had, and this chap stopped and he could see that I was a Republican soldier. He knew this by my lack of uniform, that it was a Russian gun and that I was going in the right direction.

With a few words of Spanish and a few words of English we managed to communicate. I warned him that I was the last Republican soldier between him and the enemy and to proceed with caution, and if possible get off the road. I asked him if he could be kind enough on his way back to give me a tow with the gun and a lift back.

About 20 minutes later I heard the sound of a car engine behind me, and I thought I hope to God it is him coming back, and it was. So we lashed the gun trail to the armoured car and I jumped up on top and rode back. We got to the divisional staff where one officer said to me (he could speak English): 'You will have to surrender the gun because the enemy is likely to break through to the Mediterranean and we want everything to be sent to the central front, because in Catalonia we can get reinforcements.' I did the sensible thing, I didn't argue, I surrendered it.

I then attached myself to a Polish machine-gun team and met one or two chaps of the British Battalion. We clustered around this gun and it was dark. I put my head down on the ground because I was tired and dozed off. Then I heard a bloody drumming on the ground and I thought, good God what's that? So I sat up and said, 'Boys, stand to'. Suddenly one of those Dabrowski [Polish] chaps yelled out a challenge (they had loud voices). Cavalrymen have good ears because they answered the challenge and they went through us – two horsemen who were obviously carrying despatches. Afterwards we went back to sleep.

The following morning we were told to make our way over the Ebro, up on the hills and to go along to Mora de Ebro. I was very amused when I was explaining what happened to the number three gun to Bill Alexander, and he asked me one of the most ridiculous questions I have ever been asked: 'Did you get a piece of paper with a signature on it?' I looked at him in amazement. I said of course not, these men had no time for such frippery as that. What they wanted was to get the gun and get it through to the central front.

Then we had to get across the Ebro, which because it was summer was at a very low ebb. We managed that, we got over the other side and machine guns opened up on us. We realized that the enemy was very close. We marched all night and then ran into another cavalryman. We were standing around near this farmhouse and I put my hand up to stop this chap and to ask him a question, but he didn't know in the half light if I was friend or foe, so out comes a bloody cutlass. I never moved so fast in my life! He was coming right at me and I got out of the way. Obviously those chaps had to be really alert, travelling as they were at high speed on horseback. Then we got to the reorganization point at Mora de Ebro and we were there for a few days.

I was on sentry duty with orders not to let anyone go towards this bridge from the Republican side because the engineers were placing charges to blow it up. Then a car drove up and for some reason we had all acquired a hatred for [Denis] Sefton Delmer, who had reported in the press that we [the

British Battalion] had been wiped out. This had caused a hell of a lot of anguish so I said, 'Where are you going?' They said, 'We are coming up to see what the battle is like and we are going forward'. I thought if one of you is Sefton Delmer I don't give a damn; the whole lot of you can go and get killed. If that had happened it would have been a great disservice to the Republican cause because the chap that was speaking to me had an American accent. I said to him, 'Excuse me, would you mind telling me your name'. It was that great correspondent of the *New York Herald* [actually the *New York Times*]. I think his name was Matthews [Herbert L. Matthews] and he had been a staunch reporter in support of the government. I said 'Would one of your companions be a man called Sefton Delmer?' No, he replied. I said I was just about to make a terrible mistake, I was going to let you go forward. If he was present I would not mind him getting bumped off. He laughed and he said, 'Oh no. We represent the American Press'. I told him the bridge was about to be blown. The enemy was very close so he would have to go back, I was to stop anyone going forward. They turned back but I could have been responsible for the death of some very good men.[6]

Reginald Saxton

British doctor. Served with medical units in Spain, August 1936– October 1938.

At the Ebro I was actually there with my mobile laboratory. The frontline was along the Ebro, along the two sides of the river. It was a very well-planned offensive from our side from Catalonia, and it was supposed to have been coordinated with the corresponding attack from the other side, and there were the fascist forces in the middle. We set up a hospital in some caves on our side of the river to receive casualties at the beginning of the attack. We had this hospital in this cave and the cave was on two levels inside. It had been levelled up inside and was very nicely protected by this enormous hill over the top of it. It was lit up with electric lighting, which an American engineer did for us. On one level there was a ward and an operating theatre, and on another level another ward. In the end we found that we were using one ward for Republican soldiers and the other ward for prisoners of war, and in the valley just below the caves were canteens and feeding arrangements, ambulance parks and a tent or two. It was quite well arranged.

Then we had the first casualties brought back across the river to us in this cave. Our transfusion and laboratory was there. It was quite a temporary affair, and as soon as some territory had been cleared on the other side of the river we took this laboratory and mobile service and went across a pontoon bridge. It was very exciting in a way, going across the pontoon bridge, which the Spanish engineers had organized so well across the River Ebro. They had spare pontoons concealed in various places not far away, where there was vegetation or something to hide them from the aviation because there were a lot of planes. Every day the Italian planes would come over and try to destroy this pontoon bridge, and indeed they hit it on numerous occasions. But since it was all in sections, all standard-sized boats, when one was sunk, that evening a similar pontoon was floated into position. The next morning things would be going across again.

We went across it at night and there were planes all around even then. We got across and drove up to a farmhouse along very narrow roads. We had to stop every now and then to cut down a tree because the road was not wide enough for this very wide vehicle. Then we set up our little hospital in the farmhouse. We were digging ourselves shelter there and our driver was digging a trench beside a car. He was a very energetic, strong young man. He dug us a nice shelter, a trench beside the vehicle and he also cut down lots of branches from the trees to camouflage it for when the wounded came in.

The wounded came in spurts but we did have quite a lot because it was a very fierce battle. There were certain fortified mountain peaks and tops of hills, which the enemy held on to with great tenacity, and our men with very little cover were trying to force their way up to the tops of these hills and were being killed in great numbers. There were stony slopes with very little shelter. It was very hard going. It [the battle] more or less ground to a halt. They were throwing in more and more reinforcements and we were hoping that we would hear from the Madrid side how the attack would draw the enemy away, but they didn't and so that battle once more came to an unhappy conclusion with a retreat again across the River Ebro. We went back a different way, over a bridge that was still intact, a railway bridge I think. Again we went back under cover of darkness and retreated into Catalonia.

The wounded were evacuated by great ambulance trains that were fixed up with tiers of bunks on either side, and enormous numbers could be accommodated. They had long coaches with bunks down either side. Motor ambulances were also used but they could not take the numbers. Some of the roads were bumpy, so any patient with an injury found it uncomfortable to be bumped up and down along the terrible roads.[7]

Patience Edney

Volunteer from St Albans, England. Served as a nurse with the British Medical Mission in Spain, August 1936–October 1938.

On May Day 1938 we had a celebration in the village. We had a spitting competition. The Spaniards were very good at spitting, as were some of the Americans, the Texans. They could aim at a particular point, as could the Spaniards. It wasn't something that I cared for but it was a well-known thing. We had a target at the side of an ambulance to be spat at. It was a very good competition, the crowd was cheering them on and the Texans won.

We knew we were going to have this big fight: we were organizing to go across the Ebro, it was an open secret. We were longing for it. We wanted to go back to recover the ground we had lost. One day we were suddenly sent for, a lot of us from different sections. We were set up away from the Ebro in a big cave, very uneven. We got 100 beds in there. It was rather dark in the day. The cave was an irregular shape and on very uneven ground. In the valley below it we had a tent, which was not so safe at nights to sleep in as the cave. The stretcher bearers had to carry people up, it was quite a steep place.

The battle started and it went on for three or four days. We got people only at night because the shelling was enormous – they could not move in the day – so we got people hours after the battle. They had been wounded and some we could not save because they were too bad. On the road up to us there were lorry loads of the last call-up of children, 15 and 16 year olds, going to the front. We saw what had happened when they got to the front. All these terrible smashed-up people streaming in, and hearing those kids singing as they went up. It was terrible when I thought what was going to happen to them, it got me down frightfully.

It was uncomfortable and very dark in the cave. There was one head case, a Spaniard, who made marvellous speeches, a commissar. Spaniards make marvellous speeches. He went on and on. He was a miner and when the miners went on strike the government put them down with soldiers. He was talking about this and fascism and it sounded awful in this cave. We had so many injured. I was on nights most of the time. This darkness and the seriousness of it got me really down, and I thought nothing is worth this, nothing is worth all this misery and horror.

A chap had come in with bundles of stuff. He was sitting on the side of a bed smoking a cigarette and talking to a chap, an officer, who had his arm strapped up and was going to go back. They were talking, laughing and smoking and I was in this terrible state, running round with people dying, and I could hear these children singing on the road. I went over and said how can you be talking and laughing. Can't you see what is going on? Can't you hear those children singing. The chap, a very nice man, a marvellous man, replied that he was just a Spaniard from the locality who had brought up some fruit for us. He heard about the hospital and brought up fruit and food. I said to him, 'Is it worth it, all this?'

He replied that he was a peasant. There was no road to their village, just a track. They were very poor and they didn't know much about what was going on. They had heard a couple of years before that there was going to be an election in which they could vote, and they went to vote. This was the first time that they voted and heard nothing more about it, until they heard that the village next to them was measuring up the land. So they went over to see what this measuring up of the land was, and were told that a popular front had got in and it was a land reform thing. They didn't know how to measure so they went and found out how to measure. They measured out their land and he was elected the local mayor. He learned to read and write and they organized everything, and five or six weeks before this battle at the Ebro he was instructed to go to Barcelona. He had a letter. The first letter he ever had. He could read it. He had a letter to go to Barcelona. He went in a car to Barcelona. It was the first time he had been in a car. He was told there was going to be this battle and roads were going to be built, and that the local authorities had to provide so much food for the army. He organized it and he did it very well. He said, 'I became a man and that is what we are fighting for'. When I heard his story I felt very bad about being so defeatist. He became a man. He had been nothing before, a landless, hopeless peasant who was not able to read or write. He knew what he was talking about. He fought, you see. He stood up and fought for two and a bit years. They stood up and fought against being taken over by fascism.

Everyone who came to us was serious and we kept them until they were well enough to leave. We got all the serious ones. We got heads, abdominals and legs. We did not get fractures, they were plastered and sent off. We didn't get the lightly wounded. We only got the dying ones, or the very bad ones. They didn't all die but some we couldn't save. I had arguments with the stretcher bearers who wanted to take my blankets for the dead. I said I must have the blankets to keep the people alive with.

... We always needed instruments for doing the dressings and we needed morphine. We used to have lots of anti-tetanus jabs and we all had anti-typhoid injections. The treatment of patients was better than in World War I. The organization was much better. A lot of things that we learnt and the things we practised were later adopted by the US Army. People were sorted out and evacuated. They had learnt about keeping the wounds open. That got through to the surgeons: the importance of opening and cleaning up wounds and leaving them open. They learnt about that in Spain.

Blood transfusions also came from Spain and were widely used. We had a marvellous blood transfusion service. The bottle bank came and was done by another two people, an English doctor with an American assistant ... It was tiresome and difficult. The very badly wounded people were so ill and their blood pressure was so low, and it was difficult to get into a vein. You nearly always had to cut down but that would be done before they went to theatre and possibly again in the theatre. We gave salines and drips. We did very well in that sort of way.

There was a Moorish prisoner that had been taken. A Franco Moor. He was very badly wounded in the neck and he hated us. He did not trust us at all. He thought we would kill him, the same as they would kill people. He was admitted among the others and he had to have a blood transfusion and the chaps got together and said they were not going to give him one, because he was a Moor. They didn't discriminate otherwise. I accepted this. But when I looked around he was getting a blood transfusion. I saw very sheepish faces. That's what was different with the Republicans in Spain. They couldn't do things like the fascists. But they did hate the Moors. They despised Franco for bringing the Moors to fight. They knew they should not be fighting the Moors anyway in Morocco. They were very clear about that.

... We didn't trust the doctors entirely politically, but they were good surgeons. The doctors did a lot of real sabotage. The medical doctors on the whole, the doctors as a profession, were nearly all pro-Franco. If they got caught on the wrong [Republican] side they had no choice, and anyway they could not resist the marvellous surgery. Surgeons can't resist surgery.

... Regarding politics, we were lucky in our particular outfit: fairly straightforward in accepting the communists as the leading force. It was easy to accept them as being the leading force. Some areas of course, in Catalonia where I had been, we had the anarchists on one side and the POUM on the other.[8]

Harold Bernard Collins

Volunteer from London. Served with the British Battalion, 15th International Brigade, December 1937–March 1938. Prisoner of war, 1938–39.

We got to Belchite mainly by lorries, the British Battalion and the American troops. Belchite was not such a high place as Teruel was. We noticed that the villages and houses were more close together. We had to go from house to house through Belchite and search every one that we came to, and one or two places that we went to we were fired on. There were fascists in the houses before they retreated. Quite a number of these houses were actually blasted to pieces. They were blown up mainly with shellfire. The fascists blew up these houses. It was only when we approached the houses that they fired on us.

Our brigade suffered casualties from their fire. We had about 10 people either taken to hospital or killed. The whole brigade was involved, our company plus the Americans and on the far right of us were the Germans and Italians, the German anti-fascist Thaelmann Battalion and the Italian Garibaldi Battalion. A number of fascists were killed, about 20 in the house fighting through the town. You had to shoot at them or be shot. If you saw anybody you would fire at them. There were no civilians about. Not in Belchite, none at all. This house-to-house fighting took about a week.

After a short while the officers in charge told us what our next trip would be: to attack towards Calaceite. It took us about two days to get to Calaceite, which was a small town and the people were still there. The fascists had gone. The people were very friendly to us. They knew who we were and would come out to meet us. In fact the people often brought us something to drink. They were very good. The shelling was still going on from the fascists and Calaceite was being shelled. We had to go to the other side of Calaceite to see if we could meet the Italians. We never met them but we knew they were there.

I remember we were the other side of Calaceite when Lewis Clive told me how far to go and what to look out for. Shells were falling everywhere and the Italians seemed to advance. He was a very good soldier, Lewis Clive. I remember we had a bottle of wine with us and he asked me to look after it for him. I put it in my pocket and when night came we had to get rid of it. We were told the next day to advance to Calaceite. Advancing down the Saragossa road, 15–20 miles away, our objective was to capture Saragossa. If we captured Saragossa it meant that the Italians were beaten, because it was their headquarters.

The next day we were called up about 05.00 hours and had to go marching down the road towards Saragossa. This officer was leading us and we got about 200–300 yards down the road when we saw half a dozen tanks there. We thought they must be our tanks because Wally Tapsell goes up to them, bangs on the side of the tanks and said something to them in Italian or Spanish. They just opened fire and poor old Wally went down, got shot down. Quite a number of people, at least 50, got killed or were hit. They had five tanks and they just opened fire on our group. The best we could do was get off the road and get away.

All that day we were fighting these five tanks and their supporters. Lewis Clive, who was in charge, directed how we should fire at these tanks. At about 18.00 hours he said we will have to fall back, so we did. We went back across the hills because we knew that if we were on the road the tanks would see us. For three or four days we walked back, making for Calaceite, but when we got there we found out that the Italians had taken it. We were told by Lewis Clive to make our way back to Caspe, which was about 20 miles down the road, to meet the rest of the battalion. We were mainly all English and Scottish lads. There were one or two Spaniards among us. We were No 4 Company and there was about 30 of us retreating.

We didn't make it to Caspe, we lost our way. We came across a river which was difficult to get across. We got across but lost the way to Caspe. Wally Carsper, who was in charge of us at the time, said to us that we had to cross a valley to get to the Caspe Road. Only five or six went at a time. Wally Carsper and Dick Moss and a group of other lads went off on the first line. We kept 100 yards apart and the next lot followed. Our group waited and saw them get 100 yards away and then we followed them. When we got about 5 or 6 yards into this valley machine guns opened up everywhere. Obviously the Italians had been watching the valley all the time. We saw Wally Carsper go down and Dick Moss, but I was too young as a soldier to know if they had been killed or not (Carsper was killed a month later on the Ebro).

We started firing on the machine guns. We had been there an hour firing away and suddenly it went quiet, and then without any warning ... about 20 Italian soldiers rushed at us with bayonets. When firing they hit one or two of our lads. They weren't after to kill us but to capture us: they were after people they could exchange for us. In this rush I thought they had missed me. I went to walk out but suddenly I had a rifle banged into my back. I was captured with nearly all the group, at least 20 of us.[9]

Bill Feeley

Volunteer from St Helens, Liverpool, England. Served with the Machine-Gun Company, British Battalion, 15th International Brigade, August 1937–1938.

I used to watch them [fascist aircraft] bomb, and you could see the bombs come out. They used to drop bombs when they were very high up. We didn't have any real anti-aircraft equipment, only machine guns mostly, because of this Non-Intervention [Agreement], but even that kept them pretty high up. They came droning up and when the bombs started coming out you had plenty of time to duck for cover. Sometimes they dropped leaflets and you would see them coming out like a white cloud. Being strafed was more demoralizing than being bombed. We used to get some good lectures by some of the military experts who had been in service in their own country. What used to interest me about strafing in those days was that the only way a fighter plane could strafe you was to fire through his prop. Obviously he could not do that at close quarters for very long because he would go crashing to the ground if he did.

Regarding tanks, an officer would give a lecture in German about people who see tanks coming at them and they would think it was impossible to stop them, which was untrue. He then pointed out the different ways to stop them. At Calaceite, for example, we set one on fire with machine-gun bullets. The machine guns were set up on a road and they kept running at us. This tank got very close and the next thing it burst into flames, caused by machine-gun bullets.[10]

Notes
1   http://morrismiller.wordpress.com/
2   Ibid.
3   Walker, Bob, Imperial War Museum Sound Archive (IWMSA), London, Ref 807/6, Reel 5.
4   Cooney, Bob, IWMSA, London, Ref 804/7, Reel 5.
5   Greening, Edwin, IWMSA, London, Ref 9855/7, Reel 5.
6   Brewer, Jim, IWMSA, London, Ref 9963/10, Reel 7.
7   Saxton, Reginald, IWMSA, London, Ref 8735/9, Reel 8.
8   Edney, Patience, IWMSA, London, Ref 8398/13, Reel 9.
9   Collins, Harold Bernard, IWMSA, London, Ref 9481/4, Reel 3.
10   Feeley, Bill, IWMSA, London, Ref 848/4, Reel 3.

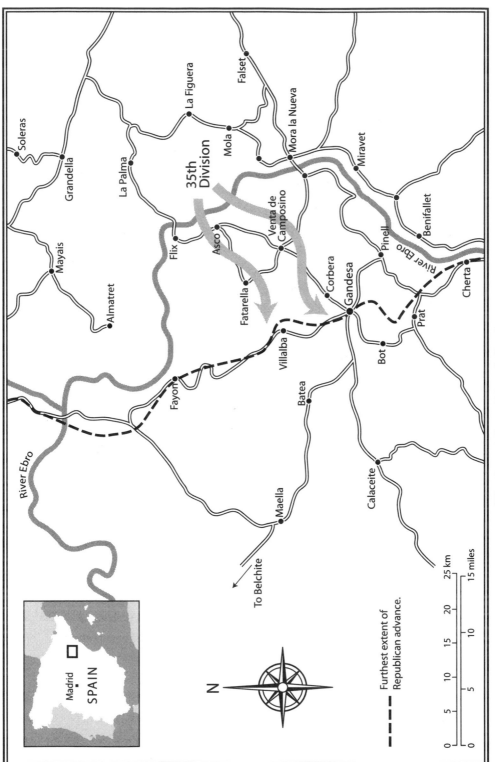

The Republican Ebro Offensive, 1938.

Away from the Fighting

Although training and combat were the main activities of the International Brigades, there were occasional breaks in the fighting for volunteers. During periods of inactivity, either enforced due to being wounded or due to a temporary halt in the fighting, individual volunteers could reflect on the nature of Spanish society, their fellow International Brigades compatriots and the character of the war they found themselves involved in.

In general, though, there was little contact between International Brigaders and Spanish civilians, and even less between male Brigaders and Spanish girls. Spanish society was in the main Catholic and conservative, which made any romantic liaisons difficult. For some foreign volunteers, of course, their work was behind the lines, carrying out non-combatant roles. Being away from the front did not, however, mean that one was necessarily safe. Nationalist bombers were an ever-present threat, especially to those living in Republican cities such as Madrid and Barcelona.

Eugene Downing

Volunteer from Dublin, Republic of Ireland. Member of the Communist Party of Ireland. Served in the 15th International Brigade, March– December 1938.

Just as the patients were of all nationalities, so were the nurses. In my ward, in addition to the Spanish girls, there was an

American, a Romanian and an English girl. During the long, hot days of that summer they did everything in their power to make conditions as comfortable as possible, never sparing themselves in attending to the needs of the wounded.

Barbara, the cool English nurse, told me one morning that I had 'a beautiful heart'. Since she was taking my pulse at the time I could only regard it as a purely medical observation and consequently derived no particular pleasure from it. In fact, it merely highlighted the lack of any comparable praise when, later in the morning, she was giving me a blanket bath. Dora, the Romanian, was very forthright and explosive, in several languages. On hearing someone boast, in Spanish, that he could learn any language in a week she burst out in a loud voice which I was sure could be heard in Barcelona '*NO POSSIBLE APRENDER UNA LENGUA EN UNA SEMANA*'.

The American nurse, who never stopped informing all and sundry that she was 'fully qualified', was indignant that she spent most of her time in routine duties instead of attending to casualties at the front. 'I keep telling them I want to be a frontline nurse.'

Of the Spanish nurses, Josefina was the real centre of our lives, the calm, even-tempered, soft-spoken one who never erupted, whatever the pressure, into streams of explosive language and wild gesticulations.[1]

Patrick Curry

Volunteer from Manchester, England. Member of the Communist Party. Served as a rifleman with the British Battalion, 15th International Brigade, and as a motorcycle despatch rider with the French Battalion, 14th International Brigade, December 1936–March 1938.

In April I was released from hospital and went down to Cartagena. It was a grim town because it had taken a bashing.

People lived in caves – ghastly. It was like the London Underground during the Blitz. There wasn't a great deal of food.

I went back to the battalion until they left to go to Brunete. Three or four of us were taken out for despatch duties. The battalion had suffered badly, though replacements had arrived. I joined the French as a despatch rider because I could ride a motorbike and I spoke French. So that was it. I went down to Albacete for despatch rider training. I was then sent to Almansa. From Almansa I used to take anything from there to Madrid, or anywhere else. I mostly took messages to brigade headquarters in Madrid, to a liaison officer who was liaising with the high command. I didn't see any generals at Madrid, though [André] Marty was there at the time.

Almansa to Madrid took about five hours. We had Nortons – they could move. Then I was ordered back to Albacete; then on a job between Valencia and Barcelona. I was the only British despatch rider; the rest were French and German. The journey from Barcelona to Valencia took most of the day. I would get a meal, sleep overnight and then go back [to Barcelona] the next day ... I had very little time off because I had to service the bike, so there was very little contact with civilians. We were told to keep to ourselves anyway. We had no uniforms, I'm glad to say.

The bombing of Barcelona reminded me of the bombing by Zeppelins in World War I. Quite light bombing, but quite frightening. There were a lot of air-raid shelters and the air-raid precautions were much better than those in England. The people were mystified at first but adapted quite quickly. There was not much damage compared to say Liverpool and London during the war. Barcelona was far more damaged than Valencia because it was a main port.[2]

Bob Cooney

Volunteer from Aberdeen, Scotland. Served as adjutant and commissar with the British Battalion, 15th International Brigade, October 1937–October 1938.

I was responsible for discipline. We had a lad from Walsall who deserted because his twin brother had been killed. He made his own way back to us, he was very ashamed. So I sat him down, gave him a drink and we talked. He was a first-class lad before and he was a first-class lad after, and he's a first-class lad today. We were all afraid.

One character we had to get rid of was Alec Marcovitch, a man from Glasgow who had been expelled from the [communist] party. He was a Trotskyist but professed repentance and came out in the same party as myself. When we got to Tarazona he got very drunk and I dressed him down for defeatist talk. I was asked to go to officers' school but I refused. Marcovitch went to officers' school but he later became totally demoralized. He stopped washing and shaving. Bill Rust [the British Communist Party's representative in Spain] said the sooner we get rid of him the better, but we failed. We were stuck with him.

After the Battle of Teruel I was made battalion commissar. Walter Tapsell had been killed at Calaceite in April 1938. Before I had been No 1 Company commissar. Then I was put into No 5 Company, which was full of bad boys. Paddy O'Sullivan, ex-Free State Army, and I called a meeting and reminded them of what people back home would be thinking of them, and what the Spanish people would think of them. They passed a self-condemnation resolution, promising they would make up for their actions.[3]

Alec Ferguson

Volunteer from Scotland. Served with the Anti-Tank Battery, 15th International Brigade, April 1937–October 1938.

I recovered from my wound in October 1937 and volunteered to go on the anti-aircraft guns on the Ebro front. We got a month's training at a naval battery at Valencia. When we got to the Ebro we found that the anti-aircraft guns had been blown up, so they put us on anti-tank guns. I was horror-struck by the number of refugees – men, women and children. Villages were bombed and there was great starvation as a result of non-intervention. There was a tremendous amount of suffering but the spirit of the people was great.

In the International Brigade, when I volunteered for anti-aircraft duties, I severed my connection with the British Battalion. I served with French, Czechs, Poles and Germans. Some Yugoslavs got drunk, broke into a house, stole things, abused the old lady who owned it and raped a young girl of 15. They were court-martialled ... a firing squad shot them. Well, this young Jewish man, a Welsh miner, a good lad, thought they had been unjustly dealt with. I said that the fascists were looking for incidents like that to spread among the villages. But he went up to the officers and called them bastards. He got two days in jail for that. Discipline was marvellous in general, but I was horrified by the drinking and gambling at Albacete.

I was amazed at the bravery of Republican women fighters. They were battle hardened, fighting alongside the men. The Spanish people had desperate bravery when provoked. They were hard-working people, very proud. But once you got to know them properly they couldn't do enough for you. Unlike in Britain, France and Germany, they had never been involved in many wars. They lacked at that time military experience. The Republican side could only draw on the lower ranks because all the officers and generals had deserted to the fascists. The International Brigades gave them that experience in the early period of the war.

Later the Republican Army with its new officer class that they had trained was so well organized, so disciplined that it could have turned the tide of war, if they had gotten enough supplies. I am convinced of that. I remember one captain, a Basque, a miner who had been in Guernica. He fought as bravely as his men, he inspired them. When they had to withdraw he stayed behind, manning a machine gun.[4]

John Longstaff

Volunteer from Stockton on Tees, England. Served as a runner with the British Battalion, 15th International Brigade, September 1937–October 1938.

We took probably about 100 or so prisoners at the first battle when I went to Belchite. I was not in the frontlines as such. The prisoners were generally taken by the Spanish comrades because they had captured them. At Belchite we took them because we encircled that town and lots of fellows on the fascist side surrendered because they knew there was no avenue of escape. Some of them had been conscripted by Franco. Some of them deserted because they were in the wrong part of the country when the war started, and they wanted to get back to their own home or wherever. So some of these on Franco's side would desert and come into our lines, and at the same time, unfortunately, there was a few of our Spanish lads whose homes were under fascist rule who would from time to time disappear. We used to understand why they had gone: to see if their parents, children and wives were still alive. The prisoners that we had, certainly the ones that were wounded, would be treated in the same way as the Republican Army treated its own wounded people, and they got the same kind of food or the same amount of food. They were not badly treated at all. The reason was quite simple: we needed those people. We needed them to go back and tell the enemy soldiers what life was like under the so-called red machines of the Republican Army.

... At the same time we would give them political information about why we were fighting, and why foreigners like ourselves were fighting in Spain. The best thing that happened in Spain was to demoralize Mussolini's fascist army. We had the Garibaldi Battalion with us, who were mainly Italian refugees who had escaped from Mussolini's camps in Italy, and they set up a battalion in Spain. But the Italian Army was boasting that they were going to break through to Madrid and the whole of the Italian Army was put into this attack against the weak Republican defences. They captured quite a bit of terrain and it could have become very serious for the people of Madrid, but the 12th International Brigade, which was mainly composed of Italian soldiers, took microphones and loud speakers into the frontline, and this made a lot of the Italians desert from Mussolini's army. They would broadcast to them over the frontlines and they would sing Italian songs to them. It also demoralized the Italian Army because they actually knew they were killing their own kith and kin.

The Battle of Guadalajara was not just a great victory but the equipment that the Spanish soldiers and the 11th and 12th International Brigades had captured, made the army three or four times stronger, with ten times more firepower. All this was a great morale booster for the whole part of the Republican part of Spain ...

Fascist prisoners were not interrogated by the International Brigades. The prisoners that we took in Spain would be sent back, they would be disarmed and an escort of two or three people would escort them to hand them over to the Spanish. We didn't even know their names. Sometimes we didn't even know the officers because they would tear off their emblems showing what rank they were. I don't know where they went to. No doubt they were interrogated by the Spanish authorities. It was not our duty to do that. I can't answer what happened to the fascists. I know for a fact, though, that just before I left Spain somewhere around about the village of Ripoll there was a prisoner-of-war camp full of Spaniards. They were building roads and things like that. They certainly didn't look as if they had been mistreated, but I was not near enough to talk to them. We were not allowed near them. I can't answer the question if they were treated better, worse or equal to the Moors, or the Italians or the Germans from the Condor Legion.

Some prisoners of war were shot. On our side, yes. There was the well-known case of Jimmy Rutherford. Jimmy had been captured, had been exchanged and he was sent back to England. When he got back to England the first thing that he did was to make enquiries to be sent back to Spain, which he was. Unfortunately for Jimmy he was captured again. He went to the same prison camp that he had been in some months before, and he was recognized. So he was taken out and shot.[5]

Maurice Levine

Volunteer from Manchester, England. Served with No 1 Company, 14th International Brigade, and as a political commissar with the 15th International Brigade, November 1936–March 1938 (see plate 1).

As commissar I approached George Aitken, who was the brigade commissar on that front, and told him that a man in my opinion was no use and should be taken to the rear, away from frontline duty. To my surprise Aitken agreed. He was very understanding. He had been in World War I himself and been wounded. I thought it was very good of him because you have to be very hard during a war. You can't just fit everybody in who might feel that they can't carry on, otherwise you would have nobody left.

My other duties included seeing that there was a fair ration of food and that sort of thing. Also arranging for people to go on leave. In the early period they were given seven days' leave in Madrid, but quite a number did not come back because there were all kinds of organizations in Madrid and in Spain which were helping people to desert. One organization that was very active in this was the Scottish Medical Aid Unit. Deserters who would get to the coast would find no difficulty getting on to a British freighter and be sent home …

After a while I was sent to Albacete to work in the Cadre Department, which dealt with tracing people, where they were and interviewing the volunteers as they came into Albacete. I used to go down to the barracks where the new arrivals would come and take their details. They would be processed and then leave our hands. It became a trickle by the end of 1937 and beginning of 1938. By March 1938 I had officer rank and about the middle of the month I was told I was being repatriated. It was a big surprise to me because I would not dare to ask to be sent back home. I was repatriated along with a man named John Henderson who was badly wounded at Brunete. We had to go to Valencia, make our own way there as best we could, and present ourselves at the Delegation of the International Brigades.

By this time Franco's forces were driving through the Aragon to cut Spain in two. There were crowds and crowds of peasant refugees streaming from the interior, coming to the coast to get away from the advancing fascist forces. We showed the police our *salvo conducto* (safe conduct passes) and they stopped a lorry, a Swiss lorry, which was piled high with cases of oranges. The police told the driver to take us, but the only way to get on that lorry (there were other people in the front) was to climb on top of the load. We travelled through the night – it is a long distance to Barcelona from there. We stopped about three in the morning somewhere on the road, lit a fire and got warm. Later that morning we arrived in Barcelona, on 16 March. I remember the date because it was the commencement of a three-day aerial bombardment by the Italian Air Force, dropping bombs at regular intervals on Barcelona. That was the first time a great open city (Guernica had been bombed in one afternoon) was bombed from the air, with no retaliation, no anti-aircraft fire.

Shortly afterwards Franco's forces reached the Mediterranean. We could not move from Barcelona because all trains to the frontier, all trains anywhere, were stopped. So after three days we journeyed to the frontier with a group of about 10 Romanians, International Brigade men who also had been repatriated. We finally got to a place called Portbou. It was on the frontier of Spain and France and we crossed under the International Tunnel on a train that only ran about 200 yards and passed into France, where we were met by a representative. They must have gone there every day to the station to meet International Brigade men returning. We were taken by this man to the station buffet for lunch. I remember the meal. It was grilled chops, sauté potatoes and coffee. The coffee we had been previously drinking was made from burnt wheat. We could not get any food. There was no food available, Spain was starving in 1938. But now, just 200 yards across the border, we were sitting down to a lovely meal and real coffee. That contrast remains with me even now. It was another world, here was war-stricken Spain, starving and being defeated, and there were the democracies doing nothing …

Regarding political infighting on the Republican side, when I was at the front at Jarama and elsewhere, I never asked a soldier next to me what his political affiliations were, or what he was fighting for. I never asked that, I was not concerned. I knew that as a soldier at the front I was fighting to win the war, anything else that came afterwards was not my concern. When I first read George Orwell's book *Homage to Catalonia* I was so disgusted about this front on the Aragon, which was quiet. All that time when we were losing lives on the Jarama, at Brunete and Madrid, the front where he was, was quiet. It was a joke. Here he was criticizing the role of the Communist Party, whereas the people he was connected with, the anarchists or the CNT, wanted to ensure a social revolution. To me that was ridiculous. Here was a country at war. These people for ideological reasons were putting a spoke in the wheel, they were controlling Barcelona. When I was in Barcelona everything was CNT but they had been ousted by 1938. On arriving there in 1936 it was anarchist controlled.[6]

Tony McLean

Student from England. Served as a research clerk and military censor with the International Brigades, May 1937–December 1938.

When I was in Albacete before I got to Madrigueras, the first person I met was a very nice person indeed. A chap called Tony Highman. I knew him before when I had met him in London. He came up to me and said, 'I am pleased to see you but I am in some trouble and I must tell you that when I got to the front and I saw the Moors coming, I just ran, and ran and ran. I never knew I could run so fast. They took me to a penal camp and gave me a bad time and sent me back home'. I knew this one man, John Angus. He was only about 20 when he came out to Spain. He joined the Communist Party when he was in hospital in Spain after he had been wounded, and the very first job they gave him was to be in charge of the deserters, a terrible job. These people had to be persuaded to go back to the front, but of course didn't want to go. He said the Germans would really have liked to put these people through the hoop. A lot of them did go back to the front and some of them did get fed up at times ...

After Madrigueras I got a message to go back to headquarters because they were short of people who knew French. I left Madrigueras, went back to Albacete and was posted as a clerk. There I found myself with a little group of English clerks who could speak French. All the work we did was in French. Was I disappointed because I had gone to Spain to fight? I took the view that I did what I was told. When you join an army you accept discipline. You do what you are instructed and if you are told to go to headquarters, you go. The work was very routine, typing at first, and then they transferred me after a few weeks to the Research Bureau. Its job was to try and find out the causes of death or whereabouts of lost International Brigaders, and reply to letters from their anguished relations. We did this on an international scale and had to cover the whole of Europe. We had an enormous great file of people with all the information we could get about them, and we were in constant touch with an office in Paris, trying to give relatives information about International Brigaders. The records were very defective, especially in the first period of the Spanish Civil War. People got killed and nobody really recorded this. I worked in the bureau for a number of months.

I was determined to make myself fluent in Spanish as soon as I could. We went over to Spanish as the official language [in the International Brigades] sometime in the autumn of 1937. By then we were filling up the International Brigade units with Spaniards because not enough people were coming in, and so Spanish became absolutely essential. We then began to do all the files and correspondence in Spanish, they went over from French to Spanish. I did that for a number of months.

In January 1938 I said it was about time I went to the front, but they gave me a fortnight's leave and then I was posted to a beautiful hospital in Orihuela, in the south of Spain. Then I came back to Albacete and they said we are not going to send you to the front, we are going to put you into the Educational Department at Tarazona, which was actually the American base. I was there for five weeks organizing war newspapers. I then got a summons to join the military censorship office just outside

Valencia. There we used to handle all the incoming and outgoing mail to see if there was any funny business. I don't know how efficient we were. I think that any clever spies could have got through our fingers quite easily.[7]

Stafford Cottman

Volunteer from London and Bristol, England. Served with the Independent Labour Party (ILP) contingent in Spain, January 1937–June 1937.

The POUM Headquarters was fairly primitive, nothing very ornate. It was more like a third-class hotel. It was very clean and pretty basic. No thick carpets. This was still in January 1937.

We then went in groups to the Lenin Barracks just outside Barcelona. There we were given our first meal and a uniform, which consisted of corduroy-type trousers. Boots were a bit like a rugby boot without the studs. A donkey jacket, which wasn't very smart looking. We must have looked a pretty rough crowd. We had drill and were taken each day to have training. We were there for a fortnight and mainly had drill training. A Spanish captain marched you up and down. It was not really technical in any way. You didn't have any instructions on guns, just obeying commands and walking up and down. They were mainly Spanish officers or NCOs at the barracks. All Spanish people and international volunteers going through Spain went to the barracks before being sent on to the front. I did not have any insignia on my uniform. I don't think there was a single mark. If you see photos of the people at the front at that time they were noted for their lack of adornment, not even stars or anything.

My father was killed in a motor accident some years before this. I had my mother's blessing and she even came to see me off. She came to London. She was quite happy and stayed with family and friends that we were with before I went. We were all in touch. We maintained keeping in touch.

I had a lot of friends in the ILP Guild of Youth in the East End [of London], and they had written to me and asked if there was anything that I wanted. There was really nothing that I wanted in that sense. The one thing that I noticed was the chocolate in Spain was not as nice as the chocolate back home. I did say you could send a bar of chocolate. In May John McNair, the administrator for the contingent of English volunteers, said to me that something had arrived for me. We went down to where it had arrived and there were nine tea chests full of chocolate. We thought what could we do with it, we can't obviously eat it all? So we took a couple of bars for ourselves and then gave the rest to the hospital.[8]

Roderick MacFarquhar

Volunteer from Inverness, Scotland. Served as an ambulance driver with the Scottish Ambulance Unit and International Brigades medical units in Spain, January 1937–October 1938 (see plate 11).

Regarding smuggling people [deserters] out of the embassies, it was minor really. It saved a lot of bloodshed and it saved a great deal of unfriendly propaganda abroad, which would have done the Spanish Republican cause no good. Therefore it was a satisfactory solution to the problem of these people who were hiding in the various embassies and in various friends' houses in Madrid. They were taken out of the embassies by the Scottish Ambulance Unit down to Valencia to be shipped across to Gibraltar.

During this time they were shelling Madrid. I have stood in the central plaza in Madrid with shells dropping, and seeing passers-by being killed. I picked up a child who was only two or three years old who got a shell splinter in his stomach. There was a hospital across the square and I rushed over to their operating room and they took the child, but he died. There was this type of incident going on every day of the week. There was also the shortage of food. The Republic was doing its very best to supply a ration of food to all and, of course, they had a campaign in the countryside to grow more food. There were artists and newspaper people preparing graphic pictures to encourage people to grow more food because many of them could not read or write, and these pictures were the propaganda vehicle used to stimulate both the spirit and the purpose of the Spanish people. It was extremely effective.

There were not many political meetings in Madrid. Any political meetings took place in hospitals where pep talks and discussions took place. Also available to us were the European newspapers, in all languages, and at that time books were coming in every month from various writers on the current political situation as it was developing. It was developing at great speed so many of us became politically conscious. I was at that time a member of the Labour Party. I was asked to join the Communist Party in Spain and I refused to do so. I said this is not the place for me to join the Communist Party. I said I will do my duty here. I will do whatever I am told to do, but I will not join the Communist Party and no one pressed me to do so.

George Green, a musician who I became friendly with, asked me to join. He was a member of the Communist Party. We left the Scottish Ambulance Unit and joined the International Brigade. We arrived with virtually no clothes at all. We were semi-clothed and I remember George diving into his kit bag and handing me a jersey and a shirt. It was this kind of discipline, unity and comradeship that made a tremendous impression upon me and upon many people who went there (who were not members of the Communist Party; in fact, I would have said that the majority of them were not members of the Communist Party). They were democrats who were determined to give all they could to this struggle in Spain, which they realized was crucial to the whole future of peace in Europe.

They did so with great courage and great belief in the unity of working people. Everybody – intellectuals, teachers and land workers and so forth. In Spain the majority of the workers realized that their chance of a better and more prosperous life was dependent on the Democratic Republic surviving.

... Our first International Brigade assignment was to go up to Sierra de Guadarrama, in the hills. There was a battle there and they were trying to break through to Segovia. I was in a small hospital where there was quite a lot of wounded. The hospital was in Navasarada. We then went to Brunete in July 1937.

Brunete was a tough assignment. I was in a hospital there and they asked me to go to the front. 'We want you to take over the ambulance station at the front.' I was there for about three weeks. It was a pretty nasty time: the amount of attacks that were being mounted upon us, the amount of rifle- and shellfire and bombing that went on. The final attack on us was an attempt to break the line completely. I remember when they sent over the bombers they came over in clouds, huge things, flying low because the Republic did not have the necessary planes to combat them. They bombed and bombed. I thought we were going to have it that day. One or two were brought down. We had to pull back from that place. We got back and I went to headquarters, where General Walter promoted me to lieutenant for my work on that front.

Years later, in 1977, I went to Poland with a friend whose son was named Andrew, who lived in Warsaw and was head of the tourist industry in the city. He asked us what we would like to see and I said to visit the grave of General Walter. He said he was a hero in Poland. He took us there the next day and I found his grave. He was a very fine soldier, calm, not disturbed by events at all and very proud of how at that time his troops had behaved. At Brunete he was so proud of how his troops had attacked, held the enemy and had fought them to a standstill.[9]

Morien Morgan

Volunteer from Ynysybwl, Wales. Served with No 2 Company, British Battalion, 15th International Brigade, September 1937–January 1938. Prisoner of war, January 1938–January 1939.

Unfortunately I had an attack of tonsillitis and I had to remain on the farm while the others went on foot to the bottom of the valley, where they caught two lorries. I then had a most lovely drink given to me which was coffee with a raw egg beaten up. I always thought it was a wonderful drink, something like nectar. The following day I walked down the mountain, then rode in a lorry and was taken to Guernica. (The place painted by Picasso and which the Nazis had obliterated in a bombing attack.) We were there in some sort of a building, whether a church or barracks, I don't know, and there we stayed a few days. There was no sign of bombing when I was there, none at all. It was a peaceful village when I got there. It was clearly far from the fighting. There we had some training with rifle shooting and crawling with a rifle.

We weren't really seeing much of Spain. We were either in a building or out in the field training, or away from the towns and villages. I think the closest contact I had was when on one occasion when we were on the train nearing Barcelona, some Spaniards came along and gave us some wonderful Spanish oranges, small and beautifully sweet. The people were very welcoming. All cheering, all raising their clenched fists in welcome. It appeared to me that the International Brigade was idealized by the Spanish loyalists. They knew that they were fighting the combined forces of Hitler and Mussolini.

We didn't come across many people showing hostility. I remember when we were given our pay, I think about six pesetas. I went to the village to buy some oranges and I think I bought a peseta's worth, and I thought I would have three or four to put in my pocket, but to my astonishment he gave me about 40 or 50 oranges. I took my jacket off and wrapped them up in it.

It was very uneventful when you were in the villages. I remember up in the mountains singing 'Red River Valley', you know the one 'Home over the range where the deer and the antelope play'. Well, we had that tune but we had our own words for it. I think it went: 'There is a valley in Spain called Jarama, it is a place that we all know so well, for it was there that we gave up our manhood and where most of our brave comrades fell.' I was a teetotaller, of course, like all my family. Not even sherry passed our lips, but we were given brandy every night to help us sleep in the mountains. This was when we were not in actual action, but when we had been withdrawn from the lines.[10]

Frederick Arthur Thomas

Volunteer from London, England. Served with the Anti-Tank Battery, 15th International Brigade, May 1937–October 1938.

The propaganda about the Republicans persecuting religion and persecuting nuns and priests had quite a considerable effect on many people. Hampstead Museum had some pictures of the skeletons of nuns that had been dug up and flung out onto the street. I hated that. I can never find any justification for that kind of behaviour. I know what the church meant to tens of thousands of people in Spain. I did think it had an effect but not so much on us, quite simply because we didn't believe it. We merely thought that it was propaganda, lies.

I saw no atrocities at all. We reached Madrigueras, which was a small town where we did our two and a half weeks of training. There is a story that you will read in many books: in the church there was a high tower and when the revolt began the priest went up into the tower with a machine gun. In front of the church is a little square with a fountain and a trough of water, and the men used to bring their donkeys to the trough to drink, and the women came to the fountain part of it with their buckets and bowls for their water. The story was that he killed so many trying to get water with the machine gun but, of course, retribution was at hand and you could see on the walls the bloodstains where they finally shot him down. When I went to Spain I didn't speak a work of Spanish. I was with comrades in the same position and I never found anybody who said it is true. I was there. I saw it. It's a story that has been repeated.

There is a story about the Battle of Brunete. I told it in my diaries. I had the honesty to say that I don't know if this is true but this is the story, and it makes a jolly good one as a propaganda story. At the Battle of Brunete when the British were attacking the village of Villanueva de la Cañada, they had difficulty in taking this village and when they went into the attack, from the village came a large group of women and children running towards the British, shouting 'Please don't shoot, we are coming out'. The British held their fire and then from behind these women and children, who had been forced out at gunpoint, emerged the fascist soldiers, who promptly shot them and at the British. The British were compelled to reply and a number of women and children were killed. I never met anybody who said, 'Yes I was there, I saw it'. The stories might be true, I don't know.[11]

Charles Sewell Bloom

Commercial traveller from London, England. Served as a political commissar, runner and interpreter with No 3 Company, British Battalion, 15th International Brigade, and as an interpreter and intelligence officer at International Brigade Headquarters, December 1936–January 1938.

Peter Kerrigan was a very able man, a brave man. Our brigade commissar was Major Nathan, who got killed. Kerrigan shot

McCartney accidentally. McCartney was our military commander over Tom Wintringham. It so happened that Wilf McCartney formed the International Brigade. I joined the International Brigade because I was reading the newspaper one day. It said they needed comrades with military experience out in Spain. I thought, that's me.

Tom Wintringham was second-in-command and Peter Kerrigan was political commander of the brigade. We were going to the front and Wilfred McCartney didn't want to go back. He said he was going with the fellows to the front. Peter Kerrigan and the rest of us thought he shouldn't, and it so happens that he shot him in the arm to make him go back to hospital. That was the only way to get him back because we didn't want to give him a bad name. Later on during the war we had the [future] prime minister come out to us, Major Attlee. I was in hospital then after the Ebro battle and we formed another battalion.

During the first two weeks in the frontlines we were up there day and night. We ate and slept out in the open, which was damn cold at night up in the hills, very cold. Fellows started growing beards. When I was wounded and put into a hospital bed in Huesa, those white sheets and pillows were like paradise. When I was in the post office, I lived there. My job was looking after the post and getting this newspaper going, but prior to that I was general dogsbody looking after all these American doctors and nurses. I learnt Spanish.

We had a Fifth Column in the town of Murcia (population 60,000); some were for us and some were not. My job working with the Spanish post office was to watch out for propaganda. I met a young English lady, who was a spy. She wouldn't talk, though. She was only representing British interests, but British interests, even though they were neutral and sympathetic, in the Foreign Office they were anti-communist. I tell you another thing about her. She used to go to the market, to do the groceries for all the children who were refugees. One day I walked with her to the market and she was wearing a pair of fancy sandals. I said they are nice sandals and that I might get a pair. I asked if she got them in Spain. She said no, she had bought them in Germany about a year ago. She said she was in the 1936 Olympics and Hitler was on show. She asked me if I knew anybody in the frontline. But she wasn't a German spy, she was representing British interests.[12]

Arthur Nicoll

Volunteer from Dundee, Scotland. Served as a political commissar with the Anti-Tank Battery, 15th International Brigade, February–October 1937.

Visualize the scene: you are in Barcelona and these girls are working in a factory, getting fed on beans and lentils, and the fascist planes come over and start bombing, and they are standing in the streets and shouting at them. At the front you see your mates getting killed alongside you and you say to yourself, well, I have lost my best pal and you say to yourself, this is what it is all about. If you are prepared to do that you are going to live as La Pasionaria [Dolores Ibárruri] said: 'It's better to die on your feet than to live forever on your knees.' It's a classic statement and it describes Spain.

… I didn't have much contact with Spanish civilians, only speaking to them in the village. When our battalion was 50 percent Spanish I was the commander of the battery and we had a [anti-tank] gun that needed fixing. So we had to take it down to Valencia for repairs. The chaps who were in charge of the kitchen, the cooks, were all Spaniards. They reckoned that their cooking was the best way to get acclimatized to Spanish food. They knew how to cook the Spanish food better than an Englishman. I asked the sergeant who was in charge of the kitchen if he would go with me to Valencia because his own village was only a few kilometres from the city. I said he could go and see his folks and I would stay the night in Valencia. So we went and left the gun in a car park. He invited me to join him and I got an amazing reception. I stayed two nights in that household and they couldn't do enough for me. These people didn't have any pro-fascist feelings at all, they just could not accept them there. When we first arrived his mother said: 'I can't give you anything just now but I will make you a snack. Go to the cafe and have a drink and come back and I will have something nice for you.' The snack was eggs and chips and I hadn't seen that for ages. When we came back there was a Valencia paella. I have never tasted anything like it since. The cook made paella up in the line and it was good, really good, but his mother's paella was glorious. There was everything in it – chicken, rabbit, fried rice – and then it was all put into this big pan and boiled. They put this paella on the table and you got your plate and helped yourself to it. The wine went round all the time we were eating. A young girl was turned out of her bed so I had one of the finest beds in the house. I thought they were amazing folk.[13]

Notes

1   http://www.geocities.com/irelandscw/ibvol-EDEbro.htm.
2   Curry, Patrick, Imperial War Museum Sound Archives (IWMSA), London, Ref 799/3, Reel 2.
3   Cooney, Bob, IWMSA, London, Ref 804/7, Reel 5.
4   Ferguson, Alec, IWMSA, London, Ref 820/2, Reel 2.
5   Longstaff, John, IWMSA, London, Ref 9299/13, Reel 11.
6   Levine, Maurice, IWMSA, London, Ref 9722/6, Reel 5.
7   McLean, Tony, IWMSA, London, Ref 838/5, Reel 2.
8   Cottman, Stafford, IWMSA, London, Ref 9278/7, Reel 3.
9   MacFarquhar, Roderick, IWMSA, London, Ref 9234/5, Reel 3.
10 Morgan, Morien, IWMSA, London, Ref 9856/4, Reel 2.
11 Thomas, Frederick Arthur, IWMSA, London, Ref 9396/8, Reel 3.
12 Bloom, Charles Sewell, IWMSA, London, Ref 992/6, Reel 4.
13 Nicoll, Arthur, IWMSA, London, Ref 817/3, Reel 2.

Prisoners of War

Many volunteers with the International Brigades were captured by the Nationalists during the civil war. Their treatment and the conditions they were kept in varied, and some were subjected to mental and physical torture. The Nationalists were particularly brutal towards members of the Communist Party and Young Communist League, so any Brigaders who were members of these organizations did their utmost to hide the fact if they were captured.

On 9 March 1937 Franco issued a proclamation stating that any foreigners captured under arms would be shot. Though the British government was largely unsympathetic to British brigaders, the shooting of prisoners was beyond the pale and so it issued a 'stiff note' to Franco threatening the 'strongest possible reaction' if he contravened the Geneva Convention regarding the treatment of prisoners and started shooting them.

The Geneva Convention of 1929 was an internationally agreed set of rules that sought to limit the worst excesses of warfare, especially with regard to the treatment of prisoners, non-combatants and property. For example, it stated that enemy soldiers in uniform who were captured were not be be mistreated in any way, including not having their property stolen, being physically or mentally abused, and certainly not being executed. Nevertheless, Franco delayed rescinding the order until April 1938. By that time Benito Mussolini wanted Republican prisoners to be exchanged for the large numbers of Italians who had been captured.

In general British brigaders who were captured were not shot (though there were exceptions) and the Italians in particular treated them more or less correctly. However, no mercy was extended to those foreigners who had been captured and then repatriated to their homelands, and who had then returned to Spain to fight for the Republic. One such person was Jimmy Rutherford, who had been captured at the Battle of Jarama and repatriated, but who had returned from Britain and had been captured a second time. Like all freed British prisoners, he had signed an agreement not to return to Spain following his repatriation. As a result, he was shot on 24 May 1938. After this, the British Communist Party did not allow volunteers who had been prisoners to return to Spain.

Conditions within Nationalist prisoner-of-war camps were rudimentary at best, and the food was invariably poor and sparse. As a result the prisoners suffered a variety of illnesses, especially dysentery brought on by unhygienic living conditions. In addition, the guards were often hostile, made worse on many occasions by the prisoners' unwillingness to adhere to camp rules and regulations, in particular their refusal to give fascist salutes. The result was frequent beatings from their guards.

Frank H. Mills

Volunteer from Hucknall, Nottinghamshire, England. Served as an infantryman with the British Battalion, 15th International Brigade, July 1937–March 1938 (captured at Calaceite). Prisoner of war in San Pedro de Cardeña camp, March–October 1938.

We were unprepared and ran into the Italian army – the Vittorio Division. It wasn't an even struggle. They had aircraft, tanks, artillery. We were prisoners of war of the Italians, which was probably better than being in the hands of the Francoists who were full-blooded mercenaries. I was carted off to a hospital for Italian officers. It was comfortable. There were five in the ward and one day the bloke opposite had a visit from some of his subordinates. They had brought him some presents, and he said,

'Take them over there to the Englishman'. I was only in there about four days, then it was back to the prison. We were swapped at Santander, then got a train to Dieppe and a boat to New Haven. And then we got a bill for £13 from the Foreign Office. We used to get the bill regularly, until they got fed up sending it.[1]

Jim Haughey

Volunteer from Lurgan, Northern Ireland. Served as an infantryman in the British Battalion, 15th International Brigade, May–October 1938. Prisoner of war, October 1938–April 1939.

The captain of the bunch that captured us ordered his men to shoot us. Our hands were tied and a bandage placed over our eyes. This I refused in the good old traditional style. While our grave was being dug I asked this captain would it be possible to see a priest, as I was a Catholic. As he was a Catholic himself, he said yes, after a conference with his superiors. This saved our lives as it was taken for granted that my fellow prisoners were Catholics also. But he was so enraged because we wouldn't snivel or whine for mercy that he bent a Colt 45 [pistol] over my head. I lost all interest in proceedings for a few hours after that.

It would be impossible to describe the humiliations we suffered after that until we arrived in the concentration camp. There were 36 different nationalities including Irish, British and Americans. Here I had my head dressed and settled down patiently to await the day when we would be liberated. There were 400 of us in a room which would hold 50 comfortably, no smokes, no books, one toilet and one water tap for 400 men. An abundance of lice, very little food: beans twice a day. For the last three months before we were released we were fed on bread and water, nothing else.

There were some Basque and Asturian priests in the camp. In one part of this 200-year-old building there were some nuns who were prisoners also. There are several hundred priests and nuns in Franco's prisons because they want to tell the truth about this 'saviour of Christianity' who is merely the tool of Hitler. I hope and pray that some day the truth will come out about this. Veronica dear, it would take hours to describe all I have seen and experienced in Spain.[2]

Carl Geiser

Volunteer from Orrville, Ohio, United States. Served as an ammunition carrier in the Abraham Lincoln Battalion, April 1937–April 1938. Prisoner of war in San Pedro de Cardeña camp, April 1938–April 1939.

Finally we were taken to a field and ordered to strip. Behind a table sat a Gestapo [Nazi secret police] agent with a ledger. As each prisoner was identified, an assistant using the callipers called out the length, breadth and depth of his skull, the distance between his eyes, the length of his nose, and described the skin colour, body type, wound scars and any disability. Next each prisoner was instructed to stand in front of a camera for a front and side view and close-up of the face. We were now 'scientifically' classified.[3]

Tommy Bloomfield

Volunteer from Kirkcaldy, Scotland. Served in the Machine-Gun Company, 15th International Brigade, December 1936–February 1937. Prisoner of war, February–May 1937. Repatriated to Britain in May 1937. Returned to Spain in February 1938 and served until December 1938, when he returned to Britain.

On 13 February there were 120 men of No 2 Machine-Gun Company. Of those 120 men, 29 of us survived as prisoners. We were assembled as prisoners and one of us put his hand in his pocket to get a cigarette. They shot away his hand. Another of us, a man named Stevens, was wounded in the neck. He was dying. A priest went over to him with a crucifix, and an officer standing beside him said: 'He's English.' The priest snatched back his crucifix. That told me there was no God.

On the way back to the prison camp, Ted Dickinson, our second-in-command, had dressed a wound in our company commander's arm – he had been hit by a dum-dum bullet [where the bullet 'mushrooms' on impact, thus causing greater internal damage]. They gave him the choice of fighting for fascism or dying. Dickinson marched up to a wall, like a soldier on parade, did a military about-turn, said, 'Salut, comrades', and was immediately shot dead. He put backbone into me.

The 27 men left alive were mentally tortured throughout their imprisonment: 'Tonight you will die. Tomorrow you will die. This afternoon you will die.' We realized, gradually, that they couldn't kill us, because we had been under observation when we were taken prisoner. The bitterness I felt. During all the time of my imprisonment I never had a wash. We picked body lice off the insides of our clothes. They even carried on with their mental torture just before we were released. They held a military tribunal; it sentenced two of us to death; four were given solitary confinement for life. The rest of us were given 30 years. Before we left, they gave us three razor blades to shave 27 men.

The Salvation Army tried to give us a meal, but they wanted the cameras on us. We refused. We were escorted through France. French police and CID [Criminal Investigation Department] took charge of us. They photographed us and took our fingerprints – and that was that. Six of these 27 men went back out again. Young Jimmy Rutherford, 18 years of age, was captured a second time and shot. Basil Abrahams from London, Bernard Thomas, a minister's son from London, and myself were among those who returned. Why were we prepared to repeat these experiences? Well, inside you were knitted up – tight inside you – you couldn't help yourself. You went back out, you walked during darkness, from dusk to dawn. You walked across the Pyrenees, yet you knew full well where you were crossing.[4]

Bob Doyle

Volunteer from Dublin, Republic of Ireland. Served with No 4 Company, British Battalion, 15th International Brigade, August 1937–March 1938. Prisoner of war in San Pedro de Cardeña camp, April 1938–February 1939.

We were resupplied with weapons and got sent back into action. After an all-night march we were approaching Caspe, on the central part of the Aragon front. We were marching to stop a formidable fascist advance. I was in the Attlee Company and we were marching in extended formation on both sides of the road, a 3–5 yard gap between each man as a precaution against artillery shelling. It was 31 March 1938. We had sent out a patrol but it didn't come back. Nevertheless we continued to advance. We could hear a terrific roar of mechanical equipment coming from the valley and I was told to take my gun to an advanced position in a bend in the road. Frank Ryan was beside me. I took up the position and nearly the whole of the company passed. The noise from the valley got louder and louder. Suddenly, from the ditches, hedges and bushes, we were surrounded by Italian soldiers. Then motorcycles mounting machine guns passed through us and cut off the others in the battalion. The Italians ordered us to put our hands up. Then their artillery opened up and they told us to get down. The first tank was only 20 feet from us, but some in the rear of the battalion managed to escape. About 150 of us were captured.

We walked with our hands up for a mile. We passed through massive lines of equipment and soldiers of the Black Arrows, the crack mechanized division of the Italian Army. As we passed through the lines the soldiers were inciting the officers to pour petrol on us. They spat at us as we passed. As our hands dropped an officer would press a pistol to our foreheads to keep our hands raised.

They put us up against a barn and beat up a couple of us. They asked for any communists, socialists, Jews and machine-gunners to step forward. No one did. I knew of the horror of the Civil Guard, and at that moment a lorry load of them pulled up in front of us, armed with rifles and jumped out. An Italian officer spotted Frank Ryan and asked who he was. Ryan replied, 'captain'.

They told us to get in line – we were certain that they were going to shoot us. There was a spontaneous attempt by all of us to get into the front rank to be shot first. However, they marched us another kilometre and put us in a well-guarded barn. They were deciding our fate as we could hear arguments between the officers. The next morning they took us to a barbed-wire enclosure by a river, where they tried to get information from Frank Ryan about the brigade. He said he would only give them personal details but no military information. With this the Italian interrogator slapped him across the face. We had to restrain Frank from retaliating.

Then we were taken to a church and crammed in there for two days. We were given no food and very little water. We had to use the space behind the altar as a toilet. We were then transported to the barracks in Saragossa where there was a compound crammed with Republican prisoners. The first thing we were told was that we would have to give the fascist salute. A big argument ensued. We were in the hands of the Spanish fascists, not the Italians, and they told us we would be shot if we didn't salute. We eventually reached a compromise and said we would give the British Army salute. But Frank Ryan wouldn't compromise despite having a pistol put against his head.

The next morning we were given a good meal prior to being paraded before the world's reactionary press: the *New York*

Times and *Daily Telegraph*. Alfonso Merry del Val [the son of a former Spanish ambassador in London] was accompanying the reporters and he recognized Jimmy Rutherford, now called Jimmy Small. Jimmy had been captured previously by the fascists and as a consequence he was shot by them three months later. After the interviews with the press we thought our names might be published and we might escape with our lives. At that time the war had turned [against the Republic] and Franco wanted to show that he was humane in the treatment of prisoners. He had even jailed Moors for committing crimes such as rape.

After the appearance of the journalists we were taken by train to Burgos, accompanied by Spanish soldiers and officers carrying sticks and beating us every time we became disorderly. We were then herded 10km to San Pedro de Cardeña, an old monastery. We remained there for 12 months. Some 700 of us from the Ebro arrived there, all nationalities, even Moors. They used to beat the Moors in the courtyard.

If you showed any indiscipline they would smash you with rifle butts and sticks. The guards also confiscated any improvised chess sets, invariably preceded by a beating. They would blow a bugle in the morning and before you could get up off the floor they would rush in with rifle butts.

After a few days there the Gestapo arrived in a black Mercedes. They were dressed in civilian clothes and carried out verbal interrogations. They measured head dimensions to prove that we were sub-normal. In my case I was described as being 'athletic'. Anyone who was Jewish or a bit abnormal was singled out. We were photographed both naked and clothed. Some of us had very few clothes because if you had any good clothing, such as boots, they would be taken off you. I had no trousers, for example, and wore a bit of blanket instead. After the interrogations they took Jimmy Rutherford away and then Frank Ryan. Colonel Martin, who was from the Foreign Office and liaised with the prisoners, told us that Rutherford had been shot and Ryan had his death sentence commuted to 30 years.

Gestapo questions included, when did you have your first woman, was she a prostitute, and why did you come to Spain? We answered without fear, but the German [brigaders] were interrogated at pistol point, beaten and forced to sign documents saying that they wished to return to the Fatherland. No doubt if they did they were killed. No torture was carried out on us, but most of the Germans tried to escape because they knew what their fate would be. We had some Czechs in the camp, and after the Germans took over the Sudetenland [October 1938] they were beaten and told that they were now German.

Those who tried to escape were locked up in dungeons. Our treatment was brutal, demoralizing and part of a deliberate strategy to make us out to be sub-human, that we were not normal for fighting in the International Brigades. Several prisoners died, they just pined away. Seriously ill prisoners were given no treatment, they were left among us and then taken to a so-called hospital. Then we were told they had died. We were then forced to make a coffin out of fish boxes (we were fed on sardines and beans only).[5]

Douglas Eggar

Student and policeman in London, England. Served as an infantryman with the British Battalion, 15th International Brigade, November 1937–March 1938. Prisoner of war, April–October 1938.

I was a prisoner in San Pedro de Cardeña. Conditions were very unpleasant, with mice and rats on the floor. We got taken out early for breakfast, and if you were last in the queue you often got a whack across the shoulder with a stick from a guard. But in truth there was nothing very dramatic about it … When we were released we were being exchanged for prisoners on the other side. There were a lot of negotiations. Some of our prisoners were stateless, such as German Brigaders. The fascists were not happy about releasing them. Their argument was that they didn't mind releasing Britons or Americans, but they were not going to release any Germans or Italians. When I was released, in October or November 1938, my condition wasn't too bad. The Italians who ran the prison let us write letters home. We also got books and papers sent out to us as well. One chap who did a lot for us was a right-wing chap at the Foreign Office, but I can't remember his name.[6]

William Kelly

Volunteer from Scotland. Served with the British Battalion, 15th International Brigade, January–March 1938. Prisoner of war, April 1938–February 1939.

We went to Albacete for six weeks of training (I had no military experience at this time). While we were there Belchite fell, which allowed the fascists to break through. So all the International Brigades were rallied at Albacete and marched to the front. All through the night we saw Spanish soldiers retreating. I was in No 1 Company, the Attlee Company. We were marching up the road towards Calaceite. The road was littered with discarded ammunition, canteens, webbing equipment, things we desperately needed. We could not carry two rifles, though.

Then we saw Italian trucks in the distance. My friend Bob recognized them by their broad headlights. We carried on. The commander, Frank Ryan, sent out two scouts. But about 30 minutes later there was no sign of them coming back. Just as we were going to continue, up comes an Italian tank, then another. As we went to jump off the road an Italian appeared in front of me with a rifle, telling me to surrender. I didn't understand him at first – my Spanish was very basic. Bob said: 'He's telling you to get your hands up.' The Italian was shaking, and I've often thought what would have happened if I had grabbed his rifle. But I wasn't so brave at that time.

Most of our recruits were young, 19 or 20 years old. We didn't know what was going to happen. We'd heard so much about the fascists shooting prisoners. We had communist leaflets in our pockets, but as soon as I could I threw them away. An Italian officer came up and spoke to Captain Ryan. He said we should sit down and not panic, because if we panicked it could cause a tragedy, because they [the Italians] were as nervous as we were. After that an Italian staff car came up and this brigadier got out. He asked Ryan where the last line of the International Brigades was. Ryan refused to answer. Then Ryan said: 'Excuse me, brigadier, these men haven't had any food for quite a while. Is there any chance of getting some food for them?' The brigadier said yes, and about an hour and a half later the Italians came down with loaves, mussels and potatoes.

They took us to Gandesa and put us in a church. We were there for two days. We got nothing except bread and water. After that they sent us to Saragossa, which wasn't too bad. After three days they sent us to San Pedro de Cardeña prisoner-of-war camp, just outside Burgos. There was nothing in the camp and the guards tried to intimidate us. We were in the British section, but there were also Germans, Dutch, Italians and Greeks.

I was interrogated by two Germans. They asked me if I was William Kelly from Glasgow, with a wife and three children. I said yes. I was asked if I had any political affiliations when I came to Spain. They knew a lot about me, so I said I was a member of the Communist Party. I said that they were well informed about me. One said: 'We're well informed about every one of you.' He said I was going to be repatriated, but if it was up to him I would never be repatriated. I think they got most of their information though the British Foreign Office, either that or there was a leak in the party because they knew so much. I was repatriated in February 1939.[7]

Harold Bernard Collins

Volunteer from London, England. Served with the British Battalion, 15th International Brigade, December 1937–March 1938. Prisoner of war, 1938–39.

We were lucky to be in the hands of the Italians because their attitude wasn't as bad as the Moors. Every now and then some Moorish cavalrymen would come along with sticks, they'd push through the Italians and they would hit us. Some of the sticks really hurt, but the Italians kept them away. An Italian officer came up, had a word with the Moors and told them to get away.

We weren't fed until the next day, when they gave us some bread. We were all given a loaf each. We were then told we were going to Saragossa. We were interrogated. They asked us who we were and where we had come from, who sent us here. I told them the story that I came to Spain on the spur of the moment after spending a week in Paris with a group I had gone with to have some fun. We didn't tell them that we were anti-fascists. We told them we were passing the time.

The Italian officer could speak very good English. The Italian troops could only speak Italian or Spanish. In fact the Italian officers were part of a brigade which I recognized as a mobile brigade. The Italian Black Arrows they called themselves.

The officer conducting the interrogation seemed very friendly. I told him what we had done, how we got to Spain and he seemed to believe me. He gave me a cigarette while we were talking. He asked us where we had come from and the towns we had been at. Asked about Albacete and places like that. I told him the truth. I didn't tell lies at all, other than getting to Spain. I was asked about the location of units or information like that.

I told them that most of them went on to Caspe and we had lost them on the walk back during the retreat.

We were paraded through the streets of Saragossa, marched along the streets as prisoners. We were told we were going to another place, another camp, San Pedro de Cardeña. The Spaniards there were really rough with us. They would lash you with sticks. If you did not answer them correctly, they would lash you. They would not worry where they hit you – they would hit you either across the head or the face with these sticks ...

Some lads were badly hit, either across the face or the head. In fact they shot one or two chaps. They took them to Burgos headquarters for some reason and they picked them out and executed them. Jimmy Rutherford was taken off to Burgos with Frank Ryan, who was the leader of the Irish people out there. Rutherford was shot and Ryan was sentenced to death (later commuted).[8]

Garry McCartney

Volunteer from Glasgow, Scotland. Served with the Machine-Gun Company, British Battalion, 15th International Brigade, March 1938–February 1939. Prisoner of war, March 1938–February 1939.

First thing in the morning before we went down to the courtyard to eat a horrible concoction of whatever they called it, soup I think, and in the evening before we retired, there was a count by the fascists to ensure that the correct number of prisoners were still there. Between night and morning escapes were tried (the fascists didn't want to be in our quarters all night because we were lice ridden). We prisoners had the responsibility of ensuring that everything was as it should be. It was the fault of the guards who were on duty that night [of the escape]. There was an open corridor on each floor, and the three guards on each floor would be aware that people had moved out of a window or down a stairway. The six guards who were on duty were very closely questioned regarding from which floor the escape had taken place. Kennedy, a lad from the Port Glasgow area, was so severely beaten up by the fascists that he was in hospital for two weeks.

That particular escape was not discussed by our [Escape] Committee, but the escape of two of the comrades was arranged. We had the knowledge that it was taking place. We collected what money we could among the prisoners to expedite this adventure. The person who acted as interpreter, a Dutchman, was one of the people who had decided to escape. A member of the Communist Party, we gave him valuable information in respect to the number of prisoners that were in San Pedro, the kind of situation in which we found ourselves, and the names of contacts in Britain with whom he should get in touch with in relation to our own situation. Not only ourselves, but information of this kind was given about all the national groups to this comrade. He was not successful. Four days later he was brought back along with the other person who had escaped. They were brought back in chains, displayed in front of us and beaten up. It was a pitiful sight to see. When I say chains I am not speaking of just handcuffs. There were chains around them and they were brought back in a lorry. We never saw those lads again. They were completely isolated from the rest of the prisoners and I don't know what their fate was. They were brought back as an example of what would happen to anyone else who tried to escape, but it did not prevent other efforts being made, not all of them successful.

There were three lads who were successful because we never saw them again. The interpreter, who escaped with the full knowledge of the Committee, made his approach to the Committee and indicated that because he was an interpreter he had freedom of movement. He could move from the prison over to the commandant's office without question, no guards stopped him, and he could walk in the grounds. As he had these privileges he decided to make use of them, and as walking past a guard did not evoke any kind of suspicion day or night it was easy for him to make his escape. But unfortunately he and the lad with him were taken prisoner. It was a terrible time because the reign of terror that followed was just dreadful. We were taken down as an international unit into the courtyard for mass and to listen to a sermon from a priest who had a gun at his hip.

He would have all the Spanish prisoners in front. He would give a tirade against the Internationals and ask the Spaniards to look at us because we were the scum of the Earth, and such like. This was the kind of verbiage that was given. The guards' eyes were on us all the time during these sermons; for not standing to attention or talking to one's neighbour our names would be taken. In the early hours of the morning we would be taken out of our quarters to the courtyard, with its whitewashed walls, and made to stand at attention as close to the wall as possible all night. The guards used wooden riding crops on anyone who tried to lean against the wall, though this never happened to me, fortunately. However, I did receive beatings with the wooden riding crops when moving from the courtyard back up to our quarters, or even inside our quarters. One lad, Morris, who was next to me in line during the count one evening, still had his beret on. This was unforgivable when the fascists were present. One had to take one's headgear off as an indication of respect to them. This was part of the discipline and if it was not adhered to a beating would result. Morris was unaware that he still had his beret on, and he received three or four strong lashes from a riding crop before he realized the reason why it was happening. As a matter of fact I had to tell him, 'Your cap'. I received a beating for speaking, so this was the kind of terror that happened regularly following the escape of these two comrades.

In San Pedro we received two small loaves per day and in the morning we had some soup (which many of us didn't look at let alone taste). At dinner time we had one small bowl of beans and in the evening the same small bowl of fish. The meal at night was small sardines cooked in grease and olive oil and served with head, tails, guts, the lot. This was our staple diet for 11 months, except on one occasion at Easter when we were given a few green vegetables. That was the only change during all that time except for the time when Christmas gifts arrived from the British people. A truck load of parcels had arrived from Britain and for two days we had a new diet: chocolate, sweets and tobacco for the first time. Every prisoner from San Pedro shared in that distribution.

We were all interrogated by the Gestapo. We were fingerprinted and the same kind of questions we had answered way back, when we were first taken prisoner at Calaceite, were asked again to see if they coincided with what we had said earlier. We were also given a medical examination. The indignity was terrible because we were photographed in the nude, not all of us but most of us, and I had my privates callipered. It didn't happen to all of us. I didn't think I was built different from anyone else but my forehead was also callipered. This was the indignity that one had to suffer, and then the intelligence tests were given. I don't understand the reasons for this. I asked myself, and members of the Committee asked themselves, why were these things being done to us and why were such silly questions being asked. The only conclusion that I could come to was that they were trying to prove to themselves that we were a depraved race of people, or that they were the master race. There was always two of them present during these interviews, both in civilian clothes, and they spoke languages fluently. During the period I was in prison I must have had about eight interviews with the Gestapo.

I was sent home at the beginning of February 1939. We received the information from Colonel Martin [the British military attaché in Burgos] that we were at long last being repatriated home in an exchange of prisoners between the Republican government and the Franco authorities. The Italian prisoners would be exchanged and we would be exchanged under a covenant of the League of Nations. When we left San Pedro we had a forced march to Burgos ... We marched, we did not walk. We did this to show the fascists soldiers ... that the forces of the Republic were a disciplined body of men, that we were not the scum of the Earth as had been depicted, and that we were not careless or slovenly in our soldiering. We were a very disciplined force of men.

So we marched through Burgos to the station in military style. We were then taken on a train journey to San Sebastian. When we got off the train loud speakers were calling to all and sundry: 'Come and see the Reds. Come and see these people who came to Spain to rape and loot.' (It had already been carefully pre-arranged.) And we were a bit apprehensive about just what was going to happen to us because the crowds of people just rushed forward. The guards didn't care if we were being attacked. It was a long walk from that railway station to the prison where we stayed for two weeks, but in the course of that walk we managed to speak to the civilians and cigarettes and sweets were handed to us. Signs of the clenched first were given by many of them, so the carefully planned programme that had been designed by the fascists backfired.

San Sebastian was a civilian prison camp. We could see the Spaniards and talk to them through our cell windows. The quarters where we were located had not yet been completely fitted with pipes and the like. The pipes were there but not connected. We could knock on a pipe to indicate to the Spaniards above that we wished to talk and vice versa. This happened frequently and we exchanged all kinds of information ... We could only assume from what they told us that they were political prisoners, and were under sentence of death. There was a number of priests who had associated themselves with the

Republic and had been incarcerated in that jail, many of whom were shot. I spoke a little bit of Spanish, enough to give information and receive information.

We were in a basement and our hands could reach the level of the common courtyard where these Spaniards used to walk. On occasions they would gather round a window and one of them would get down and pass through tobacco and the like to us as a gesture of comradeship.[9]

Notes
1   *Guardian* interview, 10 November 2000.
2   http://www.geocities.com/irelandscw/ibvol-JHLetter.htm.
3   http://www.geocities.com/irelandscw/ibvol-MoR1.htm.
4   http://www.dougiekinnear.pwp.blueyonder.co.uk/scw.htm.
5   Doyle, Bob, Imperial War Museum Sound Archives (IWMSA), London, Ref 806/4, Reel 3.
6   Eggar, Douglas, IWMSA, London, Ref 9426/4, Reel 4.
7   Kelly, William, IWMSA, London, Ref 819/1, Reel 1.
8   Collins, Harold, Bernard, IWMSA, London, Ref 11296/4, Reel 2.
9   McCartney, Garry, IWMSA, London, Ref 809/6, Reel 5.

Withdrawal

By the middle of 1938, with Nationalist forces seemingly near to victory, the Soviet government was considering abandoning the Republicans, the more so because Moscow had failed to establish an anti-German alliance with Britain and France. Indeed, Soviet Foreign Minister Litvinov informed the British ambassador that a Franco regime would be acceptable to the Soviets as long as it did not become a German or Italian satellite state. The Soviets' representative on the Non-Intervention Committee therefore agreed to the drafting of a plan for the withdrawal of all foreign combatants from Spain.

Seeing his regime being abandoned by its main backer, on 21 September 1938 the president of the Republic, Juan Negrín, announced at the League of Nations that his government had taken the decision to withdraw all foreign combatants from the Republican zone. This was a rather desperate attempt to win the support of Western governments. It failed. Nevertheless, the evacuation of the International Brigades was put in motion, though only 4,640 had actually left Spain by January 1939. The remaining 6,000 demobilized volunteers remained in Catalonia. The Communist Party called on them to re-enlist when the Nationalists invaded that region – 80 percent did so. In December 1938 Franco launched his offensive against Catalonia. A month later, on 26 January 1939, Nationalist troops captured Barcelona, sparking a mass flight of refugees to the French border. Seventeen days later Britain and France recognized Franco as the legitimate ruler of Spain. On 9 February 1939, the last International Brigades members crossed the border into France.

Harold Fraser

Volunteer from Glasgow, Scotland. Served with the Machine-Gun Company,
British Battalion, 15th International Brigade, August 1937–October 1938.

We had four anti-tank guns, a sort of miniature 75mm. They had beautiful range-finding telescopes, crosshairs, the lot. They were very effective ... They had a maximum range of 6 miles, but they were most effective between a mile and 1.5 miles. However, when we used them at the front we fired them at almost point-blank range. My friend Sam Pearson was killed on one of the guns. Another bloke who was supposed to be on the gun ran away, so they put Sam on the gun as a replacement. It was hit by a fascist gun. Sam's death was a great loss to me.

We were bombed in this valley. There was nothing we could do about it. We just laid down and took it. We were being withdrawn, the fascists must have known. We looked like ghosts. That was the end of the war for us. We were taken to the border, next to Andorra. We were taken by train, then we marched to get on to another train, which took us to a place in France (Ripoll). There the police served us omelettes, bread and butter – it was marvellous. They wouldn't let us out of the station, though. We were packed on a train and then sent north. I remember arriving at Dover and going on to Victoria Station [London]. At Victoria there were a lot of journalists. One came up to me and said: 'You were in the British Battalion.' I said yes, I was a machine-gunner. Then he asked me if I had met any Finns and could I remember their names. I said no, and then I realized that he wasn't a journalist at all but a Finnish detective working for Mannerheim [Field Marshal Carl von Mannerheim, right-wing Commander-in-Chief of Finland].

I didn't get a job for some time after. When the war [World War II] broke out I was working for Plessey at Ilford. They were a component makers. During the war I became first secretary of the first trade union at Plessey. We were under the essential work order so we couldn't enlist.[1]

Patrick Curry

Volunteer from Manchester, England. Member of the Communist Party. Served as a rifleman with the British Battalion, 15th International Brigade, and as a motorcycle despatch rider with the French Battalion, 14th International Brigade, December 1936–March 1938.

When the Nationalists broke through Republican lines and reached the Mediterranean coast in April 1938, the road between Barcelona and Valencia was cut. This meant that I was effectively stranded in Barcelona. Bill Rust ordered me to go home. My arm was bad by this time, which made riding a bike a problem. Rust was the liaison between the Communist Party in Britain and the battalion in Spain ...

Bill Rust knew I was doing very little so I might as well go back to Britain. I got a boat from Barcelona to Liverpool. It was a cargo ship that was running the blockade, not very big. My passage was arranged by the party. The crew were all British. On the voyage home we docked at Cádiz and Malaga, Nationalist ports. When we pulled into a Nationalist port we hid. Actually we kept pretty well below deck except at night. I was on the ship for around 10 days. When we docked at Liverpool I went straight to see the Communist Party in Liverpool, where I was briefed by Frank Bright. I was given £2 and then sent back to Manchester. I found a job quite easily, I was an electrician, and continued to be a member of the party. I was sad to leave Spain because I could see it was the end. I was under no illusions.[2]

Sydney Quinn

Volunteer from Lisburn, Northern Ireland. Served with the Royal Artillery in 1935–36 and during World War II. Served with No 1 Company, 14th International Brigade, and the British Battalion, 15th International Brigade, November 1936–October 1937.

I moved to London to find work. I got a job in a hotel. I died 1,000 deaths for those fellas out there. I got married then I was called up. In World War II we had the same problems. The fella on the floor sees all the mistakes, and he pays for them with his life. I joined the Royal Artillery. In Belfast this newly promoted major took us out, the whole battery. He took us along a restricted road, narrow with steep inclines. It took six hours to disentangle us. I was a duty driver, and because of my service in the International Brigade I was told that I would never get promoted. After the war getting a job was no trouble. But I didn't have any skills. I've had to scratch all my life.[3]

George Leeson

Irish seaman and London Underground worker. Served with No 2 Company, British Battalion, 15th International Brigade, December 1936–February 1937. Prisoner of war, February–September 1937. Spanish Aid Committee delegate in France, 1937–1939.

There was a dip in the ground that was completely invisible, and through which the enemy could have walked and popped up in front of us. It wouldn't have been too bad if we had a right flank, but our right flank was empty because [Bert] Overton's No 4 Company had deserted and run back to the sunken road. We had eight Maxim [machine] guns (usually we had around five because they jammed and we sent them back to the armourers on the sunken road). Two Maxims and 12 riflemen should have been taken out and sent to the right flank. The Franco-Belgian Battalion further on the right had been forced back 300–400 yards, so we were exposed.

After continual enemy artillery bombardments and heavy machine-gun fire, which lasted all day long, there was a complete cessation of fire on the enemy side. You think, what's the enemy doing? He was attacking, because they didn't want to hit their own troops. We saw men running down the side of a hill, and we mowed them down. But the enemy was grouping in the blind spot and eventually we were surrounded and captured.

I was exchanged in mid-September 1937 and crossed into France. I wanted to go back. But then Jimmy Rutherford was executed and they wouldn't let anyone who had been captured and exchanged go out again. So I worked for the Spanish aid organizations …

I kept travelling to the border [with Spain] where groups of wounded came across … The British vice-consul was there, a chap with a bowler hat who spoke terrible French. I saw the head of the [French] Popular Front in Perpignan and said we should arrange a meal for the lads. I said the British government would pay. So we gave the lads a slap-up meal. I was sitting at a table with the vice-consul and a member of the Anti-Fascist Committee. I had to keep interpreting for the vice-consul. The waiter came round with a huge bill, and the vice-consul said, 'What's this?' I said, 'You're not going to disgrace me by saying that the British government can't afford to pay, are you?' We got him to pay for the lot!

… The Germans, Austrians and Italians who had fought in Spain, and who could not go back home, we had them up in Belleville, a working-class district in Paris. They were living in shabby hotels. The shopkeepers in Belleville were marvellous, they gave them meat, bread and vegetables. There was a tremendous solidarity movement. The refugees only had a daily allowance of five francs, from the French Spanish Aid

Committee. In June 1939 the French government cleared them out and put them in camps in southern France. Most of these camps were in the Vichy zone in World War II, and a lot of the refugees broke out and joined the French Resistance.

By June 1939 my job in Paris was finished so I returned to London. During the war I was not accepted into the British armed forces, I was called up and passed my medical, but I was never called up to serve. Occasionally I was stopped in the street by the police and asked if I had my call-up papers. I said yes and would show them. I wrote to the Admiralty to say I would volunteer, but they wrote back and said they couldn't accept volunteers. This type of thing happened to other Brigaders. A decision had been taken to keep out agitators. During the war I did a lot of organizing for the Communist Party in north-west London, speaking on behalf of the war effort. After the war I went into teaching.[4]

John Longstaff

Volunteer from Stockton on Tees, England. Served as a runner with the British Battalion, 15th International Brigade, September 1937–October 1938.

When I got back to England, I had only been back a day and I was asked by the IB [International Brigades] Organization to go and speak to Mrs Guest, the mother of David Guest. She didn't believe that her son was dead, and as I was there when he got killed, it was essential that I explained to her that not only had I seen him die but I actually had to help bury him. It is understandable for a mother or a wife to believe that their husband or son is alive, probably wounded in some enemy hospital or held captive.

It was essential that we knew where a man had come from in England or Scotland. The IB in that area would be given the job to go round and explain to the family of the volunteer who had died. This was to put the minds of the relatives of the dead lad at peace. This task was done by the volunteers of the International Brigades Office ...

It was not the practice of the Spaniards to put up the names of the people that had died. We didn't put up names in the International Brigades, either. We would have the names of those buried in the area, which would be put on one grave stone (made of wood). We only had a few places where we had proper military cemeteries. When a man died he was generally buried where he was killed, unless of course he died in hospital. Then you would be buried in the International Brigades place wherever the hospital was located. I knew where our graveyards were in Spain, but where I actually fought there were no graves at all.[5]

Maurice Levine

Volunteer from Manchester, England. Served with No 1 Company, 14th International Brigade, and as a political commissar, 15th International Brigade, November 1936–March 1938.

I encountered no opposition on returning to England. Both [John] Henderson and myself had passports. When we arrived at Folkstone we were told to go to a certain exit and there were two men there, no uniforms, just dressed in civilian clothing. They looked at our passports and they knew we had just come from Spain. They only uttered one sentence, 'Two more bloody reds back'.

Now I know, of course, that I was on the records of MI5 [British Intelligence] because I had a great deal of discrimination in World War II in the army. 'Two more bloody reds back', and off we went.[6]

James Brown

Volunteer from London, England. Served with No 1 Company, 14th International Brigade, and the British Battalion, 15th International Brigade, December 1936–August 1937.

One night I found myself talking to a Frenchman out in the field. He had been out there in the 14th Brigade. We went back to Mondéjar but very, very few went back to Mondéjar. We were there for a time and one day a chap came up to me and said are you in the 1st Company, I said yes. He said you are going home. At Brigade Headquarters I saw Jock Cunningham and he said, 'I would like to thank you on behalf of the Republic. You have done your duty and you can now go home'. This was partly because I had lost an eye. When I saw the others going home, some had one leg.

We went to Albacete, got on the trucks and then we went to Valencia. They put us on a train and then we went to Barcelona. We could not get out. It appeared that the Chief of Police was out of town and we could not leave without his permission. So we went to the British Consul to see if they could help us. We told them we wanted to go home. A chap there said he could not help us but told us to keep off the streets, and that's all the help we got from him.

Eventually we got out of Barcelona and on to a train to Perpignan. We got out at Perpignan with a policeman each side of us who took us to the nick [jail], we got arrested. They marched us to the Police Headquarters where a woman questioned me and gave a most searching examination. She wanted to know my age, religion, school, date of birth, parents' names, mother's maiden name, their profession, grandfather's profession and so on. I made out I could not understand the way she spoke English, which confused her a bit. This questioning went on for ages.

They gave us 24 hours to get out of France. We went to this house opposite the police station and said, 'Look we have been given 24 hours to get out of France'. They said they would put us on a train to Paris. You go to this address in Paris. Here is some money, get a taxi and they will take you there. We went in a box car at the back of the train. We got to Paris, found a taxi which took us to this house. A little man told me to take my clothes off. He gave me a Norfolk jacket that would have suited George Bernard Shaw in his youth, with pleats down it, very old fashioned, knickerbocker style. I was also given a pair of striped trousers and a pair of wooden shoes with white-glazed button tops. And this rather strange outfit was topped by a jaunty looking cap called a Le Jocky. We got on a boat train at Dunkirk and got to Dover at 04.00 hours. Coming through there was a plainclothes policeman who dragged us out of the crowd. They never beat about the bush but asked what fronts we were on in Spain. I said, 'What are you on about, I have been to the Spanish exhibition'. 'Well how did you lose your leg?' 'I got run over in Paris.' After a time they let us go.[7]

Albert Charlesworth

Volunteer from Manchester, England. Served as a runner and postman with the British Battalion, 15th International Brigade, December 1936–September 1937 and December 1937–October 1938.

That's right, I deserted. After two days in Barcelona I realized what I had done and went to the Brigade Office and asked to be sent back to the battalion. By the time I had got back to the battalion they had come back across the Ebro and were in a position on the banks of the river. I reported back to the battalion. I saw Sam Wild and told him what had happened and as a punishment I was digging trenches for two days … By the time the battalion moved off to the Ebro towards the offensive

I had at least 150 boils on my body so I reported sick. I was sent to the cookhouse and they started to treat me, then I was bundled off to hospital … I wasn't sleeping so they were giving me sleeping pills, but these did not make me sleep, so they bundled me off to another hospital on top of a hill, a specialist hospital. There I was put on a diet. Slowly but surely the boils started to go away. It was some weeks before I was released from hospital and then I went to Barcelona for a rest.

In Barcelona there was nothing about. I got a meal which consisted of one sardine on a plate. I was moved from Barcelona up to a place called Ripoll. This was the back end of 1938. The battalion moved up to Ripoll in dribs and drabs and we then learned we were being sent home. We were at Ripoll for two or three weeks. We went down to Barcelona for the farewell parade. We were on our way home, and were put on a train in Ripoll up to the border. When we got to the border we got out of the train and there was a barrier across the platform. On the other side of the barrier we could see British Army staff. They checked every single person through the barrier and General Holdsworth was in command of the operation. They made sure we got on the train on the other side, which was a French train, and we were locked in that train for the journey through France …

Sometimes at the big places the Salvation Army was there with food, but we were never let off the train at any point until we got to the French coast. There we were counted and marched onto a ship on the cross-Channel ferry and then we got a meal. When we came off at Dover there were various policemen and MI5 all waiting. One of my friends was taken away by MI5 because his name was Kempe and he used to smuggle diamonds.

They didn't actually check us for anything except our names. I suspect they had a wanted list and those on the list they just pulled out. Some weren't even asked their names, they just knew them before they got off the boat. When we got to Victoria [Station, London] there was a welcome waiting for us. We were put on coaches and driven to the East End of London. We were given a hell of a reception. We were welcomed, given a good meal and after the reception there were several speeches made and then we were allocated accommodation. I know that I went with two other comrades to the house of a school teacher and his wife on Hampstead Heath. I was there for two nights and given clothing and the like, and then I went to Manchester.[8]

Walter Greenhalgh

Volunteer from Manchester, England. Served with No 1 Company, Marsellaise Battalion, 14th International Brigade, and the British Battalion, 15th International Brigade, December 1936–October 1938.

When I went back to Manchester I started organizing, trying to raise funds for Independence Aid. I appeared at a meeting with Alan Sutton once at the Ashton Empire and he gave a speech saying, 'The war is over, it has been lost and Franco has won but we have got to remember that this was a battle that was well worth fighting for'. This annoyed me and I interrupted him and said the battle is only lost when the last shot has been fired, and if we accept this then we will always accept that we are going to lose. We have got to not accept that the battle is lost but to re-double our efforts.

Since then, the fact that I went to Spain has always been held as a black mark against me. That said, in the last war [World War II] I had a very important position. I was with personnel selection at the War Office but was restricted to the rank of staff sergeant. Then I served a number of years on Brent Council. Members of the Labour Party never really trusted me.[9]

Garry McCartney

Volunteer from Glasgow, Scotland. Served with the Machine-Gun Company, British Battalion, 15th International Brigade, March 1938–February 1939. Prisoner of war, March 1938–February 1939.

After two weeks we were taken by bus from San Sebastian to Irun, then we marched over the international bridge with Spanish guards marching halfway and then we were met by French guards. We marched onto the French side of the bridge and realized we were free. We turned round and called to the Spaniard guards, '*Viva Republica!*' There were hundreds of people on the other side of the bridge ready to greet us, which they did with wine, cigarettes and food (though we were still under the control of the French guards). We were given a hot shower, a change of clothing and very soon put on a train that took us to the ferry across the English Channel. Then we got a train to London where party comrades met us. When we arrived in London we were taken care of by the London Co-operative and were taken to the Co-operative stores. We were given a complete change of clothing: shoes, socks, underwear, a suit and an overcoat. Willie Gallagher met us and invited us to the Houses of Parliament where we had a meal, and the Scots lads then left the following day for Glasgow. I went home with them.

In Glasgow hundreds were at the station to greet us. We were interviewed by the press and marched from the central station down to one of the regular meeting places in the city. We had a short meeting, joined our families and went home.

I tried to join up in the first week of World War II. I had a fairly long interview and told the authorities of my experiences in the Spanish Civil War, because I was asked if I had any military experience. I was told that due to the fact that I was doing work of national importance (I was working in a coach building shop, constructing military trucks) I could not enlist. I wasn't too happy about it. I felt there were other reasons why I was not accepted. I finally broke into the Home Guard and did what I could as a volunteer.[10]

John Peet

Volunteer from England. Served with the Machine-Gun Company, British Battalion, 15th International Brigade, and as an interpreter with the International Brigades, September 1937–December 1938.

When I got back from Spain in December 1938 I took part in something called the International Brigade Convoy. About 25 brigaders were loaded into a bus and travelled all over England, Scotland and Wales, addressing meetings. By this time we were appealing mainly for food ships for Spain and emphasizing the political significance of what had been happening in Spain. We held successful meetings practically everywhere we went.

I remember the unlikely sort of support we were getting in, I think, Southampton, certainly somewhere on the south coast. The local Aid Spain Committee had organized, as in all the other places we visited, a big meeting. When we came into the meeting we were slightly astonished to find a large Union Jack draped behind the stage (during this period there was a tendency on the part of the British left to reject the Union Jack rather sharply as a symbol of imperialism). However, we knew this was a broad meeting and so we sat down on the platform as usual. Then we found out that the man who was chairing the meeting was the chairman of the local Conservative Party. He was adopting the line that was being taken at that time by practical members of the Conservative Party, who saw that with the world war coming the loss of the Spanish Republic would be disadvantageous to Britain and to Britain's supply lifelines through the Mediterranean. At the start of the meeting the Conservative gentleman who was chairing it got to his feet and said we should open proceedings with the singing of the national anthem. This confronted us with a rather unusual problem, because it had been the habit in radical circles in those times to remain seated at the close of a theatre performance when the national anthem was played. So we sat there rather petrified for a second or two and then we looked towards Bob Cooney, the senior man present. Cooney, with great presence, finally leapt to his feet and sang 'God Save the Queen' at the top of his voice. We all leapt to our feet and joined in, taking the view that this was a broad national movement, and that it was no shame to sing the British national anthem because we were at that stage appealing not simply to the working-class movement but to the people of Britain as a whole.

Indeed, in 1939 a leading Conservative said: 'It is a paradox of history that Gibraltar might have been saved for the British Empire by the heroism of a handful of Glasgow communists fighting to defend Madrid.' I have in my mind that it might have been said by Churchill, but I have never seen it quoted since.[11]

John 'Bosco' Jones

Volunteer from London. Served as an infantryman and runner with the British Battalion, 15th International Brigade, November 1936–October 1938.

My father made enquiries at King Street [Communist Party headquarters, London] about me. I had been writing letters home but when you were in the frontline in action you never wrote any letters, and, of course, when the battalion was called in I was listed as missing. They didn't even know I was in hospital in Madrid. So I was down as missing and that is when my family got alarmed. My dad went to King Street and [Harry] Pollitt said he would enquire to find out where I was. They must have found out where I was and that I was okay.

I ended up in Albacete and it was decided that if anybody had been through Jarama and Brunete they were veterans. Some of us went into what they called the Clement Attlee Company. They were called the veterans and it was stated that after so many months you could go back to England, so it was my turn to go. I was a young lad but if I had been older I would have gone back on propaganda tours. Some men did leave and came back but I had a right to go back to England. I had done my bit. I came back home in the autumn of 1938.

Physically I looked marvellous. I was brown as a berry but inside I was shaking like a jelly. My nerves had partially gone. I went to my doctor and told him what I had been through and that my nerves were bad. He told me to get a job doing something a little bit dangerous, such as a window cleaner. So I went off and got a job as a window cleaner. Going up and down ladders I had one or two falls, and I think that helped me to recover. It was only after a few months of doing this that I was better again.[12]

Maurice Levitas

Jewish volunteer from Dublin, Republic of Ireland. Served as a rifleman with the British Battalion, 15th International Brigade, December 1937–April 1938. Prisoner of war in San Sebastian and San Pedro de Cardeña, April 1938–February 1939.

We were walking up to an established frontline to relieve somebody else, when down the centre of this road came these Italian whippet tanks in great numbers. My little group had a machine gun and had small arms, and we moved over into the field. [However, capture was to prove unavoidable.] We were surrounded by Italian fascists. We had been ordered to dig what we had taken to be our graves, and we had already been subjected to some questioning. We certainly expected to die there.

Some time after my capture they [his parents] received a letter from the (International Brigade) office in London informing them that I was 'missing, believed dead'. It is not strange that after receiving it, my father sought information from anyone who came back from Spain. Someone actually told him that he had witnessed my last breath. But when the *Daily Worker* printed the list of names of prisoners returning to Victoria Station they knew that I still lived. Of course, they came with so many others to meet the returning prisoners, but that evening I was still in Paris. Only next morning, clad in a suit provided by the Co-operative warehouse, (after first meeting Dave Goodman, who waited for me in the courtyard of the flats complex), did I return to the flat in No 78 Brady Street Mansions, walk through an open door to find my mother with her back turned to me and preparing a midday meal for the family. My embrace, I could see as she turned, was a happy surprise for her – but no shock – I was expected but not so soon that day.[13]

Notes
1   Fraser, Harold, Imperial War Museum Sound Archive (IWMSA), London, Ref 795/5, Reel 5.
2   Curry, Patrick, IWMSA, London, Ref 799/3, Reel 2.
3   Quinn, Sydney, IWMSA, London, Ref 801/3, Reel 3.
4   Leeson, George, IWMSA, London, Ref 803/4, Reel 3.
5   Longstaff, John, IWMSA, London, Ref 9299/13, Reel 11.
6   Levine, Maurice, IWMSA, London, Ref 10360/4, Reel 3.
7   Brown, James, IWMSA, London, Ref 824/5, Reel 4.
8   Charlesworth, Albert, IWMSA, London, Ref 9427/4, Reel 3.
9   Greenhalgh, Walter, IWMSA, London, Ref 10356/3, Reel 2.
10 McCartney, Garry, IWMSA, London, Ref 809/6, Reel 5.
11 Peet, John, IWMSA, London, Ref 800/9, Reel 7.
12 Jones, John 'Bosco', IWMSA, London, Ref 9392/6, Reel 6.
13 Levitas, Maurice, IWMSA, London, Ref 16358/5, Reel 5.

Reflections

Sam Russell

Volunteer from London, England. Served with No 1 Company, 14th International Brigade, with the British Battalion, 15th International Brigade, and as a correspondent for the Daily Worker *and as Communist Party representative in Spain, November 1936–January 1939.*

We could have won if the democracies, particularly the British government, had allowed the legally elected government of Spain to purchase arms internationally, as was the right of any government to do so, but they were prevented. The French tried to send arms but the British government bullied them. Through Chamberlain and Anthony Eden they made it clear that if the French became involved in any war as a result of supplying arms to Spain, the British government would not come to their assistance.

Spain has remained always in our minds and in our hearts. If the Republican government had been given its rights by international law to buy arms on the market we wouldn't have lost the war. The experience in Spain didn't change me politically. The change came for me when I was in the Soviet Union, with Russian leader Nikita Khrushchev's secret speech, the Soviet invasion of Czechoslovakia [1968] and Hungary [1956].[1]

Dave Goodman

Volunteer from Middlesbrough, England. Served with the British Battalion, 15th International Brigade, January–March 1938. Prisoner of war in San Pedro de Cardeña from March 1938.

In the long run, the resistance of the Spanish Republic doomed the plans of Hitler and his allies. With hindsight, that was worth fighting for.[2]

Chris Thorneycroft

Volunteer from Oxford, England. Served as an infantryman and armourer with the Thaelmann Battalion, 11th and 12th International Brigades, and as a mechanical engineer, October 1936–April 1938.

The experience of resisting forces heavily equipped with aircraft and modern artillery was unique, unless you were a Nazi. [The pro-Republic movement] helped develop a spirit when the spirit of countries was being trampled underfoot. We could have had concentration camps all over this country quite easily. And it didn't happen. It wasn't a defeat. It was a strategic withdrawal.[3]

Bernard Knox

Volunteer from England. Served as an infantryman with the 11th International Brigade, October 1936–February 1937.

Back home, I watched in utter despondency as the British government persisted in its policy of appeasement and the prospect of victory in Spain receded fast as Hitler and Mussolini gave Franco a steadily increasing preponderance in weapons and troops. The sell-out at Munich in 1938 plunged me into despair; it seemed to me that Chamberlain and his sinister Foreign

Secretary Halifax were intent on making England a junior partner of Hitler's Third Reich.[4]

Alun Menai Williams

Volunteer from South Wales. Served as a nurse and first aider with the Thaelmann and George Washington Battalions, March 1937–October 1938.

One of the proudest moments in my life was being in Spain helping to fight fascism, while in England fascism was the fashion of the day. *No pasaran!* (They shall not pass!) We failed because the democracies let us down. We fought for our ideals. New generations are apathetic politically because they don't trust the politicians.[5]

Michael O'Riordan

Volunteer from Cork, Republic of Ireland. Founder member of the Communist Party of Ireland. Served with the Abraham Lincoln Battalion, 15th International Brigade, December 1937–September 1938.

Well, the Republicans lost the battle because we didn't have enough equipment. The Soviet planes came through all right, small ones, Mosquitoes we called them, and they came to Madrid. A lot of the Soviet stuff had to come by sea, they came via the Mediterranean, but the Mediterranean was controlled by Italian submarines who sunk the surface ships. That is not remembered by many people! The Mexicanskis were the only rifles we had, except towards the very end, there was some Czech rifles came in because at that time Hitler was going to march on them, and they got some rifles out of Czechoslovakia. But they were got too (by the Italians), not many, but the thing was that (we were) short of grub (food), short of militia and so on. And the realization that the Republic had forced its hand as long as it could. That does not mean they were capitulating, but they were panting as they were fighting, you know.[6]

Bob Edwards

Volunteer from Liverpool, England. Served with the Independent Labour Party Contingent and as an Independent Labour Party forces organizer in Catalonia and on the Aragon front, 1936–1938.

The Spanish Civil War, if properly supported, would have been the first defeat of fascism and we very nearly won that war. In the early months of the war, we were winning easily. We attacked Saragossa and could have taken it, but we had a shortage of ammunition and supplies. We released prisoners from the heart of the town. We had the men but not the equipment, and that was true throughout the whole of the war.

The governments of the West concocted the principle of non-intervention, which Germany and Italy signed up to but then ignored. There were 70,000 Germans and 55,000 Italians fighting in Spain. Up in Aragon we were not fighting Spaniards; we were fighting Moors, Italians and Germans.

I saw enough blood in the Spanish Civil War to last me all my life. Millions died in three years. I went back to Spain in 1959 and was arrested by the secret police. It's a long story, but afterwards when I went back to the hotel the staff lined up to welcome me. They had photographs and asked me if I recognized any of those who had fought in Aragon. Half of the staff had relatives who had died in the Spanish Civil War.

Overwhelming masses of Spanish [people] were supporting us. The Spanish Civil War was a social revolution: no black market, prostitution was abolished, no bullfighting, the workers were put in control of factories and large estates were formed into collectives. But then they decided to halt the social revolution and concentrate on military means. We could not have won militarily but we could have won the social revolution. George Orwell came to the same conclusion.

Orwell was tall, quiet, suffered from bronchitis and developed TB. He suffered in the mountains where it was bitterly cold. He was very courageous. In one incident, I remember, he had been training Spaniards. We were being attacked and he was with a machine gun. The gun overheated and couldn't be used so the Spanish crew stood up, waiting to die. He stood up with them. I said, 'Lay down you bloody fools'. He had such feeling for the Spaniards. We did have problems convincing them to take cover, though. Sometimes the war was a comic opera. We had no maps. I said you can't fight a war without maps.

Returning to England, I thought a world war was inevitable. In 1939 I went to America to help the trade union movement. We had withdrawn the International Brigades by then. None of the Germans or Italians [fascists] withdrew. I came back to England because I could see war was coming. I linked up again with the Chemical Workers Union. I wasn't eligible to be called up because I had been an officer in a foreign army. They wouldn't have had me.[7]

Alec Ferguson

Volunteer from Scotland. Served with the Anti-Tank Battery, 15th International Brigade, April 1937–October 1938.

I left Spain in December 1938. I had no trouble getting back to England and getting a job, though jobs were hard to come by at that time. The war stayed with me because I had been bombed. Every time a plane came over I ducked for cover. The old fear came back. I couldn't get Spain out of my mind. For years I was determined not to go back. But I went back in 1959 to find out how the people had survived. It was still a struggle for them, the workers were poorly paid. When Franco died I was happy and relieved.[8]

Charles Sewell Bloom

Commercial traveller from London, England. Served as a political commissar, runner and interpreter with No 3 Company, British Battalion, 15th International Brigade, and as an interpreter and intelligence officer at International Brigades Headquarters, December 1936–January 1938.

When I was in the frontline at Jarama we had air raids over us. They were German aeroplanes and of our aeroplanes, a few were Russian. In fact we knew it was a practice run for the future bombing of Britain. For some to have the audacity to say there was no German and Italian intervention is like saying black is white. Enemy propaganda said we went to fight for £5 a week, which was also a blatant lie. We didn't wish to be heroes, dead or alive. We found in the Republic in Spain a democratic government that a rebel general was trying to overthrow. Franco won in Spain by an act of treason. A League of Nations formed international law, which became non-intervention.[9]

Fred Copeman

Volunteer from London, England. Served with the Machine-Gun Company and as commander of the British Battalion, 15th International Brigade, October 1936–December 1937.

The ammunition problem was the key to it. When you look back on the Spanish Civil War, all the heroism and the thousands that died, the facts are that ammunition was supplied at a certain time for a certain time and then was stopped, and it always coincided with a victory for the Republic. The Republic won every bloody battle but never won a victory. Those at the time said it was bloody awful and fought it, and I was one of them ... The major war [World War II] was a colossal thing. The Spanish Civil War was just a punch-up in a backyard in comparison. We did our best because we were carried away with an ideal, which was a good one.[10]

Alfred Sherman

Jewish volunteer from London, England. Member of the Communist Party. Served as a machine-gunner in the Major Attlee Company, British Battalion, 15th International Brigade, January 1937–March 1938. Prisoner of war, March–October 1938.

Spain was a special case; a few more good divisions and I still think the tide could have been turned against Franco. The Basques were zealous Catholics and were fanatically anti-Franco. There was even a Loyola brigade [Ignatius Loyola, 1491–1556, an aristocratic soldier wounded at the siege of Pamplona, who founded the Society of Jesus]. And, of course, there were Germans fighting Franco, too. The Spanish Civil War was never a black and white affair. Bloody complicated.[11]

Notes
1   Russell, Sam, Imperial War Museum Sound Archive (IWMSA), London, Ref 9408/7, Reel 7.
2   *Guardian* interview, 10 November 2000.
3   Thorneycroft, Chris, IWMSA, London, Ref 12932/3, Reel 3.
4   http://www.english.uiuc.edu/maps/scw/knox.htm.
5   *Socialist Worker* interview, 22 July 2006.
6   http://www.geocities.com/roav1945/osheroff.html.
7   Edwards, Bob, IWMSA, London, Ref 4669/4, Reel 3.
8   Ferguson, Alec, IWMSA, London, Ref 820/2, Reel 2.
9   Bloom, Charles Sewell, IWMSA, London, Ref 992/6, Reel 4.
10 Copeman, Fred, IWMSA, London, Ref 794/13, Reel 8.
11 *Guardian* interview, 10 November 2000.

Chronology

1936

17–18 July   Throughout Morocco and Spain, military garrisons (aided, in places, by the Guardia Civil and the Falange) rise in revolt against the Republican government.

19 July   The rebels (or Nationalists) seize power in Morocco, Navarre, Galicia, Old Castile and Seville, but fail at Barcelona and Madrid. General Francisco Franco takes over command of the Army of Africa.

20 July   Prime Minister Giral appeals to the French socialist government for arms supplies. General Franco sends emissaries to Hitler and Mussolini to ask for military aid and technical assistance. The nominal leader of the revolt, General Jose Sanjurjo, is killed in an air crash.

20 July–
27 September   Siege of Alcazar. Nationalist troops holding out against Republican militia units are relieved when troops from the Army of Africa, led by Colonel José Varela, storm Toledo. The raising of the siege of the Alcazar does much to enhance General Franco's reputation.

21 July   El Ferrol, the main naval base in north-west Spain, surrenders to the Nationalists. As a result the Nationalists capture a battleship, *España*, two cruisers, *Republica* and *Almirante Cervera* (with another two, *Baleares* and *Canarias*, under construction), and a destroyer, *Velasco*.

23 July   The Committee of National Defence (the Nationalist government) meets for the first time in Burgos.

26 July   The Comintern agrees to send volunteers and funds to aid the Republic. Adolf Hitler agrees to send military aid to the Nationalists.

27–30 July   German and Italian transport aircraft carry the Army of Africa from Morocco to the mainland.

14 August   Nationalist forces from the Army of Africa, led by Colonel Juan Yague, capture Badajoz. The two parts of Nationalist Spain are now linked.

16 August–
3 September   Catalan troops, led by Captain Bayo, land on Majorca on 16 August. However, the Nationalist garrison, with the help of Italian fighter aircraft and bombers, contain the Republican advance. On 3 September they mount a counterattack on the Republican bridgehead. The Catalan troops rapidly withdraw to the beaches and re-embark aboard the ships that had brought them while under cover of the guns of the battleship *Jaime I*.

24 August   The new Russian ambassador, Marcel Rosenberg, arrives in Republican Spain. He is accompanied by a large number of Russian 'advisers'.

28 August	The Nationalists bomb Madrid for the first time.
4 September	Socialist leader Francisco Largo Caballero becomes prime minister. His government is a coalition of socialists, communists and Left Republicans.
6 September	Italian aircraft arrive in Majorca and set up bases from which to bomb the Republic.
9 September	The Non-Intervention Committee meets for the first time in London.
13 September	The Nationalists capture San Sebastian.
16 September	The Nationalists capture Ronda.
18 September	Comintern establishes the International Brigades.
1 October	General Franco is proclaimed Commander-in-Chief (Generalissimo) and Head of State in Burgos.
10 October	The Republican government announces the creation of the Popular Army, to incorporate both the army units that have remained loyal to the government and the party militias.
12 October	The first Russian aid for the Republic arrives.
15 October	The Popular Army establishes a system of commissars (political officers) for each unit.
25 October	A large part of Spain's gold reserves are transferred to the USSR to pay for Russian 'aid'.
2 November	The Nationalists capture Brunete.
8–23 November	The Battle of Madrid. The poorly armed militia units of the Popular Army, led by General José Miaja and aided by Russian tanks and aircraft, halt the Nationalist advance and save the city. Further assistance to the Republican cause comes from the first International Brigade units to reach the frontline.
15–17 November	The German Condor Legion goes into action for the first time, in the Madrid sector.
18 November	Italy and Germany recognize General Franco's government.
19 November	Buenaventura Durruti (a leading figure in the Anarchist Movement) is wounded fighting at Madrid. He dies the next day.
6 December	Nationalist aircraft bomb Barcelona.

13 December– **15 January 1937**	The Nationalists try to cut off Madrid from the rest of Republican Spain by launching an offensive towards the Coruña Road, which runs 25 miles (40km) to the north of Madrid. The offensive ends in stalemate.
17 December	The POUM is ejected from the Generalitat (Catalan Government) by the communists.

1937

17 January–	The Nationalists attack and capture Malaga.
6–24 February	The Battle of Jarama. Another Nationalist attempt to capture Madrid. When the fighting ends, the Nationalists have driven a salient into the Republican frontline but had again failed to isolate the capital.
8–18 March	The Battle of Guadalajara. Two Nationalist armies advance towards Guadalajara, 34 miles (55km) from Madrid, and at first push back the Republican troops. Then the Republicans counterattack and force the Nationalists back.
31 March– **19 June**	Battle for Bilbao. Nationalist forces begin an offensive that results in the capture of the Basque stronghold of Bilbao.
3–8 May	Street fighting breaks out in Barcelona as the CNT and POUM battle the communists.
15 May	Largo Caballero resigns as Republican prime minister.
17 May	The socialist Dr Juan Negrín becomes the Republic's prime minister, but his new government is dominated by communists.
16 June	The POUM is outlawed and its leaders arrested.
6–26 July	The Battle of Brunete. Republican troops around Madrid launch an offensive to cut off Nationalist forces besieging the city from the west. After some initial gains the Nationalists counterattack and force the Republicans almost back to their start lines.
14–25 August	The Battle for Santander. Nationalist forces advance towards Santander. The poorly trained and armed Republican troops offer token resistance. The Nationalists enter Santander almost unopposed.
24 August– **30 September**	The Republican Army fails to capture Saragossa.
21 October	Gijon surrenders to the Nationalists. The whole northern coast of Spain is now under Nationalist control.
31 November	The Republican government moves from Valencia to Barcelona.

15 December– **20 February 1938**	The Battle of Teruel. The Republican Army captures Teruel and is then almost surrounded in the town by a Nationalist relief column. The Republicans retreat and the Nationalists re-occupy Teruel.

1938

16–18 March	Barcelona is subjected to round-the-clock bombing by Italian aircraft based on Majorca.
1 May	Dr Negrín tries to sue for peace but General Franco demands nothing less than unconditional surrender.
24 July– **18 November**	The Battle of the Ebro. The Republicans launch an offensive across the River Ebro to relieve pressure on Madrid. Initially successful, massive Nationalist counterattacks eventually force the Republicans back across the Ebro.
21 September	Dr Negrín announces that the International Brigades will be withdrawn from the war.
22 September	The International Brigades are withdrawn from the frontline.
15 November	The International Brigades parade through Barcelona before being disbanded.
23 December– **26 January 1939**	The Battle for Barcelona. Having cut the Republic in two, six Nationalist armies launch an offensive against Catalonia. The Republicans retreat, which quickly turns into a rout. Tarragona surrenders on 14 January. The Republican government flees to Gerona. Barcelona surrenders on 26 January.

1939

5 February	The Nationalists capture Gerona.
28 March	The Nationalists enter Madrid.
29 March	Hostilities cease.
1 April	General Franco announces that the war is over.

Glossary

Accion Española – Monarchist party

Acción Nacional – See Acción Popular

Acción Popular – Conservative Catholic party formed by Professor José María Gil Robles as Acción Nacional. Forced to change its name by the government April 1932 and chose Acción Popular. It was later part of Confederacíon Española de Derechas Autonómas.

Camisa Azul – 'Blueshirts' – Irish fascists fighting with the Nationalists

Carlismo – Monarchists

Carlists – Monarchists

Comunión Tradicionalista – Carlist organization, merged with FE de las JONS

Confederación de Obreros Nacional-Sindicalistas – Workers' organization of the FE de las JONS

Confederacíon Española de Derechas Autonómas (CEDA) – An umbrella organization for Catholic rightist organizations (among them Acción Popular) founded in 1933

Confederación Nacional del Trabajo (CNT) – anarcho-syndicalist trade union

Esquerra Republicana de Catalunya (ERC) – Catalan socialist party

Falange de la Sangre – Militia of the FE de las JONS

Falange Española (FE) – Fascist party formed October 1933 by José Antonio Primo de Rivera, Julio Ruiz de Alba and Alfonso García Valdecasas

Falange Española de las Juntas de Ofensiva Nacional-Sindicalista (FE de las JONS) – Fascist party formed in February 1934 when Falange Española and Juntas de Ofensiva Nacional-Sindicalista merged

Falange Española Tradicionalista y de las Juntas de Ofensiva Nacional-Sindicalista (FET) – Right-wing party formed with the merger of FE de las JONS and the Carlist Comunión Tradicionalista, later absorbing the other rightist parties

Federación Anarquista Ibérica (FAI) – Federation of anarchist groups in Spain and Portugal

Federacion de Juventudes Socialistas (FJS) – Socialist youth organization, later a part of Juventudes Socialistas Unificadas

Federación Ibérica de Juventudes Libertarias (FIJL) – Anarchist youth organization

International Brigades – Units made up of foreign volunteers fighting for the Republicans

Izquierda Comunista – Communist party, later a part of Partido Obrero de Unificación Marxista

Izquierda Republicana – Republican socialist party

Juntas Castellanas de Actuación Hispánica – Right-wing anti-Semitic organization formed 1931 by Onésmio Redondo Ortega

Juntas de Ofensiva Nacional-Sindicalista (JONS) – Right-wing party formed when Juntas Castellanas de Actuación Hispánica merged with the group around the magazine *La Conquista del Estado* led by Ramiro Ledesma Ramos

Juventud Comunista Ibérica (JCI) – Youth organization of Partido Obrero de Unificación Marxista

Juventudes de Acción Popular (JAP) – Youth movement of the CEDA

Juventud Nacionalista – Youth organization of the Partido Nacionalista Español

Juntas de Ofensiva Nacional-Sindicalista (JONS) – Fascist Party, later a part of Falange Española Tradicionalista y de las Juntas de Ofensiva Nacional-Sindicalista

Juventudes Socialistas Unificadas (JSU) – Socialist youth organization
Legion Condor – German unit fighting with the Nationalists
Los Amigos de Durruti – Anarchist opposition group within the CNT, FAI and FIJL
Los Legionarios de España – Militia of the Patrido Nacionalista Español (PNE)
Margaritas – Monarchist women's organization
Movimiento Sindicalista Español (MES) – Fascist party formed in 1933 by José Antonio Primo de Rivera and Julio Ruiz de Alba
Mujeres Libres – Anarchist women's organization
Nationalists – Those fighting against the Republican government
Partido Agrario – Catholic party, later a part of Confederacion Espanola de Derechas Autonomas
Partido Communista de Espana (PCE) – Pro-Soviet Communist Party
Partido Nacionalista Español (PNE) – Right-wing organization formed April 1930 and led by José Maria Albiñana
Partido Nacionalista Vasco (PNV) – Basque separatist party
Partido Obrero de Unificación Marxista (POUM) – Anti-Soviet Communist Party
Partido Republicano Radical – Republican socialist party
Partido Socialista Unificado de Cataluña (PSUC) – Catalan Pro-Soviet Communist Party
Partit Comunista Catalá – Catalan Communist Party
Pelayos – Monarchist youth organization
Primera Línea – Organization of the most active members of the FE de las JONS who were young and healthy; also used as the party militia
Renovación Española – Far right Carlist party formed in February 1933 and led by Antonio Goioccha
Republicans – Those fighting for the government against the Nationalists
Requetes – Monarchist militias
Sección Femenina – Women's organization of the FE de las JONS
Segunda Línea – Organization of the most active members of the FE de las JONS who were not fit for the Primera Línea
Servicio Investigacion Militar (SIM) – Political police force controlled by the pro-Soviet communists
Sindicato Español Universitario (SEU) – Student organization of the Falange Española
Sindicatos Libres – Right-wing workers group in Barcelona. It was expanded into a national movement during the Miguel Primo de Rivera dictatorship and lost its influence after the fall of the dictatorship
Unión General de Trabajadores (UGT) – Socialist trade union
Unión Militar Española (UME) – Conservative officers' group
Union Militar Republicana Antifascista (UMRA) – Republican officers' group
Union Monárquica Nacional (UMN) – A fascist and monarchist organization formed April 1930 by supporters of the Miguel Primo de Rivera dictatorship
Unión Patriótica Castellana – See Unión Patriótica
Unión Patriótica (UP) – Right-wing organization formed April 1924 as Unión Patriótica Castellana. An organization much inspired by Italian fascism that was the political front of the dictatorship of Miguel Primo de Rivera y Orbaneja (1923–30)
Union Republicana – Republican socialist party

International Brigaders by Nationality

England – Bill Alexander, Charles Sewell Bloom, James Brown, Albert Charlesworth, Harold Bernard Collins, Fred Copeman, Stafford Cottman, Geoffrey Cox, Patience Edney, Bob Edwards, Jack Edwards, Douglas Eggar, Bill Feeley, David Gilbert, David Goodman, Walter Greenhalgh, Thomas Walter Gregory, Jack Jones, John Jones, Lou Kenton, Frank Lesser, Maurice Levine, John Longstaff, Bernard Knox, Bernard McKenna, Tony McLean, Morris Miller, Frank Mills, Joe Norman, John Peet, Sam Russell, Reginald Saxton, Alfred Sherman, Frederick Arthur Thomas, Chris Thorneycroft, Frank West, Richard White

Canada – Bill Wood

Denmark – Age Kjelso

Irish Republic – Eugene Downing, Bob Doyle, George Leeson, Maurice Levitas, Michael O'Riordan, Jim Prendergast, Frank Ryan, Bill Scott

Northern Ireland – Jim Haughey, Tom Murphy, Sydney Quinn

Scotland – Tommy Bloomfield, Tom Clarke, Bob Cooney, Patrick Curry, Alec Ferguson, Harold Fraser, William Kelly, Peter Kerrigan, Garry McCartney, Roderick MacFarquhar, Arthur Nicoll, Tommy Nicholson, Bob Walker

United States – Canute Frankson, Carl Geiser, James Lardner, Abe Osheroff, Dave Smith

Wales – Jim Brewer, Edwin Greening, Billy Griffiths, Morien Morgan, Alun Menai Williams

Acknowledgements

The author would like to thank the following people for their help in the production of this book:

A big thank you to Aruna Vasudevan, Publisher at New Holland, for giving me the opportunity to write about the International Brigaders. I owe a big debt of gratitude to my wife Karen, who spent hours at a keyboard going through the first-hand accounts. Without her help I would not have made the deadline. I would also like to thank the following individuals for assistance in collating the accounts: James Carmody of the The International Brigades Memorial Trust, Hayley Murphy of the Marx Memorial Library, Margaret Brooks and Laura Warren at the Imperial War Museum, Terry Norman who runs the Ammanford website, Jonathan Miller who created the Morris Miller commemorative website, and Ciaran Crossey who runs the Ireland and the Spanish Civil War website. Finally, I would like to thank Julia Shone, Project Editor at New Holland, for her patience and attention to detail.

The publishers would like to extend their grateful thanks to the Imperial War Museum, London, for its generous help in compiling this book and also to the individual copyright holders for accounts reproduced in this book.

Photographic Credits
Plates 1, 2, 5, 6, 7, 8, 9, 10, 11, 12, 13, 14 and 17: International Brigade Archive at the Marx Memorial Library
Plates 3 and 4: © Hulton-Deutsch Collection/ Corbis
Plates 15 and 16: © Bettman/Corbis

Index

Indexers note:
Where a country is indexed, its citizens are implied. Page numbers in *italic* refer to maps.

Index

Index